"LOOK
AT MY
UGLY FACE!"

"LOOK AT MY UGLY FACE!"

MYTHS AND MUSINGS

ON BEAUTY AND

OTHER PERILOUS

OBSESSIONS WITH

WOMEN'S APPEARANCE

SARA HALPRIN

VIKING

VIKING
Published by the Penguin Group
Penguin Books USA Inc., 375 Hudson Street, New York, New York 10014, U.S.A.
Penguin Books Ltd, 27 Wrights Lane, London W8 5TZ, England
Penguin Books Australia Ltd, Ringwood, Victoria, Australia
Penguin Books Canada Ltd, 10 Alcorn Avenue, Toronto, Ontario, Canada M4V 3B2
Penguin Books (N.Z.) Ltd, 182–190 Wairau Road, Auckland 10, New Zealand

Penguin Books Ltd, Registered Offices: Harmondsworth, Middlesex, England

First published in 1995 by Viking Penguin, a division of Penguin Books USA Inc.

10 9 8 7 6 5 4 3 2 1

LIBRARY OF CONGRESS CATALOGING IN PUBLICATION DATA
Halprin, Sara.
Look at my ugly face: myths and musings on beauty and other perilous obsessions with
women's appearance/Sara Halprin.
p.   cm.
Includes bibliographical references and index.
ISBN 0–670–85393–3
1. Beauty, Personal.   2. Feminine beauty (Aesthetics).   3. Ugliness.
4. Creative ability.   I. Title.
HQ1219.H295   1995
305.42—dc20   94–26999

This book is printed on acid-free paper.

Printed in the United States of America
Set in Stemple Garamond
Designed by Ann Gold

FOR
HERBERT DALE LONG
WHO LOVES
THE MANY WAYS
I LOOK

CONTENTS

CONTENTS

PRELUDE

LOOK

AT MY

UGLY FACE

SUN PU-ERH

Sun Pu-erh was the Taoist name of a woman who lived in China in the eleventh century. She was the beautiful wife of a wealthy merchant, who sought the path of awakening and knowing. Her teacher, an enlightened man named Wang Ch'ung-yang, told her that if she would go to Loyang, a place of power, and cultivate the Tao, she would attain immortality. She said she was willing to go anywhere, but then he looked at her face and said she could not go:

> You will meet with perils along the way. You will be the target of men who desire your beauty. They will rape you and molest you. And rather than be shamed, you would take your own life before they touch you. Now, is that not wasting your life to no purpose? . . .

Sun Pu-erh left the meditation hall and went directly to the kitchen. Telling the servants to leave, she filled a wok with cooking oil, heated the oil until it was hot, and then poured in cold water. The oil sizzled, and sparks of hot liquid shot out of the wok. Sun Pu-erh closed her eyes and let the liquid hit her face, burning the skin in numerous places; even after healing, the burns would leave scars and marks all over her face. She then returned to Wang Ch'ung-yang and said, "Look at my ugly face. Now will you allow me to travel to Loyang?" Wang Ch'ung-yang clapped his hands and said, "I have never seen one as determined as you are or willing to sacrifice so much. . . . You shall go to Loyang."

Sun Pu-erh then traveled a thousand miles by foot to Lo-yang, disguised as a crazy beggarwoman. Once there, despite her scarred face and crazy behavior, she was still threatened by would-be molesters, but the gods protected her, unleashing a hailstorm against the men. So she continued her studies undisturbed, living in great poverty until she attained immortality.

When she joined the company of immortals in the garden of the Empress of Heaven, she was placed last, the position reserved for the one to whom the greatest honor is due.

For Sun Pu-erh, beauty and ugliness were roles to be assumed and dropped at will, in the service of her ultimate goal, enlightenment. To her, appearance was simply a tool. However, as a woman living in a patriarchal society, she had to contend with the way appearance was used to define her by others. Although Sun Pu-erh was not attached to her physical beauty, it placed her at risk, and in that way it became an obstacle to her spiritual development. The ugliness she achieved by scarring her face and by letting the rest of her appearance deteriorate was something she delighted in, not because she enjoyed pain or self-mutilation, but because this was her way of finding freedom.

Sun Pu-erh's satisfaction with her hard-won ugliness sets her apart in her single-mindedness from women whose identities are shaped by their wish to look attractive or by despair at being ugly. She is unusual in her willingness to endure pain and disfigurement, to challenge her teacher's decision, and to persist in her path of danger and hardship.

We are taught by our contemporary culture to desire and seek beauty, and to shun ugliness, yet we know very little about our relationships with these complex and powerful concepts. This book is about the roles of beauty and ugliness, about the way these roles are connected with an obsession with appearance that haunts women's lives. It is about ways we can work with these roles creatively, finding and reclaiming the power behind the roles.

ON BEAUTY, UGLINESS, AND CREATIVITY

Women are expected to be naturally beautiful, effortlessly beautiful, and men, as artists, as writers, as connoisseurs, make art out of the artless beauty of young women. This expectation has prevailed for many centuries. In fact, women have striven for as many centuries to make ourselves beautiful, and have been the objects of satire, even ridicule, for so doing.

When looked at in this light, Sun Pu-erh's disfiguring of her face was a radical act, an act of rebellion and of creation. She might be considered an early performance artist, who used performance to achieve the goal she had in mind. Sun Pu-erh was interested in transformation, the attainment of enlightenment and immortality of body and mind. She did not pursue the cultural and philosophical implications of women's beauty or ugliness.

But appearance has much to do with how women are received in the world. Both beauty and ugliness are problematic for us. We are endangered, raised on pedestals, and trivialized for being beautiful; on the other hand we are insulted, ignored, shunned for being ugly. White women are expected to follow a standard of white beauty that implies purity and chastity, whether or not we are interested in these qualities. Women of color are judged according to white standards of beauty. Lesbians are judged by heterosexual standards of femininity. All women, as we age, must come to terms with a universal standard of youthful beauty, in a world that increasingly worships youth and denigrates age.

Most of us, men and women, strive for beauty and shun ugliness. Women, though, hold ourselves responsible for being beautiful, and we are held responsible by our culture. We may follow or defy fashionable standards, but we are very much aware of them and of ourselves in relation to the standards. Who is the inexorable judge who says, You, you are beautiful, and you over there, you are ugly? And who is the spirit seeking to be beautiful? Although men, notoriously, look at women, women also look at men, at other women, and at ourselves, in mirrors, windows, and as we are reflected in the reactions of others, in our dreams and waking fantasies. There is pleasure in our looking, and a yearning for something we may not normally articulate.

In this book I use myself, my experiences, fantasies, and dreams, as the central subject for investigation, to find out what it is about beauty that so draws me, what the power is in ugliness that so repels and yet fascinates me, and what possibilities there are for creative transformation in these ancient concepts.

I am not usually a beautiful woman, and I'm only occasionally ugly. As a young girl I daydreamed that I was the most beautiful woman in the world, so beautiful that people would stop on the street in awe of me. They would offer me anything I wanted. I dreamed of the man who would "discover" me. He would be intelligent, talented, and powerful, taller than I was, and he would wear a tweed jacket with leather elbow patches.

It was many years before I was able to identify that interesting man of my fantasies as an aspect of myself that needed development and support. I thought of myself as being intelligent and talented, but not at all as powerful, nor as independent. Eventually I came to question my own standards of beauty, and to realize how they are influenced by culture.

My interest in my own appearance and in the appearance of others is so great it could be called an obsession, an obsession I share with many others in this visually oriented culture. While I admire the Taoist immortal Sun Pu-erh and would like to emulate her, I know that a great gulf separates us. I am not yet ready to give up my interest in appearance. This has been a source of embarrassment for me, as it has seemed contradictory to my other concerns and beliefs, my feminism, my spirituality, even my professional identity. Worst of all, it has seemed trivial, as so many preoccupations of women have seemed trivial, like cooking, raising children, sewing, keeping house. Fortunately, we have finally arrived at a time when many of us are questioning our own categories, asking what is really important, and why the activities labeled "womanly" are so often also labeled "unimportant."

Over the years of gathering materials about this subject, as I have explored issues of appearance in my practice as a therapist and as a filmmaker and critic, in workshops and in classes, in literature and popular culture, I have come to realize what a huge and complex issue appearance is for women of all cultures, all ages, all ethnicities. How we see ourselves, how others see us, how these visual standards affect our lives—these are not trivial concerns for most women.

I invite you to come along with me on this journey into the world of beauty, ugliness, and transformation. Fairy tales and myths, stories and popular culture and conversations with other women are the vehicles I use for exploring this territory. If you are never quite satisfied with the way you look, or if you wish you didn't care so much; if there is something about your appearance that causes you to be labeled or stereotyped, or if you wish you could be seen for what you really are, then my guess is that the spirit that lurks behind issues of appearance is moving within you, seeking expression and fulfillment. There is something vital and creative behind these concerns about how we look.

The body of this book is divided into three sections. The structure is based on the polarity of beauty and ugliness, and the unifying field of creativity, in which both roles can be seen to exist. In the first section, on beauty, I look at issues of power and cultural standards of beauty, at the use of beauty as a metaphor, at the dangers and violence associated with beauty, at beauty as obstacle to spiritual development, at beauty as material commodity. There is not one myth of women's beauty, there are many. I am interested in the diversity and contradictions, the many-layered complexity of this mythology, and its potential value as well as the problems it creates.

The concept of women's beauty has been used to diminish our power, limiting us to our ability to be ornaments in the lives of men. But we have, deep in our collective psychology, memories of the power of beauty, of beauty as ritual and decoration, memories that linger, much changed, in fairy tales, in popular culture, and in dreams, of a time when the beauty of women, men, and nature was associated with the power of the Goddess.

Some of the stories and icons examined in this section are very well known, like the fairy tale of "Little Snow White" and the movie stars Audrey Hepburn and Marilyn Monroe. Others are less known, for instance, the Tibetan story of Nangsa Obum, a woman who, like Sun Pu-erh, followed a spiritual path. Some stories are from my own life, or were told to me by other women. The function of these stories and examples is to expand the concept of women's beauty and to open out possibilities for seeing beauty where we have not seen it before, as well as understanding the limitations and pitfalls of attachment to beauty.

The second section of the book is about ugliness. Some aspects of ugliness are symmetrical to aspects of beauty, especially when we consider stereotypes of beauty and ugliness. There are oppositional pairs, such as the beautiful maiden and the ugly old woman, or the pair found in the fairy tale of "Beauty and the Beast" or in the reverse story of "Gawain and the Lady Ragnell." But ugliness has a power and fascination all its own, rooted in disavowed and hidden aspects of human nature. These aspects emerge in fairy tales in the form of monsters and bestial figures, often beautiful people under some kind of spell or curse. The magical power of ugliness is shown in the South African tale of "Mulha," in which a young woman comes under the spell of an ogress.

Again in this section I use my own and other women's stories of ugliness to expand and make personal the figures and motifs found in popular culture. In studying ugliness I have come to understand the need to reclaim the power of ugliness, also to understand that it is no more of a fixed, permanent state than beauty. Beauty and ugliness exist in relationship to each other, and it is only by understanding this that we can begin to play with these culturally assigned roles and transcend the stereotypes associated with them.

In the third section of the book, on creativity, I look at some playful and serious ways of transgressing conventional boundaries of beauty and ugliness. Disguises, cross-dressing, and transformation in the mass media are the subjects of this section, which looks at old fairy tales like "The Girl Who Pretended to Be a Boy" and "Allerleirauh," at the movie *The Wizard of Oz,* and at television news, concluding with a chapter called "Storytelling." I return here, near the end of the book, to my own family story—which begins below in "The Personal Thread"—to illustrate the effect of my study of appearance on my life, and to suggest how the act of storytelling, applied personally, can be transformative. There is a playful, trickster spirit at work here, influencing relationships of identity and appearance.

It is the relationship between appearance and identity that is at issue. The judgments we make based on appearance are ridiculous if not informed by something other than appearance. What is that something other? Is it behavior? Is it character, or personality, or soul? What is it that the Zen Buddhists mean

by asking students to meditate on the following koan or question: What was my face before my parents were born?

This Zen koan refers to the concept of Original Face, a paradoxical concept of appearance that is detached from appearance. By meditating on that question deeply, I consider my mythical identity, the part of me that is independent of my genetic inheritance. Occasionally, I realize the meaninglessness of the question, and I feel, momentarily, free. In the Coda, called "Original Face," and in the appendix on inner work, I suggest some guidelines for the reader's meditation or work alone on the deepest aspects of your concerns with appearance.

In exploring the many layers of women's concerns with appearance this book is itself a many-layered story of women's beauty, ugliness, and creative powers, which we can all collaborate in telling and retelling.

THE PERSONAL

THREAD

Woven through this book are the threads of my personal history, stories of my family that I grew up with, pondered, even changed to suit my own changing life myth. Because the topic of women's appearance is so subjective, so personal, so much a matter of attitude and perspective, I offer my own stories as a way of reaching out directly to my readers, to tell who I am and where I come from, so that you may understand my ideas in their own particular context, and form your own ideas based on your lives and your stories.

My story has little of glamour or tragedy, but like all of our stories, it has been lived in the context of personal dreams and history, which are filled with images of glamour and tragedy.

MY FAMILY—FROM SURVIVAL TO FASHION

In my mother's family, the men were rash and the women survived. My great-grandfather Nathan, a tall, red-bearded blacksmith, was the only one in his Jewish village to stand up against the Cossack raiders. He died of the beating they gave him. Then his wife, my great-grandmother Sarah Mayasha Halprin, emigrated from Lithuania to America, to New York's Lower East Side, where she worked plucking chickens, saving money to bring her five children over to join her, one by one.

I don't know how Great-Grandma Sarah looked in her daily life. I have two photographs of her, one posed formally with my grandmother Rebecca, my great-aunt Flora, and her grandson, my uncle Louis, as a baby on her lap. I am impressed by a timeless quality in all three women.

My other photograph of Sarah is as a very old woman, in bed, looking tired and immensely sweet, which is how my mother remembered her. Her hands, swollen and gnarled from the years of plucking chickens under cold water, lie idle on the bedcovers. My grandma, Rebecca, whom I called Grandma Bee, was also tired, sweet, and bedridden when I knew her.

Behind their sweetness was a toughness and temper of women who survived great hardship with greater determination. These were women whose large bosoms were visible signs of large hearts, women of courage in the old sense of the word, meaning heartfulness. For them, the beauty of their youth was simply a passing phase, which gave way to the dignity of motherhood and then old age. Their substantial figures proved their ability to find and cook good food for their families and themselves.

When I look at my old family photographs I see images of women who were pillars of support for extended networks of family and friends. To speak of the beauty of my foremothers is to redefine beauty as endurance, courage, and compassion, the beauty attributed to biblical mothers. But to speak only of their beauty is to ignore the other side of their strength: their terrible tempers, their hard hands used to discipline too many children, their narrowness of outlook, hemmed in by hardship and ignorance.

Living through the Depression as a teenager, my mother experienced many hungry times. When she graduated from high school and got her first job as a secretary, she gave most of her salary to her mother, but she kept some money to buy clothes. Clothes and appearance were matters of obsession for her for most of her life. But to say that she was a clotheshorse, as I often did, is to misunderstand the meaning and function of clothes and appearance in her life.

For my grandmother, appearance signified social status. She made her children's clothing and her own, and insisted on good fabric and careful stitching. Dressed like a lady rather than a Jewish immigrant, my grandmother had less fear of being attacked on the streets, or disrespected by policemen.

My mother never learned to sew and rejoiced in the ready-made choices available to her in the stores. For her, clothing was fashion, designed to enhance the beauty that was nurtured by eating as her ancestors had never eaten, and by abstinence from hard labor. Unlike her grandmother's, my mother's hands were smooth, not roughened and red from plucking millions of chickens. My mother was ten inches taller than either her mother or her grandmother. Beauty, to my mother, meant the fairy-tale possibility of transformation from an immigrant's child into a woman of privilege and leisure.

I still have two of my mother's dresses, made specially for her when she was her most fashionable, an attractive executive secretary in Manhattan, who was often taken to fancy events by her bosses. One dress is made of tropical-flowered transparent chiffon, high cut in front and backless, designed to cling to the figure and draping down to a fishtail that sweeps the floor. In the roaring seventies I once wore that dress to the May Week ball at Cambridge University, having had it altered for my much shorter figure. It was the sexiest dress I ever wore, and, of course, I managed to spill a plate of ice cream right down the front!

The other dress is too delicate to wear, as it is made entirely of handmade lace that shreds at a touch. It is like a spider's web in brown and beige, a classic twenties garment, made for dancing the Charleston and for grand garden parties. I imagine my mother as a slim young woman; she was very overweight from the time of her pregnancy with my younger sister until she died at seventy-five. Wearing that lace dress, with, of course, a modest silk slip underneath and all the right accessories, she must have felt as delicate and precious as a valuable piece of porcelain.

But my mother was not destined to be collected by a rich lover of porcelain and beautiful women. Instead, at the age of thirty-two she married my father, an attractive man of the same age with no wealth and no prospects, who had just been drafted into the Air Force. The year was 1942. I was born a year later.

For the next thirty years my parents struggled along in a difficult relationship, in which money and jealousy were always issues. My mother ate to console herself. By the time my younger sister was born, my mother was a fat woman. I have a picture taken of our whole extended family shortly after my grandmother died. My mother was hiding behind my father, hoping that her obesity wouldn't show. This was to be her preferred pose in photo after photo through all her years of Weight Watchers and late-night bingeing.

My mother once ate a gallon of ice cream at a sitting, hoping to cure herself of her addiction. It didn't work. Now, remembering her endless stories about the family and herself, which we found so tedious as children, I understand better my mother's craving for sweetness, for comfort, for the affection and community she missed so terribly. I remember my mother as a large woman who found no outlet in the world for her largeness of character and ambition.

Growing up, my sister and I felt terribly oppressed by our mother's obsession with clothes and appearance—our clothes and our appearance, and hers when she was slim, which she never tired of describing. I think that until the day she died my mother thought of herself as a slim, beautiful young woman, living in a body with which she hardly identified, a body that was large, heavy, and in her old age, riddled with cancer.

Rebelling against my mother, I developed a personal myth

of beauty, which I thought was eccentric, free from the dictates of fashion and convention. I didn't realize that my ideal of eccentricity was itself culturally shaped and biased, influenced by images in movies and illustrations in books, an ideal of aesthetic elegance that took deep root in me. I thought elegance was simple and natural, and I longed, as a child, for clothing that exemplified this look. Margaret O'Brien's clothes in *The Secret Garden*, even though they were complicated, with endless buttons and laces, seemed to me to fit this ideal, and I also admired the pinafores in illustrations of *Alice in Wonderland* and *Little Women*.

Laura Ashley clothes, originally made of cotton or corduroy and based on nostalgia for the flowing lines of an earlier femininity, did not appear in American or Canadian stores until I was in my late twenties. They succeeded the London-based "Dolly Rocker" fashions of the late sixties and early seventies, which I had worn, convinced that I was a pioneer of liberated fashion. I embraced Laura Ashley's clothes with the fervor of my early admiration for English and New England heroines, just as, in earlier childhood, I had loved my buckskin "cowgirl" skirt, with its fringe and its association with a bold female spirit. But I didn't realize that it was the spirit signified by the clothes that I loved and longed to emulate.

My generation was the first in our family to attend college, the first to pursue professional careers. Our parents, like their parents, encouraged us to forget our ethnic origins, to assimilate into mainstream U.S. culture. From nursery school through graduate school, nothing I studied was related to my family background, but it didn't occur to me that it should be. By the time I graduated from college, my intention, successfully carried out, was to *look* as if I belonged in the academic and professional circles where I felt at home intellectually. And yet something in me stayed aloof from these circles, felt like a different identity, one which was not reflected in my appearance. This disconnection between appearance and identity was to become a topic of great interest later in my life.

Eventually a pattern emerged from the disparate threads of my academic, professional, and personal lives. As a university teacher, a documentary filmmaker, a therapist, and a student of the Tao, I have spent many years studying and working with issues of appearance. The root of my interest was my family background. My deepest learning about appearance has come, not from formal studies, but from unexpected sources.

TEACHERS

My very first teachers were stories, in books and in movies. I fell in love with books at the age of six when I got my first public-library card, my ticket to the world of fairy tales. That was the same year I saw my first movie, *The Secret Garden*, a movie about beauty, ugliness, and the cycles of nature. I dreamed that the MGM lion leaped out of the movie screen and charged down the aisle toward me as I sat frozen in my seat. As a child and young woman I remained frozen so far as movement was concerned, spending most of my time sitting and reading, writing, or watching movies. The benefit was good grades and scholarships, my ticket into the intellectual world.

As a young woman in the mid-sixties, studying literature and philosophy at Edinburgh University in Scotland, I had the good fortune to meet Beatrice Huntingdon Macdonald, a portrait artist, then seventy-five, who lived in an elegant Georgian flat overlooking Queen Street Gardens. Beatrice had a Renoir in her hallway and a small cartoon by Leonardo on her mantelpiece, next to a bowl by Hokusai. The walls were covered with her oil portraits and her late husband's landscapes.

Each year Beatrice's old friend Violet Dreschfelt, a sculptor, came from Majorca to spend the summer in Edinburgh, and the two would preside over the Sunday-afternoon teas to which I was regularly invited. Those two women provided me with a foundation for understanding art. For them, art was the outward expression of the inmost self through a medium such as oil paint or clay. The deepest lesson I learned from them, which I wasn't able to articulate for many years, was that beauty and ugliness are simply two aspects of perception, each containing some element of the other.

The summer I was twenty, Beatrice painted my portrait in oils, and insisted on making a gift of it to me. Although she called it "Portrait of a Young Girl," I remember thinking that it was a portrait I would grow into. There was a quality about it I admired but felt wasn't yet me, a sense of someone simply looking out from a very deep place, an old woman with a young face, sitting by the river as it flows. I am still growing into that portrait.

That same summer Beatrice painted another in a series of portraits of Violet. It was a formal portrait, in silhouette, showing Violet with her dark hair drawn back in a chignon, her deep, dark eyes shadowed and distant, her aristocratic, European-Jewish nose shown in all its beaked splendor. Right after finishing that portrait, Beatrice saw Violet one morning with her hair loose, just after she had washed it. She insisted on sketching her right then. This was to be the last portrait of Violet, who fell ill and was unable to return to Edinburgh another year. After Beatrice died at the age of ninety-nine, a retrospective show of her work was held in Edinburgh, and the catalog was sent to me, with a photo of this portrait of Violet. Even in the black-and-white catalog photo Violet's splendid old face blazed out at me, framed by a wild cloud of dark hair, her skin deeply tanned like old leather by her many years in the Spanish sun.

I remember one of Violet's anecdotes, about how she had cherished an Etruscan vase she kept on her patio, and how disturbed she was when a cleaning woman innocently removed its antique patina. Since then, I have viewed wrinkles and lines on old faces with appreciative eyes, as gifts of time.

The last time I saw Beatrice she was ninety-three, weakened by illness, and still working, although her fingers were so cramped with arthritis she had to place the brush in her hand and then use her wrist to direct it. In the afternoons she rested, and sometimes talked to me about her past. One day she showed me a photograph of herself as a small child. She told me how the photographer had said, "Look at the birdie," and how she had looked and looked, earnest and curious to see the bird. I saw my old friend in the miniature photograph in its velvet case, her head cocked like a bird, looking and looking at the world, which was then new for her, and which remained new for her whole life.

I still have a photo of Beatrice pouring tea, which I snapped during one of our Sunday afternoons. She looks in that photo very much the same as in the one of her as a child, curious, bright, caring passionately for all that was near her. I see in these photographs the way a life can be shaped by one image, which remains constant, collapses time into a photographic instant, makes a fairy tale or myth of a life.

Beatrice looked at all around her with her heart informing her eyes, just as she listened to the classical music she loved (she studied cello with the great musician Julius Klengel in Vienna before she turned to painting). Toward the end of her long life it was clear that she was looking for something that could not be seen with physical eyes, or heard with physical ears, something she sought in the writing of Teilhard de Chardin and Simone Weil, in the counsel of spiritual friends, in the solitude into which she retreated in her last years. In her letters to me she referred to that something as a light in a dark place, as clarity. I think she was seeking enlightenment, and she refused to die until she found it.

From Edinburgh I went to graduate school in New York, then embarked, along with my first husband, on a promising academic career in Toronto. We were a handsome young couple, leading attractive, privileged lives, and eventually we had a wonderful son. Like many other women in our youth-oriented culture, I was entirely unprepared for motherhood.

Childbirth was a traumatic event, and subsequent surgery left me heavily scarred and with a weakened back. At the time, I was more concerned with the effect on my appearance than with the damage to my health. I had taken great pride in my slim body, and now I was ashamed to be seen in a bathing suit. I felt I had aged twenty years. This wrenching change in my appearance corresponded to a crisis in personal identity that had been building over many years. At the same time, I was caught up in a new fervor of feminism, which affected many women in the great wave of the early seventies. I questioned my roles as wife, mother, and university professor, and I found no satisfying answers.

In one stress-filled year I left my first marriage, quit my tenured job as a university teacher, and embarked upon a complicated career as writer, mother, filmmaker, part-time teacher, lover, explorer of life. I bounced around like a rubber ball from one role to another, trying to find the right one. While I learned a great deal about myself and about women's roles, especially from the women who formed my community of support and challenge during those years, my body, not nearly so flexible or elastic as rubber, rebelled. Severe physical symptoms related to my postpartum surgery and subsequent stress led me to explore alternative forms of treatment: shiatsu, chiropractic, t'ai chi.

I had led a sedentary life for many years. My t'ai chi teacher Moy Lin Shin taught me the value of fluid movement. At first, all I could focus on was how to take steps in t'ai chi without falling over. Gradually I became aware of the depth of knowledge my teacher had to offer. Master Moy's teachings come from an ancient northern Chinese Taoist lineage called Wu-chi, or Return to Earlier Heaven, which uses principles of internal alchemy to transform the body. These teachings recommend that we cultivate the body first and then the mind, learning to use movement in the pursuit of stillness. This leads to the integration of body and mind, which allows us to follow the Tao, the mysterious force of nature. Beauty, in this Taoist system, is an external sign of inner development, and is not a goal or value in itself. It emerges spontaneously from right living.

Early in our acquaintance, Master Moy offered me the excellent advice that I should follow the path of the heart. This is a Taoist concept, which I have also come across in the writings of Carlos Castaneda about Mexican Indian shamans, and in Arnold Mindell's process work which was the basis of my training as a therapist. The path of the heart is a simple idea, which requires simplicity of the person who would follow it. But I had been trained to be complicated! My teacher's advice seemed mysterious to me, and, leaving Toronto a few years later, I pursued some intricate and far-flung pathways before returning to my studies with him.

On one of my paths, as a documentary filmmaker, I collaborated with other women to explore issues of appearance and identity. I made several films about women, but one, my film about a bearded woman, changed my thinking about gender and appearance. In *Keltie's Beard: A Woman's Story,* Keltie explains to the camera in one long close-up how she came to the decision to let her facial hair grow, rather than having it removed as the women in her family had always done. She speaks of seeing a billboard in a Toronto subway saying, "Get rid of ugly facial hair. You too can be beautiful." "But," Keltie says calmly, "I already knew I was beautiful." She was sixteen at the time.

In the film Keltie speaks of her trip to Africa. Before that trip, she had only and always suffered criticism, abuse, even assault because of her beard. "The best I got was silent toleration," she sighs. In Africa, the market women of Kenya considered Keltie's beard a tribute to the women of her family, and they honored her accordingly.

I've often wondered how Keltie, a white Canadian woman, had the courage to defy the standards of her own culture so completely. Knowing her, I can speculate that the loving support of her mother and sister was a strong factor, and that a changing climate of public opinion about women's options was another, although Keltie was certainly in the forefront of change. But I think there were other factors, less easy to define, such as Keltie's love for her beard as part of herself. She calls it pubic hair, since it first appeared in her puberty, and she speaks of its softness. Whether or not Keltie continues to wear her beard, her decision to appear in a film allows those of us who hear her story to reflect on the decisions we all make about our physical appearance.

My work as a filmmaker and critic of literature and film, together with my personal search for an identity transcending appearance, led me to an interest in psychology. This pathway led to another teacher, Dr. Arnold Mindell, who developed from his clinical practice as a Jungian analyst the theory of process-oriented psychology now known as process work. Process work is distinguished by its focus on following the moment-to-moment process of the client, based on the client's sensory-grounded descriptions of his or her experience, on attention to nonverbal communication, and on the relationship of client and therapist. There is an underlying attitude that our problems contain the potential for growth and development, and that this potential may be unfolded by working with problems as evolving processes rather than fixed states. Like Jung, Mindell uses principles of ancient Taoism as well as field theory from modern physics. Mindell extended Jung's work by introducing movement and bodywork into his therapeutic practice as well as work with relationships and groups.

Mindell, with his interest in childhood dreams and life myths, helped me to understand the terrifying lion of my childhood dream as my own creative energy, emerging from the illusory territory of the movie screen, aiming straight for the frightened little girl who could neither move nor scream. In my study of process work I learned how to use and understand movement as a form of nonverbal expression. This helped me to shift from an identification of myself as a motionless spectator, and to encompass the aspect of myself that charges like a lion to grab my prey.

Above all Arny Mindell articulated for me the overriding importance of loving support as a background for personal and social change. Understanding this made it easier for me to accept such support from my family and friends. I was able to extend my childhood dream of the MGM lion by jumping on the lion's back and riding it right out of the movie theater, up into the sky, as it spread its mythical wings and flew on the current of my imagination. The process work that enabled me to convert my terror into creative energy also inspired me to become a therapist.

After a five-year clinical training at process work centers in Zurich and Portland, Oregon, I was certified as a process-oriented therapist. In my work with clients, as in the rest of my life, I use process work concepts to extend the meaning of identity. We are more than what we think we are in each moment. For instance, using concepts of roles and field theory, we can see the roles people play in terms of group dynamics as well as individual psychology. Understanding that there are multiple channels of perception and communication, such as seeing, hearing, feeling, and movement, helps us to pick up on unintentional signals. The idea of edges, which act as boundaries to our identities, suggests why people often resist change. Edges define all that we think we are not, and all that we might become, if we dared. Fear of going over edges keeps us locked in roles, afraid to experiment with other roles in the field. We can work with an edge by noticing that it exists, by changing channels of perception, imagining what it might be like to go over the edge and try another role.

For example, a client who dreams of being pursued by a monster is, in her waking life, identified with being meek and quiet. She is unhappy with her own appearance, and has a tendency to criticize herself fiercely. I help her to play the role of the powerful monster, and also to understand the value in her role of quiet meekness. As she begins to fill out these and other roles available to her, the field in which she lives becomes friendlier, less menacing, because it is less unknown. She becomes less fearful of random violence, and more resourceful in learning ways of defending herself. We discuss together the ways that we see her fear in relation to the culture we live in, one where women often suppress our wilder side, and need support to express it.

Together, we work with her edge toward acting powerful, using different channels of perception: movement, sound, body feeling, relationship. I work on my own edges to being powerful and also to being meek. She and I take turns becoming monsters and mice, lions and little girls, powerful critics and nurturing mothers. As she worries less about how others see her, her appearance changes dramatically—she looks like a powerful, vital woman.

My task, as therapist, is to carry the thread of awareness through the maze of our work, understanding that my own reactions are as essential to my client's work as her own, but I am also able to drop my concerns in order to follow her process. As we work together, picking up and dropping the different roles that emerge between us, as I help her to follow the flow of signals, in speech, gesture, imagery, and body feeling, in our relationship, in the world around us, we both move toward wholeness.

By wholeness I mean the ability to have access to many roles, being able to acknowledge even those parts of ourselves and others that disturb us and seem foreign to our nature. The woman who identifies with beauty may neglect her uglier side and be unaware of the power hidden in ugliness. The woman who sees herself only as ugly is missing her great longing for beauty, which must also be a part of her. Those of us who identify only with our momentary appearances neglect the importance of body feelings, of movement, of relationship, of our many ways of communicating with the world around us.

These concepts of beauty and ugliness are figures from our dreams. We should follow them so long as they haunt the imagination, feed them like hungry ghosts until they no longer claim attention, or are transformed into the deeply spiritual values they always were striving to express.

The influence of my teachers and of friends and lovers in my life balances the force of cultural hypnosis, the trance-inducing images of the mass media, the relentless pressure to be feminine in a misogynist setting. My teachers have offered me the tools and support to become a teacher and role model in my own right, which means that I can validate and evaluate my own experience of growing up female, Jewish, white in the United States, of living in the family I had, in the culture around me, in my time. Their teachings also have given me the means to step aside from my personal experience and to see it as one ordinary life among many, one set of roles among many possibilities, a perspective I offer to you.

From this perspective, beauty and ugliness take their place in a great range of roles that I have played and may continue to play, at one time or another. What is most important to me is the practice of following and unfolding the Tao, the mysterious and inexpressible flow of experience, on the path marked out by heart.

BEAUTY

She is very beautiful, as fresh as a mermaid emerging from the sea, with deliciously dark skin, gleaming, as golden as if she had just returned from a summer in the Islands. She is not fat but abundant. Her flesh is light: tender and slightly puffed like an infant's. The minute she opens her mouth, the minute she speaks, you realize that this flesh was needed around *the voice, to nourish it as the good earth nourishes its fruit, so that it might achieve its full depth, its marvelous velvet sound.* —Marguerite Duras, "Leontyne Price"

Beauty is a demon that breeds and proliferates when admired. —Carlos Castaneda, *The Eagle's Gift*

I

BEAUTY

AND POWER

I. THE GODDESS

Once upon a time, women were free to develop, unrestricted by concerns about appearance.

Each Halloween, from age six to eleven, my best friend, Claire Teitelbaum, and I would go trick-or-treating in the housing project where we lived, in the Bronx in New York City. For years our mothers dressed us in pink tutus with starry wands, and we were sweet little fairies. But when we were nine, we rebelled and planned our own Halloween costumes. We would be cavewomen! We got unbleached flannel and spotted it with black paint to make skins. We made clubs from papier-mâché, combed our hair over our faces, and set out to terrorize the neighbors. Our mothers mourned our transmutation and the

—— neighbors were suitably scandalized. Claire and I had a wonderful time, and I think we created a rite of passage for ourselves of great importance. We would no longer be the appealing pink fairies of our mothers' dreams and our culture's expectations.

We had no idea that the time of the cavewomen we were reaching back to was a time of goddess worship, of reverence for all the powers of women, creative and destructive, based on biology and culture, a time before beauty became an assigned role for women. We didn't know the ancient history of Halloween, All Hallows' Eve, taken over by the Christian church from the pagan Celtic holiday of Samhain, the magic time between summer and winter when a crack opens between the world of humans and the spirit world, and all manner of beings cross over, when it is possible to become unknown aspects of oneself. And of course we didn't, couldn't know of the profound acceptance of cyclical change, of life, growth, death and rebirth, that characterized the worship of nature gods and goddesses prior to patriarchy. We didn't know any of that, but, as children always do, we reinvented our archetypal past in play. We were radical in our fantasies, challenging the role of the beautiful woman before we knew from experience how constricting it really could be. Without the mature and single-minded focus of Sun Pu-erh, we just wanted to be free! Although we had never heard of the Maiden Goddess, Claire and I, in our childish imaginations, were recreating her as best we could.

Thirty years later, living on the other side of the North American continent, I came across a book translated from Sumerian cuneiform, c. 2000 B.C., the oldest writing yet discovered, preserved on tablets of hardened clay. What I found in *Inanna: Queen of Heaven and Earth* transformed my understanding of the importance and history of women's appearance.

INANNA

Inanna, heroine and goddess of Sumer, leaned back against an apple tree, gazed at her own vulva and said to herself, I am wonderful.

> When she leaned against the apple tree, her vulva was wondrous to behold.
> Rejoicing at her wondrous vulva, the young woman Inanna applauded herself.

Then, filled with her sense of wonder at herself, Inanna visited Enki, God of Wisdom, and drank with him. One by one he offered to her the all-important Me (the holy laws of Sumeria), which Inanna happily accepted, loading them onto her Boat of Heaven, and left. Later he repented, but it was too late. Inanna brought the Me to her people, thereby providing them with the foundations of civilization.

Inanna's story includes her courtship and marriage to the shepherd Dumuzi, her descent to the underworld, ruled by her sister, Ereshkigal, her death there, and her resurrection. It was the predecessor of many later stories of male figures, including Christ, but none of these later stories or others repeat the woman's joy in her body contained in that lovely vulvic line.

Thirty-six hundred years later, in sixteenth-century Italy, Agnolo Firenzuola, writing On the Beauty of Women, an imaginary dialogue that takes place between a gentleman and several upper-middle-class ladies, describes a woman's beauty through the eyes of the gentleman, dwelling at length on the features and proportions of the ideal beautiful face, neck, breasts, legs, and feet, and keeping silent on the subject of "the other parts," on the grounds that these are properly "kept covered." Of all these "other parts," the vulva is the one most hidden in art and literature. Twentieth-century artist Judy Chicago's celebration of female genitals in her famous "Dinner Party" still produces shudders among misogynist critics.

Women today look to old goddess-worshiping cultures for

the images of female sexuality and pride in all our appearance absent from contemporary culture.

> *Inanna spoke:*
> "*I bathed for the wild bull,*
> *I bathed for the shepherd Dumuzi,*
> *I perfumed my sides with ointment,*
> *I coated my mouth with sweet-smelling amber,*
> *I painted my eyes with kohl.*
>
> "*He shaped my loins with his fair hands,*
> *The shepherd Dumuzi filled my lap with cream and milk,*
> *He stroked my pubic hair,*
> *He watered my womb.*
> *He laid his hand on my holy vulva,*
> *He smoothed my black boat with cream,*
> *He quickened my narrow boat with milk,*
> *He caressed me on the bed.*
> *Now I will caress my high priest on the bed,*
> *I will caress the faithful shepherd Dumuzi,*
> *I will caress his loins, the shepherdship of the land,*
> *I will decree a sweet fate for him.*"

Inanna's adornment of herself for her lover Dumuzi, her use of amber on her lips and kohl on her eyes, is a ritual preparation for the pleasure she anticipates in their sexual union, Dumuzi's entrance into the "black boat" of Inanna's vulva, a union that was sacred and essential to the fertility of the land and to the prosperity of the Sumerian people.

The echo of Inanna's sacred rite of adornment persists today in advertising and fashion, but it is an echo that has been rendered profane. Sex is no longer considered a sacred act, especially in reference to a woman's pleasure, and has not been so considered for several thousand years, except in certain remote indigenous cultures, such as the Ait Hadiddu among the Berbers of North Africa, the Hawaiians before the arrival on their shores of Europeans, and some Tantric practitioners. As sex has become profane, considered impure, even dirty and therefore

bad, decoration and ornamentation have been devalued, along
with women's bodies. At the same time adornment of the body
is defined as part of women's obligatory role, a role created by
patriarchal culture. How did this happen?

THE TRIPLE GODDESS

Since early patriarchal times, when the goddesses were first rendered inferior, then supplanted by father-creator gods, a woman's beauty has never been simply itself but has been also a
metaphor for something else, something with moral overtones,
such as goodness, or evil, often both. The idea of a woman's
sexual parts as something in which she herself takes delight has
receded, so far as mainstream cultures are concerned, almost
beyond memory, so that Inanna's story now evokes astonishment in contemporary readers.

(The word *patriarchy* is used loosely and with widely different implications. What I mean by *patriarchy* is the historical
period characterized by a social structure based on families
headed by fathers; and by worship of, first, a pantheon of gods
who took precedence over goddesses, later by worship of a
single, male-identified God. This patriarchal period coincides
with most written extant records, has lasted about four thousand years, and has shaped most human cultures.)

Precisely because its influence has been so pervasive, patriarchy is not often identified as such, unless it is challenged by
an alternative idea. A large body of literature has by now been
generated by scholars and writers documenting evidence for the
previous existence of a human culture that was not patriarchal,
and speculating on its implications. This has in turn generated
ideas about the nature of patriarchy itself. Patriarchy is the context in which most of our concepts of appearance have developed. Please see the notes and bibliography at the back of the
book for further reading on this vast subject.

One main characteristic of patriarchy is the tendency to create relations of domination among people, so that one group
has power over another, power backed by institutions and tra-

dition. Throughout this period, men have had power over women, and that power has extended to prescriptions about women's appearance.

By defining women in terms of appearance, patriarchy diminishes their role. We are not credited as doers, rather we are seen as passive objects. The paradox is that great activity is expected of us and we deliver.

The dualistic tendency of patriarchal culture, a tendency to think in oppositional terms (such as black-white, good-evil, strong-weak), has led to the assumption that the only alternative to patriarchy is matriarchy, a reverse situation in which women have power over men. But the work of cultural historians, based on archaeological findings, on anthropology and mythology, suggests that something else has existed, cultures that may have been based on cooperation and partnership rather than on domination and organized warfare. Out of the many different interpretations of old myths and artifacts emerges some agreement, as well as considerable debate, about the time preceding patriarchy.

For many thousands of years prior to patriarchy, the different cultures of the world worshiped some form of a great Mother Goddess. According to the first creation myths, there emerged from the primordial unity a triple Goddess, whose triune nature was related to the cycles of the moon as it appeared, waxed, waned, and disappeared in the sky. Great respect was accorded to the mysterious three days of lunar darkness, during which time no moon appeared, a period related to death, which was considered a part of the life cycle.

The Goddess was personified as Maiden, Mother, and Crone, sufficient unto herself to procreate. Her three aspects referred to the three biological stages of a woman's life, youth, motherhood, and old age. The Goddess as Crone ministered to the dying and was considered to have powers related to death as well as birth. Later, she was associated with a son who was also her lover or consort, and still later, in Sumerian culture, the triple deity was conceived as mother, father, and son.

As the goddess-worshiping hunter-gatherer cultures developed agriculture and with it the concepts of property and lineage, they were based on matrilineal social structures, tracing descent through the mothers, and on respect for the powers of nature, symbolized by the Goddess.

Goddess worship is based on the metaphoric associations of fertility and creativity with woman's ability to give birth and nurture her young, power implicit in her as a young woman and explicit when she becomes a mother. This power of woman, still a deeply rooted concept in the human psyche, is not limited to childbearing, nor does it end with the end of childbearing, according to the old myths. On the contrary, woman's power, associated with many creative and administrative functions, expands after menopause, as the woman's great expenditure of energy for nurturing becomes available for other uses, and her "wise blood" is no longer shed, but, in mythical terms, retained.

The legendary wisdom of old women is still detectable as a relic of older patterns in traditional stories, often appearing in the guise of witchcraft. It was used as a pretext for fierce persecution by the Christian church for centuries. We are just now, thanks to the work of many feminist writers and scholars, developing a new respect for crones in our culture, although the old stereotypes of ugly wicked witches still persist. But we are still very far from the immensely powerful concept of the death-dealing aspect of the Goddess.

In Sumerian mythology, Inanna's sister, Ereshkigal, is the queen of the underworld. Ereshkigal represents the destructive side of Inanna, which Inanna must integrate in order to stand for the whole of nature. To do so, Inanna goes down through the gates of her sister's realm, where she is stripped of her garments and royal insignia, so that she enters her sister's presence "naked and bowed low."

Then Ereshkigal fastened on Inanna the eye of death.
She spoke against her the word of wrath.
She uttered against her the eye of guilt.

She struck her.

> *Inanna was turned into a corpse,*
> *A piece of rotting meat,*
> *And was hung from a hook on the wall.*

After three days and three nights Inanna's companion and protectress, Ninshubur, acting as Inanna has instructed her to do, mourns and pleads with the gods to restore Inanna to life, and Father Enki responds to her pleas. Inanna is rescued, but she must find someone to replace her in the underworld, and she chooses her consort, Dumuzi, who, alone of all her family, is too preoccupied with his royal status to mourn her death. In choosing Dumuzi to die in her place, Inanna repeats, word for the word in the poem, what Ereshkigal had said to her, thereby showing how she has integrated her sister's power into herself:

> *Inanna fastened on Dumuzi the eye of death,*
> *She spoke against him the word of wrath.*
> *She uttered against him the cry of guilt:*
> *"Take him! Take Dumuzi away!"*

In the context of the procreative and death-dealing powers of the Goddess, a woman's sexuality was viewed as her own, unharnessed attribute, dedicated to the Goddess, whose representative she was. The concept of woman's beauty developed long after the concept of her power. Beauty, enhanced by adornment, was an offering to the Goddess. Young men, consorts of the priestess/queen/Goddess, similarly adorned their bodies, and were celebrated as beautiful in their virility, beauty reflected in still-existing carvings, sculptures, and paintings.

"I turn the male to the female. I am she who adorneth the male for the female; I am she who adorneth the female for the male."—Ishtar

The global shift to patriarchy was accompanied by the explicitly sexual subjugation of women by men, depicted in many famous stories and representations of heroic rapes. It took many centuries of terror and widespread violence to replace the cooperative cultures of goddess worshipers with the warlike cultures of patriarchy. We can only guess at most of these cultural changes by tracing changes reflected in artifacts and in recorded mythology. The *Enuma Elish,* the Babylonian epic of creation, offers the most graphic description of these changes, depicting the violent destruction of the great Mother Goddess Tiamat by her great-great-great grandson, Marduk.

Marduk savagely destroyed the dragon form of Tiamat, and from her dismembered body he created heaven and earth. Out of the blood of Tiamat's sacrificed son-lover Kingu, Marduk created the "savage-man," the new warring man of the patriarchal era being ushered in. No longer was creation to be celebrated as the procreative act of the Goddess.

Creation was to become the prerogative of the male, and for this to occur, against the grain of thousands of years of prior tradition, women's procreative power and her sexuality had to be visibly harnessed to the service of man. Her beauty, which had been a celebration and offering to the Goddess, became a decorative tribute rendered to the man whose jealous and threatening god stood behind him. To justify the subjugation of women, her beauty was viewed with profound ambivalence, as a threat, a danger, as evidence of impurity, and at the same time, as the sole justification of a woman's existence.

In our time a woman's beauty is measured, not by her internal experience, which includes feeling and movement as well as her senses of sight and smell, but externally, in visual terms and in terms of the reactions of others. In late Judeo-Christian and other patriarchal contexts, a woman's beauty was specifically associated with innocence and experience, the former admirable and desirable, the latter reprehensible but still desirable. She was judged good or bad by her obedience or disobedience, especially to men, especially in matters concerning sex, and by her ability to bear and raise children. In story after story, beauty and morality are connected.

ESTHER

In the Old Testament story of Esther, Vashti, queen to Ahasuerus, was banished when she refused to heed the king's command to appear before him and his drinking buddies so that
they could admire her beauty. She was dismissed and replaced
as queen by Esther, chosen from among the fairest young virgins of the land by the king, after he had tried out many, spending a night with each one. Esther was very obedient as well as
beautiful, but she risked the king's wrath by appearing before
him unbidden, which could have brought her death. She did
this at the command of her uncle, Mordecai, in order to save
her Jewish people from the machinations of the evil Haman,
who was plotting to have them all killed. Arrayed in her royal
robes, having fasted and prayed for days, Esther won "favor in
[Ahasuerus'] sight," and so he spared her life and honored her
beauty, which he decided was good rather than bad.

In the Old Testament story Esther invited Ahasuerus to a
great banquet, and he was influenced by her hospitality and by
the good record of her uncle Mordecai. In the later Apocryphal
version of her story, there is more emphasis on appearance.
Esther "dressed herself in splendor. . . . She was radiant with
her perfect beauty, and her face was happy as it was lovely, but
her heart was in an agony of fear." The story of Esther, like
the Apocryphal story of Judith, who slew Holofernes, intro-
duces a new idea into the Bible, the use of woman's beauty as
a tool whereby she gains an advantage over a powerful man.
This idea is widely used today by Christian and Jewish fundamentalists as evidence of the ancient vanity of women, our
inherent deceitfulness, and the well-founded mistrust of us by
men, which keeps us from positions of power and responsibility.

We never learn what Ahasuerus looked like, except, according to the Apocrypha, that he was splendid in his royal
robes, and looked first at Esther with an angry face, which
caused her to faint. We never know what Esther's experience
of her body was, or whether she enjoyed her relations with the

king, or what she thought or felt about anything at all, except
in relationship to the wishes of the men around her. For many
years I believed that this was simply the literary style of the
time, that to expect psychological complexity in a biblical character was to place modern expectations on an early period. But,
after reading the story of Inanna, I realized how the early pa-
triarchs suppressed ideas and feelings that were described in
great detail by even earlier cultures. To read about Inanna's
wrath, jealousy, stubbornness, power, majesty, and lustfulness
is to read of a woman endowed with attributes that, according
to most of written literature, are reserved for men.

Even at the time of the cuneiform writings about her, about
two thousand years before the Common Era, Inanna was a
highly unusual goddess, representing behavior no longer con-
doned for women in Sumeria. She was already a relic of earlier
practices, a figure at the border of the genders, honored in rituals by cross-dressing and hermaphroditic costumes. Her
adornment was the adornment of a goddess, signifying her immense power, her symbolic stature as Goddess of Heaven and
Earth, as well as her sensuous pleasure as a maiden. Inanna was
known to the Semites as Ishtar, a name that later became the
Hebrew equivalent of Esther. But there is a great gap between
Inanna and her distant namesake, Esther.

The change in the role and status of the heroine from the
story of Inanna to the story of Esther mirrored the extent of
the change in the position of women from early Sumeria to the
biblical period. Inanna was celebrated as powerful in each of
her aspects, as Maiden, as Mother, and as Crone. Esther was
an early heroine of the Maiden stage, honored for her obedience
and decorative beauty, her allegiance to her husband, the king,
and to her uncle.

In some ways, the position of women has changed as much
again from biblical times to the present day, especially as
women demonstrate the widest range of interests and abilities,
and as we uncover the old goddess myths, hidden until recently.
But the great majority of women in the world today are far
from enjoying the full equality with men that was supported

by law and tradition in early Sumerian culture. The role of woman as decorative support to man has persisted from Esther's time to our own. The outward position of women in our period has more in common with the story of Esther than with the story of Inanna, even while our modern longings for fulfillment bring us closer to Inanna's story.

Obedience to male-imposed conditions is still expected of many women today. But obedience is not always enough. Esther, obedient to her uncle, risks death by breaking the law of her king and husband that states she cannot approach him unless summoned. Her beauty saves her. In other instances, from biblical to modern times, the beauty of a woman leads to her downfall by inspiring lust in a man, for which she is held responsible.

In a paradoxical way, women suffer from being perceived as dangerous to men, a danger that is often more in the man's mind, in his psychological vulnerability, than it is factual. This sense of danger may go back to the man's childhood or infantile experiences of a powerful and tyrannical mother. Or it may stem from early conditioning concerning women and our sexuality. A woman's beauty is associated with her sexual appeal, and sex is viewed with suspicion by patriarchal culture.

In any case, a woman whose position depends on her beauty is vulnerable to the ravages of age and circumstance.

From the celebration of women's sexuality experienced from within, which we see in Inanna's story, there was a shift to the celebration of women's beauty as viewed and judged externally, as a measure of her sexual appeal to men. Harnessed, a woman's sexuality and procreative power are the property of the man who subdues her. This is the premise on which patriarchy is founded. It became unthinkable that a woman's beauty or her access to sexual pleasure should be determined by the woman herself. This would undermine the basis of patriarchal authority. It is on these grounds that lesbians who insist on the open expression of their sexual preference are and have been condemned as a threat to society.

Although there is considerable debate about the prehistorical period before patriarchy, the idea of goddess worship has made a great impact on contemporary thinking. What is clear from a psychological perspective is that the archetype of the triple Goddess is immensely important today, as a long-neglected aspect of humanity.

The patriarchal tendency to think in oppositional pairs has tended to obliterate the strength of the concept of three, and to set up polarity and conflict as the basic model, rather than ideas of cycles and cooperation. The yin-yang symbol of the Taoists demonstrates how principles of polarity and conflict are contained in a concept of wholeness that embraces all the parts.

Patriarchal culture has set the ideal Maiden and Mother on pedestals, devalued real-life maidens and mothers, and repudiated the Crone entirely, with disastrous results of jealousy, repression, and the denial of nurturance and the dying process as central values of humanity. What we see in most extant culture is a wealth of images of young women, including the young Madonna with her child, and very little interest in mature and older women. For four thousand years the overwhelming majority of our art, stories, and myths focus, when they do focus on a female figure, on the Maiden, not the Mother or the Crone.

We also see a fine patriarchal scorn for the desperate clinging to youthful beauty seen in many aging women. What is ironic is that most women who try so hard to remain young never really identified with their own youthful beauty.

Thinking again of Inanna as a young woman applauding herself, I think of all the attractive young women I know and have known. Not one has fully applauded herself. I believe that not one has fully believed herself to be beautiful. We aspire to a role that we never claim as our own. Because we seldom identify with our beauty in our youthful freshness, because, in fact, we often consider ourselves to be ugly, and because, above all, we fear aging, many of us continue throughout our lives to strive for a beauty we have never known.

At the same time that we strive for beauty, we devalue our sexuality, once celebrated as a sacred act, and with our sexuality, we devalue ourselves. Most devastatingly, we internalize

—— the contradictory standards of the culture and pass them on to
our daughters.

I know a woman who was told as a child by her mother
that she had better be smart because she was too ugly to attract
a husband with her looks. Rather than encouraging her daughter to develop her intelligence because this is important to all
women, the mother, herself undervalued, passed on her lack of
self-esteem to her daughter. This woman, now in her eighties,
still suffers from her mother's criticism, still feels slighted easily,
still strives to be beautiful and prove her mother wrong. She is
one of many old women stuck in the Maiden stage of life, unable to come into her own wisdom and maturity, to take on
her own powers of mothering, to grow into her own eldership
and crone consciousness.

Other women have told me how their mothers have encouraged them since early childhood to believe in themselves
as whole people, not in terms of an identity based on appearance. These are wise mothers, supporting wholeness in their
daughters in a world that constantly passes judgment on their
appearance. This support and the self-esteem it nurtures is a
priceless asset.

The main lesson to be derived from witnessing the wide
spectrum of attitudes human beings have entertained about
women and men is that almost everything about gender is open
to interpretation. Women's procreative power was once understood to be linked to all sorts of creative abilities; then, over
centuries of domination, men took on the claim of being the
creative ones, and the biological act of giving birth was devalued, along with female sexuality, which was linked with appearance and a woman's ability to please and bring honor to
a man.

This was not, I think, a matter of conspiracy, but of
widespread cultural change, demonstrating men's fierce need to
assert their own creative power in the face of long and deep-
rooted reverence for women's life-giving and life-sustaining
abilities. With patriarchy the pendulum swung to an extreme.
In the absence of written records, we don't know what preceded or precipitated this swing.

It is still commonly asserted in many cultures that women are biologically incapable of many mental and artistic activities, the same activities that it now appears women originally invented, and in which women certainly excelled, such as writing, mathematics, music, and law. Women, once the bearers of medical wisdom, traditionally healers, midwives, and comforters of the dying, were barred from the practice of modern medicine in the West until quite recently, and are still a minority among doctors and surgeons.

By repudiating the concepts of wisdom, power, and the midwifery of birth and death once associated with aging women, patriarchal culture split off these functions and relegated them to powers associated with evil, the evil of so-called black magic, of witches, of horror. Death is no longer regarded as part of the life cycle, as a stage to be honored and entered into with respect, but as something to be avoided, pushed aside. Dishonored, death stalks our civilizations with increasingly ominous portents.

If we recognized our culturally diverse background of goddess worship and the cyclical principles it celebrated, we could open more options for women and men of all living cultures. This is not a call to return to the ancient rites of the Goddess, but rather an acknowledgment of those aspects of the old religion still pertinent to us now. Respecting women's powers and abilities is still a radical action today, and thinking of the needs of the entire planet is a concept described as "New," as in "New Age." But these ideas about the interrelatedness of all living beings and the significance of the life cycle go back to the oldest creation myths.

Right now women all over the world are constrained by rigid cultural standards of beauty and gender-related behavior. Hardly any woman can sustain these standards over time without sacrificing her need to express many diverse parts of her being. Pressed to fit whatever model of femininity is currently in vogue, women spend precious time and energy straining to meet impossible ideals, ignoring our own needs for growth and development. In a world that celebrates diversity, we could identify with whatever is true in the moment, whether that is to be young, supple, beautiful, brave, quiet, timid, reserved, raging, ugly, fierce, old, middle-aged, or beyond any role, simply accepting ourselves as we are.

II: CULTURAL STANDARDS OF BEAUTY

> *My hair is short and kinky because I don't straighten it anymore. . . . My skin dark. My nose just a nose. My lips just lips. My body just any woman's body going through the changes of age. Nothing special here for nobody to love. No honey colored curly hair, no cuteness. Nothing young and fresh. My heart must be young and fresh though, it feel like it blooming blood.* —Alice Walker, *The Color Purple*

The maidenly appearance of extreme, slender youth, cast in a European style of beauty, has become a global standard by which women of all cultures and all ages are measured and found wanting. These standards, such as deep-set, wide eyes, aquiline noses, long legs, high cheekbones, and shining, swinging hair are often opposed to local or indigenous standards for beauty, such as fatness, round faces, ornamental scars, shaved heads, or elaborate sculpted or braided hairdos. All standards are often opposed to individual reality. Without support and self-acceptance, we tend to internalize standards of beauty, and judge ourselves to the point of self-hatred.

As a white woman I have felt pale and anemic in the company of dark-skinned friends, splotchy when I see women with clear, smooth complexions. I have the vague sort of light skin that was unsatisfactory to me when I was young and fades as I age, but which is suffused just now with a menopausal bloom. As a middle-aged woman with an expanding waistline I often feel burdened by my aging flesh when I see young women with lithe bodies and glowing skin. As a young woman, I compared myself to movie stars and fashion models, always to my own detriment. Many of us feel dissatisfied with our appearance and compare ourselves to others with negative results. But great and institutionalized inequities of power in the world are also associated with appearance.

Our appearance, such a strong part of female identity, is routinely held against us when we don't conform to constantly changing mainstream standards of size, shape, fitness, and ethnicity. Susan Brownmiller in *Femininity* examines culturally specific standards of clothing, hair, skin, body image, voice, movement, emotions, and attitude to show how a composite picture of Western white femininity is constructed, at the expense of women's fullest development.

Naomi Wolf in *The Beauty Myth* and Susan Faludi in *Backlash* have documented in great detail the contemporary use of such standards to keep women under control and in the marketplace as compliant consumers. Both authors show how the arbiters of fashion in industry and the mass media manipulate beauty standards according to current politics and profit margins. Naomi Wolf goes so far as to say, "The beauty myth is not about women at all. It is about men's institutions and institutional power."

But for women's own sake, we must find out how the various myths of women's beauty *are* about us as well as how they affect us, and how we assume roles that emerge from our unexamined myths. For all women, youthful beauty is a role that defies time and natural process. For many women of color, the myth of white beauty is exclusive from the outset and denies the value of black beauty, Asian beauty, the beauties of many indigenous or aboriginal peoples. Myths that emphasize women's beauty often deny women's capacity for powerful action.

The myth of the beautiful white woman has been used to drain all women of power in the world and ownership of our own sexuality. Whiteness, in women, is often associated with purity, innocence, and chastity, qualities that are assumed to be morally desirable and opposed to the "undesirable" qualities associated with sexual experience. It is by upholding this complicated myth that white women actually become a danger to others, not by being beautiful, but by representing one limiting standard of beauty, which renders all others unbeautiful.

There is an idea of the beautiful black woman, distinct from but related to ancient myths of black Goddesses, which was developed by black militants in the United States in the period following World War I, and picked up again by the black liberation movement of the sixties and seventies in the United States, attracting global attention.

In her book *When and Where I Enter,* Paula Giddings documents the emphasis on femininity, distinct from feminism, among African American women in the twenties, and also the way ideas of black beauty crossed gender lines, as "both men and women celebrated the transformation from drudge to butterfly—in all its variations." She cites the writing of black men praising "Black women from all walks of life . . . [who] likened feminine beauty to the ultimate pleasure of the senses. Complexions were compared to ginger, honey, cinnamon, dusky sunsets, and the like. No wonder that Black women wanted to fill Black men's eyes with their beauty." And, she continues, black women writers "celebrated their men's celebration of them."

However, Giddings writes, "many of the products used by Black women to enhance their beauty were skin lighteners and hair straighteners [which] drew comment on the irony of wanting to approximate White standards of beauty in such a race-conscious era."

Beauty myths, explored, exploded, reassembled, carry value as well as pain. The roles associated with the myths have strength and power if used consciously, binding force if assumed unconsciously. These roles are multilayered and complex, changing even as they are presented as eternal. Above all, the roles do not equal the women who enact them. The complexities of the roles of beauty and ugliness are related to complex issues of power in the world.

My sister has skin darker than mine. We think about our skin as a dark room, a place of shadows. We talk often about color politics and the ways racism has created an aesthetic that wounds us, a way of thinking about beauty that hurts. In the shadows of late night, we talk about the need to see darkness differently, to talk about it in a new way. In that space of shadows we long for an aesthetic of blackness—strange and oppositional.   —bell hooks, *Yearning*

COLOR

The first time I remember knowing that I was white I was six years old. My grandmother died, and our family moved from the Bronx apartment building we had shared with her to a new housing project not very far away. There were several black families in our new building, and one of them had a girl who was two years older than I. We became playmates, along with two other girls in our building, and we continued to play together for four years, at which time she mysteriously disappeared into the world of lipstick and boys, along with another older, white girlfriend.

I was very much aware that my friend and her family were black and that I and my family were white, mainly because of my parents, who never said anything to me, but who made remarks to each other in Yiddish. I knew they didn't approve of my friend and her family, and that they were unwilling to say so to me. Somehow I understood that my whiteness was important, in a way I couldn't explain. I was white because I was not black, not set apart by my skin color, as I was by being Jewish.

It did not occur to me that when I went to the movies or watched television at home I never saw images of women or girls who were black like my friend, or Asian, or obviously Jewish. Everyone I saw was more or less white, like me. But I never called myself white. In my Crayola box of crayons, there was one crayon, now labeled *peach,* which was then called *flesh.* If asked what color my skin was, I would have said flesh.

When I went to junior high school I had to take two buses from our housing project to get to school. I remember several black girls, older than I was, who rode the bus. Some of them had razors in their back pockets, and I heard them bragging about getting into fights and cutting each other. I was terrified. I did my best to be invisible, and never to get in anyone's way. But my own racism was invisible to me. There must have been tough white girls on that bus too, but I don't remember them. I just assumed that black girls were tougher than white girls, and I didn't look to see if there were any black girls who, like me, were terrified and trying to be invisible.

I don't remember ever noticing that anyone was white, only that people were black. Whiteness was not something I ever noticed. It was easy to ignore. And it was easy to project qualities onto blackness that I didn't acknowledge in myself, for instance, toughness, or the ability to dance, or sexuality. I never discussed things like this in or out of school, with friends, family, or teachers.

Discussing color now, feelings about it, thoughts, memories, and attitudes, I realize the extent of unconsciousness in my own upbringing. It seems as if to be white, in my life, has been to be unconscious of color, perhaps the greatest source of division, oppression, and bitterness in the history of the United States. Fortunately, I have had access to education about racism, in reading and in listening to people of color and conscious white people who have been willing to discuss these matters. I can't pretend that I can bridge the immense gulf between white and black created by white racism in this country. But I can raise some of the concerns I have, and report some concerns of people I know, hoping that more white women will think and talk together about our own racism and how we can change.

HATTIE BROWN:
"YOU DO NOT HAVE TO ACCEPT IT."

Hattie Brown, a retired schoolteacher, has a genius for friendship, and she has maintained many friendships over the seventy-year span of her life. I have been fortunate to be included among her circle of friends for the past seven years.

When I told Hattie I was writing a book based on my own

obsession with appearance and that most women I know are more or less obsessed with their appearance, Hattie said quietly, "But I'm not."

Hattie was the third of fifteen children and the oldest girl. Her father was a Baptist minister in Harlem. She says that although she and her siblings ranged in color from light through the rich brown of her own skin to very dark, her parents didn't encourage any focus on appearance whatsoever. Hattie says, "We were too busy trying to exist for there to be any competition about beauty.

"I realized I was not beautiful. I can recall being told by other children, 'Your face is too long,' or 'You're too skinny,' or whatever. But it never came from my family."

One of her sisters was very fair, and children at school said to Hattie, "She's not your sister, she's pretty."

"I was too ugly to be her sister. I knew I wasn't pretty, but it was all right. I had 'bad' hair—my sister had 'good' hair. My mother had very thin baby hair; that was 'good' hair. But my parents never allowed us to say that. No hair is good or bad. . . . You washed and pressed your hair. You used a heated comb and oil. You went to the beauty shop when you were a young woman, not as a child—there was no money for that! My mother braided my hair, and I braided my sister's hair."

I asked if this was an affectionate ritual, and Hattie laughed and said yes.

"I thought I was too thin, and always wished I was fatter. I didn't gain weight until I was thirty-six. Food was difficult to get when I was younger—I don't recall any of my friends talking about losing weight. I've become very weight conscious in the last ten years.

"I think about women in the church," Hattie said, laughing. "Sister Brown doesn't diet, Sister Brown eats!"

When I asked Hattie about her pretty sister she laughed again: "She got over being pretty—she got beat up every day by the other kids. She knew she was no different than anyone else."

Hattie got thoughtful. She said, "You know it goes on, how

—— you're trained to feel different because you look a certain way. You do not have to accept it, to feel part of that."

Hattie's father was light-skinned, and so were all his aunts —his mother also was very fair: "Color was a very important thing to the aunts. I believe it was because of my father's religion that color wasn't important to him. An aunt would never go out with a dark-skinned man, and she would tell you it was because the children would be dark and they would have a hard time in America. They were only a generation away from slavery."

Her calm statement put our discussion in a historical perspective. Appearance in this context is a matter of survival.

We talked about light-skinned women passing as white.

Hattie remembered: "A long time ago, I went into an upscale department store. Behind the counter was this lovely, lovely young woman. I looked at her and looked away for a second, then I looked at her and she deliberately turned away. I knew she was passing and she didn't want me to recognize her and say something. I would never have said anything. They wouldn't have hired her there if they'd known." She paused. "To live that way, in fear of discovery, is a horrible thing. It's like a curse put on you by society, making you do something that is really foreign to your nature." Another pause. "African American women started to have a better opportunity to speak about these things in the sixties, and that was important, for them and for other women. To realize that black can be beautiful. What you have is what's important."

I remembered, hearing Hattie speak, the impact I had felt when powerful, self-confident African American women, like Angela Davis and Kathleen Cleaver, proclaimed, in the sixties, that black is beautiful. The slogan, the large Afro hairdos, the clenched fists and dark glasses, and the adoption of colorful African clothing and jewelry by women and men, more than any other aspect of those politically charged years, helped me to question my own assumptions about appearance. I began to get my first glimmer of understanding that issues of life and death were associated with appearance, that despite all I had been trained to believe, ideas about appearance were not trivial, natural, or based on biology.

The saying "Black Is Beautiful" applied to women and men alike. The beauty of black men was as challenging and radical a concept for white America to handle as the beauty of black women, in the twenties and again in the sixties. "Black Is Beautiful" embraced large and small, young and old. Because of these factors, and because it was, more than anything else, an act of affirmation, black beauty did not seem to be a disempowering concept for women, as white beauty has been.

Something else Hattie said lingers with me. "What you have is what's important." What I have is my own white, middle-aged-woman's appearance, much more individually mine than the ways I looked as a child, a teenager, a young woman. What I have is an inner world that more and more reflects the real diversity of the outer world.

ANDREA: MOTHERLOVE AND BROWN SUGAR

Andrea is a twenty-year-old university student, born two generations after Hattie Brown. She grew up in Portland, Oregon, as did her mother, but her grandmother was born in Washington, D.C., and Andrea has gone east for family reunions. She dreams of going east to medical school when she finishes at university.

Andrea went to a Catholic elementary school and a Catholic girls' high school, where, she says, the pressure to be well dressed, to wear the right clothes—penny loafers, polo shirts, and so on—was intense. Other girls came from wealthy families and got cars for their sixteenth birthdays; her family is middle-class and raised her to understand that nothing comes easy. When I ask if color was an issue in her high school Andrea says no, even though there were only about twenty African American girls out of four hundred in the school, and fewer Asian Americans. She thinks it is worse now, and says she hears stories of racial slurs in the school, also at the university.

Andrea says she has always felt more comfortable with

other African Americans and at school often sought them out at lunch and recess, although she has many friends who are white. She says white people have often made assumptions about her based on her skin color: that she comes from a poor family, that she lives in a bad neighborhood, that she won't amount to much.

I ask Andrea about her self-image as a child. She says she felt bad about her dark skin and nappy hair because of television images and because of the attitude of other African American children that dark skin was ugly, or less attractive than light skin, but she also says that her mother and grandmother worked hard to help her believe in her own value and beauty.

Her mother called Andrea "brown sugar," and told her that what she saw on television wasn't true, that beauty wasn't a matter of blond hair and blue eyes. Beauty and ugliness, Andrea's mother taught her, were a matter of attitude. Both her mother and her grandmother gave her only beautiful dark dolls.

When I ask Andrea what her best features are, she hesitates, laughs, then says she gets a lot of compliments on her eyes. She doesn't mention her clear, smooth skin, but when I do she says yes, she gets compliments on her skin too. Asked if there's anything she would change, she says, "I'd like fuller lips, black people's lips," and she'd like to lose a few pounds. But she also tells me that her father's eight sisters and her grandmother are all full-figured women, and that nobody worries about that or tries to change it. They all love to eat, and they have family feasts, which everyone enjoys. She and her mother, who is only thirty-seven, joke about working out and losing weight, but the joking is light and easy.

When Andrea was in high school she worried a lot about her weight. In the summer before her senior year she hardly ate at all, until her mother got worried and encouraged her to exercise more. Her mother also spent more time with Andrea, helping her gradually get back to normal eating. Andrea's story reminds me of stories I heard when I lived in Hawaii. There young women from native Hawaiian and other Polynesian families often develop eating disorders in response to the conflict between their family standards of size (huge by comparison to Europeans, Americans, and Asians) and the standards they see on television, in popular culture, and among high school peers.

Andrea says that African American men compliment her on her looks, and tell her, "Dark sisters are more beautiful," and she dimples as she tells me this. I think I've never met a young woman so confident and easy about her own self-image, and at the same time thoughtful about issues relating to appearance. I imagine that this confidence and clarity are due to her wise and loving upbringing, but also to the necessity of developing her own thoughts in situations that are racist and threatening to her.

Asked what she values in people's appearance now, Andrea says she likes dark-brown skin and short hair, large, tall men, and women of all sizes. She says her liking for short hair is probably a reaction to her childhood, when images of light-skinned girls with long hair were held up as images of beauty in the media, and she worried about her own appearance. She wears very little makeup, just lipstick and sometimes eye makeup, but she gets regular perms to straighten her hair. Andrea is not sure why she doesn't just wear her hair short and natural. She says that wearing it long and natural is too much trouble—she remembers long hours as a child sitting and watching a video while her mother patiently braided her hair.

I realize that of all the women I've spoken with about appearance, Andrea has the most positive relationship with her family, especially her mother. This relationship has buffered her and given her strong tools to deal with the racist and stereotyped attitudes that are everywhere around her.

Racial prejudice is compounded by internalized oppression, and also by the widespread and cross-cultural assumption that a woman's appearance defines her as a human being. Ironically, with something like poetic justice, women discriminated against because of ethnic appearance often develop an inner strength that is not dependent on their appearance, provided they are supported in their early development by family and/ or community.

Many of the stories I have heard from women about appearance go back to painful childhood experiences. My friend from Vietnam tells me that she was teased unmercifully as a child by other Vietnamese children because they said she had Chinese eyes. One African American woman tells me she was teased for being lighter than the rest of her family, and another African American woman tells of being taunted for being so dark-skinned. These racist taunts rest on top of the universal assumption that women and girls ought to be beautiful, or at least attractive, and they are somehow diminished if they don't match the standards of appearance held up by their culture.

There is a deep structure of history and metaphor underlying black-white relations in the United States. Asians, Hispanics, Native Americans, other indigenous peoples, all have their own mythologies of gender relations and women's appearance. There is a multiplicity of issues relating to appearance, and in every instance women and men are limited by adhering to any set of standards that says, "You are not acceptable as you are."

CHICKENS AND PEACOCKS

Jackie Phan, forty-five, a Vietnamese realtor, mother and grandmother, married to a white American man, does not want to be like traditional Vietnamese women, who, she says, "stay at home and let their appearance go." Implicit in her words is the idea that traditional women lose their independence and power when they lose their appearance. Paraphrasing an old Vietnamese saying, she tells me, "You might be a chicken, but you think of yourself as a peacock."

Jackie is a woman of three cultures, her own traditional Vietnamese culture, the white American culture of her husband, and the in-between culture of the transplanted Vietnamese, which is found in a sizable community in Portland. Moving among these cultures, Jackie must deal with several different roles for women her age. A "professional" appearance is a key to her sense of self-esteem and independence, as it is for many women.

When I say I think she is a very beautiful woman, Jackie tells me she doesn't think so. She agrees that women don't usually identify with being beautiful, and says it's a good thing, that we wouldn't try so hard to look good if we believed in our own beauty.

Jackie's mother Dao Thi Mai, a sixty-nine-year-old Vietnamese woman, lives in Saigon. When she visited her daughter in Newburg, a small town outside of Portland, I spoke with both women. I asked Mai, who was raised in a Christian family and married into a family where the children were educated in Europe, if she ever compared herself with European women. She nodded vigorously. A small, fine-boned woman who has a heart-shaped face, she admires European women, especially the French, and white Americans, for our eyes, for the shapes of our noses, and for our hair, all features she sees as outward signs of our sweet, honest, and straightforward natures.

Mai told me the story of two famous Vietnamese women, sisters, who took their husbands' places in battle against the Chinese several hundred years ago. Their names were Trung Trac and Trung Nhi. These women rode elephants into battle, and fought courageously. When the Chinese realized they could not win, they decided to humiliate the sisters by pulling down their pants. The sisters, shamed, committed suicide by jumping into the river.

This Vietnamese story of the warrior sisters has common ground with the Chinese story of Sun Pu-erh, warned by her teacher that men would attempt to molest her, and that, rather than be shamed, she would kill herself.

Mai said if she were to choose actresses to play the roles of these women she would choose women whose eyes are dark as coal, who have healthy pink complexions, oval faces, long eyebrows and eyelashes, and who are tall (five feet four to five six). She said their faces should show kindness and determination, and that their beauty would show from the inside out. This idea of linking external beauty with internal worth was repeated several times by Mai.

When I left Jackie's house, both she and her mother complimented me on my appearance. At home, I glanced in the hall mirror. For an instant, I saw what Mai and Jackie saw, a white American woman with light, fine hair and round eyes. I saw myself through their eyes—youthful, good-looking, naïve. Unconscious imperial glamour. Later, in another mirror, I saw my usual self, plump, wrinkled, matronly. The cultural filter was gone; there was no glamour. I hold on to these contradictory perceptions of myself, understanding that I am, to many, an ordinary middle-aged woman, and that to many others I represent a cultural ideal that is alluring, painful, and oppressive.

The only way I can sustain these contradictions is by realizing that they aren't just personal, and also by remembering that in some eyes, those of my husband, for example, I am attractive, sexually appealing, and special. Sometimes I can simply forget my appearance entirely, and concentrate instead on my own feelings and perceptions, but that is moving ahead to another chapter. Here I am still concerned with the range and global narrowing of cultural standards of beauty.

MIXED MESSAGES

Anuradha Deb, a psychologist, lives in Bombay with her husband and children. On a visit to Portland she spoke with me about her experience of women's appearance issues in India. In India as in Vietnam there is an ancient and complex culture, in which the role of women is carefully defined and circumscribed by centuries of patriarchal tradition. In these cultures, women are expected to be traditionally beautiful or at least attractive in order to be married, and marriage is enormously important for women. It is their destiny in life. An unmarried woman is an economic liability to her family, a millstone. If a woman is considered too ugly to be married, she is somehow blamed for her ugliness. It is a problem for which she is held responsible, and for which she pays a huge price.

These standards lay heavy burdens on women in cultures that do not value women very much at all, where the birth of a son is celebrated but the birth of a daughter is mourned, where, in recent years, ultrasonic tests to determine the sex of a fetus have led to routine abortions of females. Most women are not educated and not prepared to live independent single lives.

In India, the Crone is traditionally the most venerated of the ages of women. Once an Indian woman is safely married, and once she has demonstrated her ability to bear and raise children, she is expected to gain weight and to let her appearance go a bit, to look matronly, as befits her role. Having made the transition from maiden to mother, especially the mother of sons, an Indian woman will gain respect as she ages. Old women, provided they remain clear-minded, are consulted and treated with deference by younger women, but, except for the "elder" of the family, women remain subservient to men. Often the "elder" is the oldest woman in a family, the widow of the patriarch, and she is invested with all decision-making in important matters, both economic and social.

This is the traditional background against which the dramas of colonization and modern electronic imperialism are played out. Where the traditional structures remain in place, the traditional roles continue. Where television and Western products are available, there is a difficult and fascinating blurring of roles. In Anuradha's country of eight hundred million, perhaps twenty-five thousand have access to MTV, the channel with the biggest influence, especially on young people. From MTV, the culture of jeans and androgyny spreads, slowly in India, but inevitably. Alongside MTV there is the influence of fashion magazines, found on every newsstand, and Western movies, available alongside the huge output of the Indian film industry.

The messages are mixed. Growing up as part of an educated, Westernized, upper-middle-class intelligentsia, Anuradha and her Indian girlfriends considered the ever-present ideal of white European beauty as something unattainable, and therefore, she says, "not aspired to—but Western fashions, yes!" They judged themselves and each other by local standards of beauty, those prevailing in West Bengal, where Anuradha grew up, a part of India that remains steeped in tradition. Among themselves, as among the Vietnamese, and among many African Americans, the young Bengali women had a ranking system for standards of beauty based on skin color, and in that system fairness, lightness of skin, ranked highest.

Anuradha pointed out to me that light-skinned Indians are descended from the invading Aryan and Mongoloid peoples, and are a minority in India. The majority are descended from the indigenous Dravidian race, and are dark-skinned. She says, "The minority has become the oppressor and the majority of dark-skinned people are oppressed. So here is an example of how the mainstream need not be a majority so far as beauty standards are concerned in this country!"

MIXED RACE AND "PASSING"

People of mixed race are often treated as if they belong nowhere, treatment based on assumptions about appearance. A high school principal in Alabama, known for his racist views, was suspended without pay but not fired by a predominantly white school board for publicly saying to a student of mixed race: "Your mom and dad made a mistake, having you as a mixed child." His comment ignored the appalling history of slavery, when thousands of black women were impregnated by their white masters.

A young woman who was raised by her African American mother in a black community says proudly that she is a "black woman who has white skin and freckles." By describing herself in this way she is making clear the cultural definition of color, redefining categories. Racism obliterates the sensory-grounded aspects of appearance and replaces these with stereotyped attitudes, filters that distort and change the visible world. In related but different ways, sexism also views women through distorting filters, establishing arbitrary standards to which no woman can conform over time.

While most of us are deeply concerned about issues of appearance, many women assume these concerns are entirely personal, governed by personal inadequacies. The pressure to pass, as a feminine woman, as white or gentile or heterosexual, creates heightened awareness of the importance of appearance. Those who successfully "pass" may acquire some detachment about appearance as a measure of inner value. When I identify myself as an artist manipulating my appearance with a clear sense of my own options, I feel more confident about my own identity than I do as a woman struggling to match some standard I have not set, believing that the standard is correct and that I am in need of correction.

How is passing different from changing roles? An important question is, why would someone want to pass as something or someone else? Is power or privilege involved? Is it dangerous to be open about your background or your sexuality? Does the change in roles represent growth or camouflage?

A story recently told to me by a woman of mixed race illustrates some of the confused messages given to women about appearance. It is a common assumption that children of racially mixed couples are often very attractive. Dark-skinned women have told me of being encouraged by family and friends to marry lighter-skinned men, so that they will have "pretty" children.

Chris Moyers's mother was a Creole from Louisiana, a woman of French and African descent, and Chris's father was of European Jewish descent, from a family that converted to the Baptist faith and assimilated into white America. Chris was raised as a white Christian woman, but discovered what she calls, with a note of irony, "horrible ethnicity secrets in [her] family." She was thirty when she learned of her mother's Louisiana French Creole background, a secret her mother had guarded fiercely until then. Chris's grandmother and mother were "legally black," with, Chris thinks, some Native American heritage.

When Chris asked why her mother had never told about her ancestry, her mother responded, "Look what happened when you said you were French." At the age of six Chris had told her friends in Texas that she was French, and "they wouldn't speak to me for three weeks. I asked myself, what would they do if I were black?"

When Chris was a child she was perceived as being really pretty, and this offended her father. She remembers his saying, "I don't want her to get along on her looks alone." Chris says that he claimed this was his dislike of superficial vanity, but "what he really meant was, Someday she's going to find out that she's black. He realized that, if I stayed in that part of Texas, the opportunity to do something with my life was extremely limited." So he encouraged her to go as far as she could with her education and career, which she did, eventually obtaining her Ph.D. in sociobiology.

One of several paradoxes in this story is the automatic assumption that blackness is not helpful to a woman, that the "disadvantage" of being black outweighs the "advantage" of being pretty. Another is the assumption that a pretty white girl might be and often is encouraged to "get along on her looks alone," encouragement that often leads to great disillusion when she ages and loses her youthful beauty. No woman, white or black, wins in this racist and sexist dilemma, but perhaps the greater strength is developed by the young woman who is encouraged by a supportive adult to develop her skills and intelligence.

Would Chris's father have encouraged her to stay at home, forgo her education, marry and raise children, if she had not been of mixed racial background?

As a teenager, Chris developed a severe case of acne, "the kind that tunnels under your skin." Did she think she was ugly? "If I had looked at myself in a mirror I would have thought, Wow, that's ugly stuff on my face. But I didn't identify with it. It wasn't important." At the age of twenty-two, in order to deal with her painful oozing scars, she had plastic surgery. The surgeon said to her, "You look so self-assured and so attractive that even I had to look carefully before I saw the scars." Chris replied, "That's because I've practiced a lot. I *feel* self-assured and attractive." She says she realized early on that self-consciousness about appearance was the problem, rather than appearance itself.

Chris thinks that "this particular culture we're living in is so obsessed with appearance that it's like an illness." Black women, she says, are much more obsessed with hair than with size: "Many black women have fatness as a standard of beauty, and they are more influenced by their social milieus than by television." But hair is another matter. "Black women will do incredible things to get their hair to where it ought to be. It never is where it ought to be."

Chris discounts the importance of outward beauty, emphasizing attitude and relationship skills instead. But many women feel that if only they were seen as beautiful their lives would somehow improve. In the biography of Josephine Baker written by her adopted son, Jean-Claude Baker, he tells of how, even as the toast of Paris, Baker still took Clorox baths in order to lighten her skin. Paula Giddings writes that skin-bleaching products were common in the twenties, and cites a report in *Half-Century* magazine of a black woman who died from using bleach on her skin.

Many women and some men undergo incredible pain and expense in order to achieve ethnic and gender-biased standards. They are encouraged and exploited in this effort by cosmetic surgeons, who "correct" Asian eyelids, change Jewish or African noses, change any facial feature that doesn't conform to the current ideal, extract body fat, change breast shape and size, alter almost any aspect of the face or body.

The dangers of such operations, and their widespread promotion by the surgical industry, are increasingly well documented, along with the insistence of people, mainly women, on continuing to risk their health, even their lives, to have their appearance altered. The question that remains after the operation is, What about the role? Now that you match the standard to which you've aspired, what does that mean for you? Is your new role one that you can neither fully identify as your own nor wholly relinquish? If you do identify with the role, what do you gain, and what do you lose?

Orlan, a performance artist from Paris, has been focusing attention on the process of surgical alteration of a woman's body, using her own body as the material for a series of "surgical interventions" performed in front of video cameras. About to appear at a conference on feminist activism and art in San Francisco, Orlan told an interviewer that "the skin is deceptive. One is never what one is. You can have the skin of a crocodile and actually be a small dog. You could have the skin of an angel and actually be a jackal." I am fascinated and repulsed by her story. But above all I am struck by the courageous, outrageously personal statement she is making about appearance and reality, the mysterious and irrational dance between these concepts that makes up our agreed-upon definitions of what is and how we perceive it.

Every aspect of appearance is filled with potential and shifting meaning, but most often, instead of looking at aspects of appearance as useful information, we tend to judge according to moral categories. Looking through stereotypical spectacles, we assign this person to the role of innocent beauty, that one to the role of sinister beauty, another to the role of well-meaning ugliness, and yet another to the role of malevolent ugliness. And so on. We do the same thing to ourselves. We suffer from the delusions that these assigned roles and our interpretations of them are permanent and immutable, and that they reflect something intrinsic and equally unchanging about the persons assigned to the roles. The roles are based on standards of appearance that differ from one culture to another, but are imagined to be universal.

THE WODAABE

They devote enormous care to their appearance for the Geerewol [festival], and the young men in particular spend hours decorating themselves in front of small hand mirrors. The Wodaabe believe that they have been given the greatest beauty on Earth. It is of the utmost importance for a woman to give birth to a beautiful child; sometimes, if a man is not good-looking, he will allow his wife to sleep with a more handsome man in order to gain an attractive child. Mothers gently stretch the limbs of their young babies and

*press their noses between thumb and forefinger to lengthen
them and make them thinner. Ugliness and physical
deformities will bring suffering to the person concerned,
though these can be offset by skills in singing, story-telling
or poetry; personal charm and charisma, revealed in
dancing, will do more than anything to increase a person's
popularity.*
>   —Angela Fisher, *Africa Adorned*

In her major work on African styles of ornamentation, from
face and body paint, hair sculpture and ornaments, to clothing,
veils, and jewelry, Angela Fisher describes the belief systems
and social customs that stand behind the widely different ornamental practices she has recorded in text and photographs.
Her work shows that, far from being universal, standards of
beauty vary widely on one diverse continent, and the significance of appearance also varies widely. *Africa Adorned* offers a
visual and textual document of some very different ways in
which appearance reflects and affects gender relations and
power structures.

Various African tribes are striking exceptions to the supposedly "natural" rule of patriarchy. Among the West African
Wodaabe, at an annual festival, young men dance and preen for
hours in their ochre makeup and elaborate ensembles, rolling
their eyes and grimacing to show off their features so that the
young women, also elaborately attired, will choose them as sexual partners. Men of the Tuareg desert people are veiled from
puberty and the women go unveiled. Women and young girls
of the Berbers of North Africa paint their faces at the annual
festival where they may seek a mate, and, if it is a second
or third marriage, they may consummate the marriage immediately.

According to Fisher, these particular tribes exhibit either an
egalitarian sense of partnership or a patriarchal structure within
which women have an unusual degree of freedom. (She fails to
mention that they also do most of the heavy work.) Some of
these tribes whose women have considerable freedom live in

—— areas alongside Muslims, whose women are veiled and live under the restrictions of purdah.

In some tribes, ornamentation, especially jewelry, is worn as protection against the evil eye, as well as a sign of status. What is this evil eye but a personification of the power of jealousy, the critical gaze of one who looks, judges, and condemns?

The Wodaabe, an egalitarian, nomadic tribe, who believe that work other than caring for their herds is demeaning and limits their freedom, lavish time and expenditure on decorating themselves for the annual Geerewol festival, geared to seduction and erotic partnership. The Wodaabe are especially whimsical in their creative ornamentation, and now incorporate plastic trinkets, sunglasses, even toy guns from the marketplace into their traditional costumes.

Their lifestyle is based on a belief system that many of us in more technologically oriented cultures would love to bring into our own work-haunted lives. (This may account for the popularity of the Wodaabe as a subject for television documentaries.) When even the pursuit of beauty has become a compulsion to achieve, the leisurely ornamentation of sexually expressive youth is a reminder of how values change according to age and culture, and how pleasure, like beauty, is a rare and fleeting value.

The issue of "beauty" and "ugliness" is not frivolous. I think of two white women who are in their sixties. One, a lesbian psychologist from a working-class, radical home, has written about the compelling urge she felt to have a facelift —until she became aware that what she was dealing with was not her own ugliness but the ugly projections of others, and became instead an activist against ageism. The other, a former airplane pilot and now a powerful photographer, has made a series of self-portraits that document, mercilessly, the bruises and scars of her own facelift. . . . These are creative, independent, gutsy women, and they heard the message of society quite accurately: the pain of an operation for passing is less than the pain of enduring other people's withdrawal.
—Cynthia Rich

AGE

My own relationship with beauty has changed as I have grown older. The brief time in my twenties when I was considered beautiful was also one of the most difficult, lonely times in my life. At fifty, I notice that women I don't know seem friendlier and more open to me than they did when I was younger, or is it that I'm more open? I'm nearly invisible to many men now, and that experience carries both relief and pain, the relief of freedom from critical standards, the pain of exclusion based on those same standards. One of the curious attributes of roles such as beauty and ugliness is that the more we experience these roles consciously, rather than sliding into them, the more we explore them with awareness, the more we are inclined to go beyond them. As we experience a sense of being trapped in roles and then forced to change, we are able to understand and transcend the roles.

No role is more volatile and subject to change than that of youth. When we think of beauty in terms of age or race, the problems that arise have a tendency to blow apart the carefully created role of beauty. For how can a woman be eternally and universally beautiful? And yet, if beauty is a woman's primary concern, what is she to do once her beauty fades?

I look at my own aging image in my mirror, and I see the tracks of time. How exciting! How disturbing! What a challenge to integrate what I see with what I feel and experience. As a young woman I constantly worried about making myself more beautiful. As an older woman I am realizing in my own body what I feared as a child, that youthful beauty does slip away, but the change is not what I feared. Something is fading, and something else is emerging.

When I was about six, I remember looking at the wrinkled body of my grandmother in the bathtub, and at my own smooth young skin. I thought, Right now I'm perfect. But it won't last. And I was afraid, because I had no idea of what I would be like when I got old.

At fifty I am still afraid. I am afraid, not of wrinkles, but of pain, loneliness, and death. I still don't know what I will be like when I get old. At my best I incorporate a wide range of living, able to think of myself as young and old simultaneously. My body responds with pleasure to my t'ai chi exercises, to lovemaking, to walking and bicycling and swimming; and I am happier in my rounder, more substantial body than I have been since early childhood. I have beautiful days and ugly days, and most days in between. Having lived five decades, I have seen a few fashions and attitudes come and go, enough to know that these things pass and return. Death is more real to me now, and it inspires me to live life more fully. And I am still afraid.

An inner conflict rages, between the pleasures I take in food, in rest, in the feeling of my body, and the images I see in films and on TV and, increasingly, on the streets of my own neighborhood—an impossible pastiche of poverty, horror, and glamour, children starving, new cars, systematic and random violence, women gloating over spotless laundry, fast food, new diets, genocide.

I am tormented by the disorder of the planet and by the terrible voice of my friend's talking scale, which announces unforgivingly that I have gained twenty pounds in three years. How can I compare these two sources of misery? To compound the situation, my inner critic castigates me for being frivolous. But the comparison persists. My weight seems unforgivable in the face of global starvation. My concern with it is even worse.

My only solution is to acknowledge the connection between painful world issues and my inner conflicts. One part of me is horrified by the weight I've gained, by the spreading white in my hair, by my wrinkles and sags. Another part loves to eat, to sleep, to walk majestically and slowly down the street, a large older woman in the impressive prime of life. Still another part dreams of leaping and running and being as elastic as the Olympic stars I watch on television. And a needy, childlike part can't bear to be deprived of a single treat, craves sweets and pastries and afternoon naps. These inner parts are at war with each other, and will keep my attention turned inward until I acknowledge their demands.

My figure is entirely unfashionable, and yet an inner voice comments, "How wonderful you look! You have become substantial!" One part of me sees ugly fat and cellulite. Another part sees a goddess in my mirror.

Nowadays, it is primarily in movement, when I am practicing t'ai chi, or working as a therapist with a client, that I sense the appearance of my body as mine, as related to my inmost self. I am also developing an inner body sense, a feeling of how my body is in the moment, when I am alone, waking in the morning, sitting at my desk, or, more subtly, when I am with other people, noticing how my body reacts to our interchanges. Beauty changes shape as my experience takes on more dimensions.

One enormous change for me, which has come about gradually through my forties, is the change from being one who is looked at to being one who looks at others. Most of the time now I am responded to in terms of my actions and speech, but hardly ever in terms of my appearance. When others do respond to my appearance, I realize with some shock that I'm often seen as a mother figure.

Women my own age and some older women share glances of recognition, which I find entirely pleasurable. Men my age or older seldom seem to see me at all, and this is primarily, but not always, a relief. I understand that my new invisibility has great potential for my spiritual development, but I'm not entirely grateful for it.

It is one thing to claim invisibility as a privilege, to walk unchallenged down the streets of my neighborhood or through the aisles of my grocery store, protected from sexual harassment by my comfortable, middle-aged appearance. It is quite another to have invisibility settled upon me as a judgment, because I am no longer considered attractive, youthful, and therefore important.

There is a paradox here, for the youthful feminine appearance that is used to put women down as trivial and not to be

taken seriously is, at the same time, a prerequisite for women
in many professions if we are to be taken seriously. For women
in business and government, there is a code of acceptable dress
which, among other things, assumes a relatively slim and youthful appearance.

Youth is associated with bodily and mental fitness and
vigor, with assertiveness and determination. A woman who
dresses according to conventional standards and manages to
look fit, young and feminine, may bypass old male fears of
powerful, therefore unfeminine, women. The ancient association of old women with power lurks behind these apparently
businesslike constraints on our appearance.

For a woman used to being regarded first of all in terms of
appearance to find this regard gradually diminishing is an immense experience, certainly comparable and often related to the
menopause in terms of overall life change.

TIME AND BEAUTY

One of my favorite movie stars was Audrey Hepburn. I am
still fascinated by her image—fine-boned, with expressive,
deep-set eyes, graceful, thin, representing for me beauty with a
mesmerizing hint of ugliness. Her image defined elegance for
me—I had no idea that she suffered from an eating disorder.
Age, or rather, ageism brought Audrey Hepburn's movie career
to a premature end, as it did the careers of many other
women—Garbo, Pickford, Crawford, Bergman, Gish. A few
returned to the screen as "character" actresses, and Bette Davis
and Lillian Gish stunned the moviegoing world and suggested
what it had lost over the years when, in their advanced old age,
they costarred in *Whales in August*.

The roles offered Hepburn at forty were no longer of the
quality of those she had enjoyed as a young woman in *Breakfast at Tiffany's, Roman Holiday,* and *Funny Face,* movies in
which she often played an ingenue role opposite a much older
man, and was praised for her mature self-confidence. Older
male stars, whose sex appeal is said to long outlast that of

women, continued to get juicy roles. But what was Audrey Hepburn to do?

She chose to live out her rather short older life as a philanthropist, working for UNICEF to help starving children in India and Africa. Her photographed image, fundraising with celebrities, working directly with children, giving interviews to the media, is of a strikingly attractive older woman, who retained her elegant bone structure and expressive eyes along with her slimness and grace. Her story says a great deal about women's beauty in our culture, about Hollywood and the roles it has offered and not offered women, roles based on the centrality of youthful white beauty.

It is not a new thing to celebrate the beauty of old women as a measure of our own aesthetic sensitivity or out of traditional respect. Neither is it new to use the appearance of old women as a metaphor for ugliness and even evil, like the image of the wicked witch. What is unusual is to regard an old woman on her own terms, as an individual, to inquire about her experience, rather than making assumptions based on her appearance.

My friend Beatrice asked me once if I knew her age. "You're ninety-three, I believe" was my slightly startled reply. "I never speak of it," she said. "If people knew how old I am, they'd never allow me to live alone as I do, and that would be unbearable for me."

Suddenly the much-ridiculed "vanity" of older women who lie about their age took on another meaning. I remembered that my grandmother, my father's mother, who lived well into her nineties, dyed her hair until it fell out and then wore a wig and lots of makeup, always lied about her age, and, to the dismay of my parents, entertained male visitors in her third-floor walkup. She in her cluttered, dark apartment in the Bronx and Beatrice in her elegant Georgian flat in Edinburgh were as different as two women could be, with nearly two centuries of living to separate them. But their fears were the same.

SEEMA: "THERE IS NO NORM"

Seema Weatherwax is in her late eighties, a photographer who knew many great photographers and was photographed by them. Looking at the portraits of her as a young woman, I am struck by her great beauty, a beauty that still shines for me in her eyes and her spirit. But when I speak of this to her she is silent a moment. Then she says, "That photograph is beautiful. But I was not beautiful. I was a good-looking young woman, and I had my days." I ask if she was told she was beautiful and she says, "Well, yes, but that was mostly by men who had other things in mind." She laughs, referring to several meaningful and passionate involvements with men who were her friends and colleagues. For this elder woman, beauty is a complex issue of aesthetics, feelings, sexuality, all things she has accepted as less a part of her life now than they once were. She is a vital woman, and her life is full and rewarding. And different, very different from youth and middle age.

Seema has been a political activist for most of her adult life, a stance she came by early. When she was six, her bookstore-owner father attempted to emigrate with his Jewish family from Tsarist Russia. They were apprehended at the border and thrown in prison. Eventually her father was able to bribe their way out, and the family went to England legally. Seema and her sisters grew up in a home where artists and intellectuals from all over Europe met. Her father died when she was thirteen, and she, her mother, and her two sisters immigrated to Boston. As a young woman Seema became involved with left-wing activists of all races and ethnic backgrounds. She also learned photographic lab techniques, which were part of her working life for forty-five years. She became aware of her own racism, then, especially of her unconscious prejudice against Asians, which she had picked up from stereotyped Chinese characters in movies and from popular attitudes in England.

During the Depression, Seema and her sister Tamara traveled across the United States to California. They settled in Los Angeles, and Seema, a high-spirited young woman, had many adventures, going to Tahiti and setting up a photo studio there, working for four years in Yosemite as Ansel Adams's master printer and assistant, finally meeting and marrying Jack Weatherwax, an American of Revolutionary descent, who shared her philosophy and lifestyle, and who devoted much of his last twenty years to writing for and about African Americans. Just before Jack's death they moved up to Santa Cruz, where Seema lives now.

In Santa Cruz, Seema joined the Women's International League for Peace and Freedom and the NAACP, becoming an active member of their board of directors. Having spent a great deal of her life struggling against prejudice based on class and race, Seema says it is difficult for her to speak in general about appearance, because she thinks in terms of people she knows, and "if you know people, your attitude is different."

Since she has grown old, she says, "There's something different about beauty that I'm more aware of than I used to be. Something about character coming through. I used to look at a perfect mouth, a perfect nose, etc. But now something else comes through. I also look at older people differently—I see more beauty in older people than I did when I was younger."

Musing about stereotypes of beauty, she says, "Everywhere I go there are a great number of people who don't know I'm Jewish. I think it's because they're ignorant or not observant. I have brown eyes, curly hair, a trace of olive in my skin. As for my nose—" she laughs—"I fell on it when I was a kid! But I look like a Jew!" Why don't people think she is Jewish? "I think it's because I learned Oxford English when I was a kid in school. And the stereotype does not include this."

At eighty-eight, Seema lives in a senior retirement apartment in Santa Cruz. "We have a beauty shop in this place— the young woman who runs it has one way of cutting hair for old people—short, with a bit of a curl. From behind I look like twenty other women I know. I got tired of being institutionalized by my hair! So I've started to grow it out."

I ask if she feels freer about her appearance now? She says, "Yes. I've accepted the fact that I have a wattle under my chin.

A young child I know asked me, What is that? Until then I had ignored it, but when she asked me so nicely, I could accept it. I'm not happy with my head—I have bald spots from the time when my husband died and I had so much stress in my life. My hair fell out and it hasn't grown back. I still try to look nice—I use lipstick, try to look as decent as I can. I'm still aware of clothes—that hasn't changed since I was young. But don't use me for a norm," she warns. "There is no norm."

Betty Friedan, whose book *The Fountain of Age* is helping to change popular ideas about aging, is optimistic about older women's freedom from concern about appearance, and she refers to a general sense of "ease and comfort with one's self, which leads to new, sometimes startling frankness, and lessened conformity to the expectations and sanctions of others: the older woman becomes a 'truthteller.' "

As a woman in midlife, I am very aware of the reality of the aging process, in a way I was not in my earlier years. I also see a great difference between my experience and the experience of much older women. Cynthia Rich sets out to delineate this difference in her essay "Ageism and the Politics of Beauty":

> If you are a younger woman, try to imagine what everything in society tells you not to imagine: that you are a woman in your seventies, eighties, nineties, or older, and yet you are still you. Even your body is yours. It is not, however, in the language of the embalmers, "well-preserved," and though the male world gives you troubles for it, you like it that way. Apart from those troubles, you find sometimes a mysterious integrity, a deep connection to life, that comes to you from having belonged to a body that has been large and small, thin and fat, with breasts and hips of many different sizes and shapes, and skin of different textures.

Rich's celebration of the old woman's body is rare, and written in the context of widespread insults against old women. Given the facts that old women and children are the poorest people in the world, that their lives are in the greatest danger and held in the least value, and that there is a widespread tendency to trivialize and jeer at old women, the defensive reaction of women to seek eternal youth, and the sexualization of very young children all form a serious beauty-related and problematic pattern rooted in our cultural mythology.

The relationship of power issues to cultural standards of beauty becomes clear when we look closely at standards based on skin color and age, and the same is true of size, perhaps the aspect of appearance that has been most subject to change over the centuries.

WEIGHT

JUSTINE: SIZE AND POWER

Justine Toms gained weight in order to feel powerful. She grew up in a white family that prided itself on the beauty of its women. At fifty, Justine is a large woman, shaped like an ancient Goddess statue. She wears striking colors and patterns and large effective jewelry. Her paternal grandmother, Chickie, also loved clothes and jewelry. "She mixed good jewelry with junk," Justine says, extending her hands as if to display many rings, "and no one ever knew the junk from the good stuff."

Justine has a photo of her grandmother's women's group of the thirties, bare-breasted, wearing feathers in their hair. She found this photo after taking a similar photo of her own women's group of the 1980s, also bare-breasted, similarly adorned.

Justine's mother was a Southern beauty queen, Miss Montgomery from Alabama. After her death Justine found a note her mother had written when Justine was a child: "I don't know if Justine will be beautiful or not—sometimes she is beautiful and sometimes she's not." In her mother's mind, says Justine, women's power was dependent on their ability to attract men, an ability that depended on beauty.

In order to identify herself as a powerful adult, Justine has had to contend with her loving maternal upbringing, aimed toward a traditional role for her as wife and mother, an upbringing that she describes as a mountain she has had to climb. The mountain, like the concept of being a beautiful woman, is at once a challenge and an obstacle. It may become part of an internal landscape, or it may become a symbol for a woman's whole self.

Justine married young and gained a lot of weight during her pregnancy, weight that she did not entirely lose after she gave birth. Instead, she continued to gain weight. One day some years ago, after dieting to lose weight, she caught a glimpse of her smaller self unexpectedly in a mirror. Looking sideways at her image, she heard an inner voice of warning, "How will you be powerful now?" She immediately stopped dieting and regained the weight she had lost.

It was then that Justine began meeting with other women and learning more about what she calls "the instinctual feminine." This mysterious quality has to do with cycles, she believes, and it is accessible to both women and men, but usually is easier for women to access because of our acquaintance with menstrual cycles and childbirth. Justine believes that this quality has acted as a glue for her work as a radio producer, and she experiences it as "belly wisdom." "I feel something down low first—I don't know what it is, and that's okay."

It is precisely her largeness that Justine understands to be connected with her difficult ascension to power in the world: she is an internationally known radio producer. She says, "I've gotten to a place in my life where, if I could, I wouldn't choose anything to be different, because then I wouldn't be here feeling what I do right now."

Her body, she believes, has expanded to accommodate the growth of her soul. And she discovered this by that sideways glimpse into her mirror, which revealed her to herself as she is seen by others.

Justine now feels a change that makes her think some of her weight will begin to fall off, and that this will help her health. I think her shift in feeling has to do with Justine's recent conscious understanding of the extent of her own personal power, and her ability to occupy space in the world, to be "weighty" through her actions and her great personal effect on other people, rather than through her physical size.

Justine's story also makes me think of other women's stories that connect size and weight with psychological factors. Women who have been sexually molested as children often say they gained a lot of weight in order to protect themselves. One woman, slim now, weighed sixty pounds more than her present weight when she was in high school; she says she made a decision to gain weight after being molested by her father.

Justine represents one end of a spectrum: she is a self-confident large woman who has gained weight in order to feel powerful. At the other end, women who have a genetic tendency to be large struggle with diets, overwhelmed by the dictum that a woman must be small to be attractive. In such cases, dieting against the grain can have the undesired effect of altering a woman's metabolism so that she gains weight with less caloric intake, and the result can be obesity for a woman who would otherwise be simply large.

By understanding the transient nature of standards for beauty in women, as well as their cultural base, we can lift a great burden from ourselves, but only if we are willing to challenge the assumptions of our own culture.

Increasingly, women of color appear in Western fashion ads and beauty magazines, but most of them are women who are distinguished from other models only by their color. If they follow their own ethnic standards, these are standards that are acceptable in the West. In leanness, youthfulness, and European facial characteristics, these models are exotic counterparts of their white colleagues.

Renoir's women are seen today as overweight, as are most of the sculptures of ancient fertility goddesses. Although in many cultures the tendency of women to gain weight after childbirth and at menopause is traditionally viewed as normal, healthy, and beautiful, there is a growing global tendency to internalize the lean, youthful standards of the West and then believe they are objective, even universal.

Responding to the inexorable pressure of these visual standards, as we age we relinquish our claim to beauty, but even when we are young our claim is never secure, threatened by illness, accident, and the aging process, by issues of self-esteem aggravated by the compulsion to compare oneself with images in the mass media, and by the jealous, critical context that surrounds so many young women.

This is the problem posed for women by the concept of beauty, that it empowers few, and disempowers most.

2

BEAUTY

AS WHITE AS

SNOW

> *Once there was a lovely virgin*
> *called Snow White.*
> *Say she was thirteen.*
> *Her stepmother,*
> *a beauty in her own right,*
> *though eaten, of course, by age,*
> *would hear of no beauty surpassing her own.*
> *Beauty is a simple passion,*
> *but, oh my friends, in the end*
> *you will dance the fire in iron shoes.*
> — Anne Sexton, *Transformations*

When I was a child my access to power was through my imagination, often the only access a child can find. Yearning for a beauty I did not see around me, I escaped from the mundane and sometimes dangerous world of the Bronx city streets to the world of books. I found refuge from the city and from my family in the land of fairy tales.

I read books of fairy tales from the public library, collections by the Brothers Grimm, Andrew Lang, and Hans Christian Andersen, and I dreamed of brave young men and beautiful princesses, slender young women with hair that might be dark or golden, and skin that was always as white as snow. As I read, I dreamed of being as brave as the heroes and as beautiful as the heroines. I was never old or ugly or wicked like the stepmothers or the jealous sisters, never frightening like the ogres and trolls, but my imaginary world was made rich and awesome by their perilous presence.

My other world of escape was the movies. Television was a rationed privilege when I was a child, and its black-and-white images on a small fuzzy screen didn't hold the magic of the great screen as seen from the front row on rainy Saturday afternoons. Now, Saturday-morning TV cartoons serve as colorful and cozy alternative escape routes for children, without the great collectivity of the moviegoing experience.

When I went to see the Disney versions of the fairy tales I so loved, my fantasies were indelibly marked and altered by them. The powerful archetypes of the folktales were watered down, oversimplified by the cuteness of the Disney characters, but the stereotypes of the ugly old witch, the charming prince, and the beautiful white princess were retained in these artful animations. I devoured everything uncritically, and in turn I was swallowed whole.

Growing up with the Disneyfied myth of the beautiful white woman, wanting to become her, I was ashamed of my pubescent body, its functions, smells, and excretions. My identity was disembodied. Snow White, as Walt Disney portrayed her, was immaculate in her crystal coffin. She didn't have pimples or sweat or bleed once a month, nor did she pass urine or have bowel movements. Neither did she speak, think, or act. All she needed to do to attract her Prince Charming was to lie there, beautiful, crystalline, and dead.

As for the wicked stepmother, once she transformed herself into an ugly old witch, she too was headed straight for death, but not the romantic false death of Snow White. In a remarkable departure from the Grimms' tale, the animated Disney dwarfs pursue the old woman even as Snow White lies lifeless on the floor of their house. Accompanied by all the forest creatures, they chase her up a bleak crag in a wild storm, and she falls to her death in the act of trying to kill them all. Disney's witch queen looks and moves like a mean old woman, the one we saw as children in our most tyrannical teacher, our most dreaded neighbor, aunt, or grandmother, the woman we did not want to become.

Every child at the Saturday matinee cheered when the witch was killed. That was the real climax of the movie for us, and all that followed, the vigil around Snow White's coffin, the arrival of the prince and his triumphant departure, walking, with Snow White mounted on his horse, heading for the castle in the sunset, seemed anticlimactic. But it was essential to the globally disseminated Disney dream of victorious youth and white, passive female beauty.

Like all popular culture, Disney's *Snow White* is derived from ancient motifs and is also a statement of its time and its maker. Walt Disney was a conservative misogynist, whose work became a worldwide symbol of American middle-class ideals. The scene in Disney's film where Snow White prissily admonishes the dwarfs to wash before dinner exemplifies the repressive ideal of cleanliness as a moral value rather than a sensuous pleasure, the whitewashing of the world in a sentimental fantasy of strong, hardworking, obedient men and immaculate, hyperfeminine young women.

When *Snow White* was first released, in 1938, German filmmaker Leni Riefenstahl was winning acclaim for her documentary of the 1936 Olympic Games, held in Munich and attended by Riefenstahl's patron and admirer Adolf Hitler. When the intrepid Riefenstahl was interviewed at length for a film about her life, she insisted that her aesthetic of youthful beauty had absolutely nothing to do with Hitler's Nazism. A strong, determined woman considered by some to be the only great woman filmmaker, Riefenstahl said in her interview that, when photographing women, the only consideration is to make them look young and lovely. Babies, she remarked, presented the ideal subject for the camera, because of their unwrinkled, fresh skin.

Still actively scuba diving and doing underwater photography at the age of ninety, Riefenstahl spoke of her single-minded love of natural beauty, epitomized for her in the Olympic athletes, the snow-covered mountains she often climbed, the athletic Nuba of Africa, and the underwater sea life she was documenting. This apparently innocent love of beauty, accompanied by a "rehabilitation" of Riefenstahl by the international art world, was criticized by Susan Sontag as concealing what she called "fascist longings"—for simplicity at the expense of complex understanding, for physical perfection, for control over natural forces, for glamorous death. Sontag's essay on Riefenstahl raises complex questions about the politics of beauty. The same mythical background that fed Nazi ideals also underlies much of our contemporary assessment of beauty.

When I began work on this book I thought of "Snow White" as an example of jealousy between women based on beauty and competition. Remembering the Disney film, I also thought of its racist and sexist implications. But when I reread "Snow White" in my old edition of Grimm, I was astonished by its echo of the old Goddess myths, by the resilience and strength of Snow White, and by the suppressed force of the stepmother. I traced some of the original roots of the fairy tale, seeing how it speaks to the ages of women, how it reaches back to old images of women's power and can serve as a source for finding new images of our own power. Here is my retelling of the tale written down by the Grimm brothers.

LITTLE SNOW WHITE

A queen sits one winter day by a window framed in ebony wood. The queen is sewing shirts for her husband, and she pricks her finger with her needle. Struck by the beauty of three drops of blood on the snow, she wishes for a child as white as the snow, as red as blood, as black as the ebony of the window frame. Soon after this, the queen dies in childbirth, giving birth to a daughter who fulfills her wish. This daughter is the beautiful little girl Snow White. A year after her birth, her father marries a beautiful, proud woman, owner of a wonderful mirror. When the new queen looks into her mirror she asks, "Mirror, mirror on the wall, who is the fairest of us all?" and the mirror answers, "Thou art the fairest, Lady Queen."

One day, when Snow White has grown up to the age of seven, with a complexion "as clear as the noonday," the mirror responds to the queen's constant question, "Thou were the fairest, Lady Queen; Snow White is fairest now, I ween." Filled with rage, the jealous queen orders a huntsman to take the child to the forest, kill her, and bring back her heart and tongue. But little Snow White pleads for her life, and the huntsman lets her run into the forest, thinking she will surely die there, but at least her death won't be at his hands. He kills a boar and brings back its heart and tongue, which the queen eats.

Snow White, wandering in the forest, discovers the small but elegant home of the seven dwarfs. There she eats a little porridge from each bowl, finds the bed that suits her just exactly right, and falls asleep. The finicky dwarfs, returning home, at once discover the changes in their belongings, but their annoyance changes to delight when they see the beautiful child asleep. They agree she can live with them if she will tend their house, and she does. They go off to work every day, warning her to stay home behind locked doors, lest her stepmother come to find her.

Meanwhile, the queen, consulting her mirror, learns that Snow White is still alive, living over the seven hills with the seven dwarfs. She dyes her face, disguising herself as an old gypsy peddler, and she persuades the gullible child to let her in and try some corset stays she offers her. Lacing Snow White too tight, she leaves her for dead on the floor, but the dwarfs come home and revive the child. Twice the queen returns, first with a poisoned comb, then with an apple, poisoned in its rosy skin. Each time the dwarfs warn Snow White, but each time she is deceived by her cunning stepmother, and the second time she falls lifeless, with the apple in her mouth. This time when the queen returns to her mirror it assures her that she is, once again, the fairest in the land, and her envious heart is as peaceful as an envious heart can be.

The dwarfs and all the beasts in the forest mourn the apparent death of Snow White, who remains fresh and lifelike, still "white as snow, red as blood, and black-haired as ebony." A case of transparent glass is made for her, and she lies in it until one day a king's son comes, falls in love with the sight of her, and begs the dwarfs to let him take her away in her case. They see his love for her and agree, and on the trip a jolt dislodges the piece of poisoned apple from her mouth, so that Snow White awakens. The prince proposes, she accepts, a wedding speedily follows, and the old queen is invited. First her mirror tells her the new bride is more beautiful than she, then she discovers who the new bride is, and she is rooted to her place in rage and astonishment. "Just then," the story concludes, "a pair of red-hot iron shoes was brought in with a pair of tongs and set before her; and these she was forced to put on, and to dance in them till she fell down dead."

This is a story of the powers and struggles of women who change. It begins with a strong visual image, which had great impact on my childish imagination, and which is missing from the Disney film: a queen sewing at an ebony window, gazing at three drops of blood on the snow, and wishing for a daughter who will be white, red, and black. The queen thereby invokes the three colors sacred to the three-part Goddess, white for the Maiden, red for the Mother, black for the Crone.

These were also the colors of the process of spiritual transformation practiced by medieval alchemists in Europe: black for the *nigredo*, the dark night of the soul; red for the *rubedo*, the sacrifice; white for the *albedo*, the coming of the light. In psychological terms this is a story about the female psyche and

its development into the Self, the spiritually developed whole
being. These metaphorical terms, which equate whiteness with
spiritual light and black with darkness of the soul, also reflect
a northern European set of values, which has been imposed on
southern cultures.

In its own cultural context, "Little Snow White" is also a
story about beauty, the beauty of red blood on white snow, of
an ebony-black window frame, of a fair-skinned, black-haired,
red-lipped girl child, of beauty in nature and beauty as perceived by humans, beauty as an absolute, beauty as a process.
It is a story evocative of the Goddess, who once encompassed
in her being beauty, ugliness, life, growth, jealousy, passion,
deception, decay, and death. It is a story about appearance and
identity.

Western Judeo-Christian culture, which commonly honors
maiden and mother, ambivalent though their positions may be,
fears and shuns the Crone, who signifies the death-bringing
aspect of nature, as essential as birth and growth. This awesome
power, so repudiated in our culture, is caricatured in images of
grotesque witches, cackling and riding their broomsticks
through the air, but it was once respected, even worshiped, as
it still is in some African cultures as Oya, a powerful Yoruba
Goddess.

The Goddess motif is supported by the symbolic structure
of the fairy tale. Not only is Snow White endowed by her
mother's wish with the three colors of the Goddess; but after
the huntsman releases her in the forest a wild boar runs by,
which he kills to take its heart and tongue back to the queen.
The wild boar was an early sacrificial god surrogate, a sacred
totem of the ancient Hebrews, sacred also to the Celtic goddess
Arduinna. Sacrifices were made to ensure the fertility of the
earth, symbolized by the Goddess. Nature supports Snow White
because she herself, as the Goddess, is nature.

At the age of seven, Snow White goes to live over the seven
hills with the seven dwarfs. Seven is symbolic, according to
ancient numerology, of worldly time, a complete cycle, the union of three, synthesis, and four, stability, as in the Chinese

I Ching. It is the number of the Seven Sisters, the Seven Pillars of Wisdom, the Seven Mothers of the world. The Seven Sages, according to feminist scholar Barbara Walker, were originally wise women, who changed to male figures as patriarchy was established. In their wisdom, these ancient women valued beauty as the harmony and wholeness of the entire cycle of life and death.

Snow White's life begins with the death of her beauty-loving mother. The death-bringing Crone touches her from the start. The motherless child has no guidance or help from her father, for he marries a beautiful but proud and haughty woman only a year after Snow White's mother has died, thereby endowing Snow White with a terrible stepmother, the Crone in disguise. The Crone became a stepmother in the patriarchal folk imagination because she was no longer acceptable as a real mother, just as old age and death were no longer culturally recognized as important parts of the life cycle.

The stepmother is an example of what Jung called the Terrible Mother, an archetypal aspect of human psychology, which he recognized as related to the death-bringing aspect of the Great Goddess. This Terrible Mother was opposed, in the popular imagination, to the Good Mother, the nurturing aspect of the Goddess. This split has caused enormous suffering in women, who experience both aspects in themselves but have learned to repudiate the Terrible Mother instead of honoring her sacred and powerful qualities.

Her innocence and the love of her mother are Snow White's blessings, but they are not sufficient to protect her from the wiles of the evil queen. The dwarfs in their tidy home represent the ordered, rational, commonsensical aspect of human nature, which Snow White needs if she is to survive. However, even they cannot prevail against the wild and cunning fury of the stepmother with her omniscient mirror. Only by apparently dying, so effectively that the magic mirror of the queen is fooled, can Snow White escape her stepmother.

Snow White returns from death through the intervention of the prince, who acts out of his love for her beauty. The long period of time that passes before the prince appears is essential to the story and is found in other related stories, such as "The Sleeping Beauty" and "Briar Rose." The glossing over of this time period is one of the most glaring simplifications of the Disney film, for it removes the serious presence of death.

Snow White's apparent death, like Inanna's descent to the underworld, is a time of spiritual journeying, of preparation for profound change. The prince who rescues her represents the male principle, what Jung called the animus principle, which a woman must integrate in order to achieve wholeness. This is her creativity, her independence, her ability to think for herself and act as a whole being.

That this principle is typically represented in fairy tales by a man reflects the deep heterosexual structure of patriarchy, which has for so long denied the independent creativity of women and led us to seek validation and completion in the admiring, but also diminishing, gaze of men.

As well as integrating her creative, independent side, a woman seeking wholeness must also, earlier or later, somehow face and integrate her shadow, the negative aspect of beauty, the jealous, possessive, murderous stepmother, who ultimately represents death, the third, Crone face of the Goddess. That the Crone and the Terrible Mother are collapsed into one character in the story of Snow White says a lot about the tendency in patriarchal culture to treat Mother and Crone as merging negative aspects of womanhood.

Mothers are more exalted in their absence than in their presence, sainted when dead, but likely to be seen as critical monsters when alive. This ambivalence toward mothers is related both to the power of the mother as experienced by the child, and to the fading of youthful beauty associated with the act of bearing children. As children grow up, mothers grow old, and are subject to the fear and denial with which we surround the idea of aging and death.

More than anything else, it is the need to integrate death that marks the story of Snow White and other European fairy tales as having ancient, faraway roots in stories, such as the myth of Inanna, that celebrate the cycles of nature, the powers of women, and the wholeness of the Goddess. But many centuries divide the time of Inanna's story from the European version of Snow White. It is not the awesome, death-dealing power of the goddess Inanna that is represented by the wicked stepmother in "Snow White," but a degraded version of the jealous wrath of Inanna's sister Ereshkigal, queen of the underworld. This idea of jealous rage has deep roots and has undergone many transformations. It is closely connected with a sense of powerlessness in women, and often divides older from younger women.

The stepmother is obsessed with her own beauty, which she views as a possession. Unlike the Taoist immortal Sun Pu-erh, she clings to her beauty, and allows it to define her. But like Sun Pu-erh, the stepmother also longs for immortality. She does not accept the aging process, which decrees that a child will become more beautiful than she. She has magical powers, but she uses them for small purposes. This false mother is ultimately destroyed by her own red-hot emotions, having tried to destroy Snow White with the red-cheeked poisoned apple. In other words, having failed to integrate the maternal role, she is destroyed by its power, coupled with the power of the Crone, which she tried to use but failed to respect. Snow White takes on the positive aspects of the archetypes that destroy her stepmother. She is both maid and mother (she takes on the role of mother with the dwarfs), but she must pass through the long shadow of the valley of death in order to emerge triumphant, ready to become the queen.

BEAUTY AND MORALITY

Woman's beauty can suggest either good or evil. Snow White's beauty is of the innocent variety, while her stepmother's beauty is clearly evil. Snow White is good-hearted, humble, and obedient, while her stepmother is proud, haughty, jealous, and willing to kill to maintain supremacy. This irreconcilable difference between them is the story's most striking patriarchal aspect, for there is no hint that Snow White will take on the repudiated powers of her stepmother. "Snow White" is a Christian tale with pagan remnants, and like Christianity itself, it tends to value spirit over body and reason over passion, in short, principles assigned to the male over principles assigned to the female. But this value is only consciously asserted; the structure of the tale shows the necessity of the instincts, of bodily survival, and the importance of death.

The dichotomy between good and evil, projected onto other dualisms, like white and black, youth and age, men and women, was not characteristic of what we now call Goddess worship, in which creation and destruction were accepted as aspects of the all-powerful and all-wise Goddess, symbol of nature herself. In this light, we can see both Snow White and her stepmother as aspects of the Goddess, of the nature of women, of all of nature.

Snow White is not merely innocent. Her will to live appears in her impassioned appeal to the huntsman; her affinity with nature is seen in her eagerness to escape into the forest, the miraculous appearance of the wild boar after the huntsman lets her go, and the way she makes friends with the wild animals, a strong indicator of a spirit in harmony with nature. She is discriminating and considerate, eating a little porridge from each bowl so as not to deprive anyone of all his dinner, seeking the bed that suits her perfectly, not one that is too long or short or narrow. Her nurturing qualities appear in her care of the dwarfs' home and her good relationship with them. Her endurance and spiritual nature are seen when she remains fresh and lifelike even though apparently dead.

In fact, Snow White's affinity with nature is such that we see a conspiracy afoot: nature in cahoots with youth. What will happen when Snow White grows old, and is herself supplanted in beauty and freshness by her own daughter? Will she be a true mother or a stepmother? The answer, for each woman who plays the role of youthful beauty, will depend on her willingness and ability to change roles as she changes over time, and on the availability of different roles for her to play.

The stepmother queen's closest relationship is with her wonderful truth-telling mirror. Gazing into her mirror, the stepmother becomes obsessed with the beauty that has been used to define her by her culture. Mistaking appearance for reality, identifying beauty with power, she has no inner experience of beauty, but must rely on her mirror to know she is the most beautiful.

Once again, the story has echoes of older cultures, where the mirror was understood as a soul-catcher, or as the reflection of the soul. In that sense, we might think that the queen was once a woman with strong spiritual foundations, like Sun Pu-erh, but that she threw away her options when she mistook physical beauty for real value. Beauty for her is competitive— to be the most beautiful is essential for this tormented woman. But she fails to understand that beauty is a transient role. Because she is not cultivating the path of the heart, which leads to immortality, she cannot transcend her biological fate.

Inexorably, age decrees that her external beauty will fade while a child's increases. How unfair, she rages; I will not allow this. And she uses all her wiles, even disguising herself as the old woman she fears becoming, to kill the threat to her supreme beauty. But what a useless endeavor, which only hastens her own demise. This myth of youthful beauty is so confusing, so unfair, so limiting, so enduring.

The ancient myths of women's power, which preceded the myths of beauty, persist as shadows in our stories, dreams, and even our physical symptoms and illnesses. The disguise of the stepmother is such a shadow, for by staining her skin to disguise herself as an old gypsy the stepmother exchanges one persona, that of the beautiful queen, for another, that of the Crone, a persona with great power and resonance, which she is incapable of fully inhabiting. That is what leads to her downfall, for were she to take on the Crone's power in full, she would no longer be threatened by Snow White, who simply represents another aspect of female power. Snow White, who trusts everyone and is willing to try anything, is naïve but also extremely powerful because of her flexibility and adaptability, qualities of survival in harmony with rather than against natural processes.

The queen, unwilling to accept her own aging process, wants to stop time, a deeply destructive desire. In the end, rather than focusing on the happy married couple of Snow White and the prince, the story tells of the grim demise of the queen, who is forced to dance in red-hot shoes until she is dead. This ending echoes another fairy tale, called "The Red Shoes," which also warns of the danger of attachment to appearances.

I was a teenager when I first saw, on late-night television, the 1948 movie by Michael Powell based on "The Red Shoes." The movie, built around a ballet version of the fairy tale, haunted my adolescent imagination. In the movie as in the ballet, the central character dances herself to death, but in the fairy tale, she escapes death by persuading a woodchopper to cut off her feet, to release her from the satanic curse of the red shoes, in which she cannot stop dancing.

As Clarissa Pinkola Estés points out in her discussion of a similar story, red shoes can be symbolic of menstrual blood, which runs down a woman's legs. They refer to rites of passage, menarchal or menopausal. We may not be aware of such symbolism—I was not as a teenager—but it takes firm hold on our imaginations. Estés emphasizes that the denial of passage or change curses a woman and kills her spirit. But who is responsible for such denial? Is it an individual woman or is it her culture?

Although she meets a terrible end, the wicked, desperate queen in "Little Snow White" does achieve an ironic kind of immortality, for her role does not die with her. The role of the stepmother lives on in the lives of women who identify beauty with power, and resent the beauty of younger women as a challenge to their own supremacy.

THE JEALOUS MOTHER

I have spoken with many women about this issue of the aging woman whose jealousy turns her against a younger woman, most often her own daughter. Women who suffer as their youth fades may look at their blooming daughters with hatred, which can hardly be acknowledged.

A mother's jealousy is still a forbidden topic in most families, a secret that reveals itself in relationship problems, in illnesses, and, more consciously, in therapy. It is the shadow side of the good mother. I have worked repeatedly with the destructive effects of maternal jealousy in clients who carry their jealous mothers around inside themselves and are, in consequence, extremely self-critical, a problem I know from my own experience.

My mother, who was in her thirties when I was born, tried repeatedly to relive her beautiful youth through me. My wedding day was traumatic for both of us. I think, now, that my mother woke up that morning and realized for the first time that it was my wedding, not hers. She acted resentful and sulked all day, provoking friends and family. She had no useful models to follow, and no memory of a wonderful wedding of her own, as she was married in a registry office during the Second World War. I was hurt and furious that she couldn't be nurturing and supportive of me on the day that I was doing what every good daughter is supposed to do, getting myself married in the religion of my parents.

Had I been able to visualize my fury, I might well have imagined a pair of red-hot iron shoes for my terrible mother to dance in. Instead I swallowed my anger and it cast a shadow on my relationship with my mother for many years. Now, when I think back through that episode, I realize how much I depended on my mother for support, and how I was unwilling to take on her negativity, to judge for myself what was right for me, to question the standards of marriage and religion I inherited. Had I been able to do so, I would have had things out with her long before the wedding, and the wedding would have been a very different event. Above all, had I been able to understand her jealousy as zeal, or passion for something she had missed, I would have valued that quality in myself and lived my youthful passion more fully than I did.

I find in my practice that young women who feel oppressed

and intimidated by their jealous mothers are relieved to discover that they are not to blame for being younger and fresher than their mothers, an irrational but commonly held belief. The difficulty in healing such wounds from early childhood is that they run so deep. Several of my clients, brought up with a constant litany of criticism from their jealous mothers, sometimes accompanied by physical and sexual abuse, are now unable to react to criticism, assuming as they do that the criticism applies to their entire persons, that they are in fact ugly and wrong. Before they can deal with criticism, they must first heal the wounds of abuse. Gradually, it becomes possible to notice how those of us who have grown up with jealous criticisms repeat these criticisms unconsciously, especially to our daughters and to other women.

The jealousy of women toward women is based on a psychology of powerlessness, which developed over many centuries in which women have, literally, been deprived of power. The outcome is a frequently encountered situation in which a woman is shamed and humiliated by another woman, even endangered by her, as in cases where mothers or mothers-in-law can exert power only over younger women, or in social situations where women feel they can show their strength only by denigrating other women.

Who can console the jealous mother for a loss that is widely accepted as condemning her to invisibility? We have accepted great divides between mothers and daughters as a consequence of our mutual powerlessness under patriarchy, but now it is time to heal the breach, if not with our actual mothers and our actual daughters, at least with the mother and daughter within. To do so would mean healing from the wounds of childhood, accepting the privileges of youth and beauty and the privileges of maturity and experience. It would mean understanding such privileges as passing pleasures, to be enjoyed and left behind when done, grieving missed pleasures and letting go of them, looking jealousy in its green eyes and finding the passion in ourselves that we project onto others. This is a tall order, and it usually requires a pattern, a model, something or someone to follow into the unknown territory of jealousy and longing.

What might the fairy tale of Snow White look like if the older idea of the Crone as wisdom and power were reasserted? My hesitation to dare rewrite such a time-honored story is countered by my knowledge that it is in the retelling, the honoring of our own narrative impulses, that our stories remain vital and true to changing cultural needs. By doing this we uncover the element of the story that is fresh and vital; for instance, the understanding of the older woman's jealousy as a need to accept and integrate her own aging process.

SNOW WHITE AND THE CRONE QUEEN

Once there was a queen, wise and beautiful, who ruled over her land with the help of a magical mirror. Each morning the queen would stand in front of her mirror and ask: "Mirror, mirror on the wall, who is the fairest of us all?" The mirror would reply: "My lady queen, your beauty is the inspiration of us all, and I hope your wisdom will recall the need to share your bounty."

Then the queen would attend to the needs of her people, from early morning to late at night, rejoicing in her own beauty and the love it won her. As the years passed, she grew very weary, but her pride and her mirror helped her to carry on.

One night the queen had a dream that her sister, who lived in another country, came to her and said she had conceived a child, a daughter who would be white as snow, red as blood, black as the ebony wood of the window frame. The sister said she would die in childbirth, and asked the queen to raise her child as if she were her own. As nothing followed to confirm or deny this dream the queen ignored it and went on with her busy life, guided, as always, by her mirror.

But one morning the response of the mirror was different. A newcomer had arrived in the queen's land, having traveled for seven years in the lands beyond the seven hills, a maiden white as snow, red as blood, and black as ebony wood, whose heart was as true as her beauty. The maid claimed she was the daughter of the queen's elder sister, and that she by right was the heir to the throne now occupied by her aunt. The queen's

mirror spoke the truth, that a new beauty had come to rule the
land, and the queen, in a fit of jealous rage, smashed her magical
mirror into smithereens.

Now there was no one to tell the queen what was beautiful
and what was right. Her heart consumed with rage and jealousy, the aging queen sought to destroy her niece, Snow White,
with every means at her disposal. Because Snow White had
many powerful allies, the queen could not simply order her
guards to throw the maid in prison. So she had to rely on her
wits, which were considerable. She realized that the only way
to win Snow White's confidence was to persuade her that she,
the queen, had something to teach the younger woman. What
better subject than the cultivation of beauty, something the
queen knew a great deal about? She disguised herself as an old
crone, an expert in cosmetics and costume, and designed a cunning and irresistible garment for Snow White, a deadly garment,
which would render the young woman beautiful and a corpse,
for it was poisoned. As she helped the young woman to don
the white wool robe, fastened the red leather belt tightly around
her supple waist, and knotted the black silk scarf around her
lovely neck, the queen whispered into Snow White's ear: "Go
now into the Darkness, and come back if you can!"

Snow White died in her poisoned robe, and her spirit descended deep into the Darkness, where she met seven wise
women and learned their sacred, secret arts. Meanwhile her
body remained fresh and lovely. Her followers, seeing that,
kept it in a crystal coffin, and guarded it jealously from the old
queen, who had retired into her private chambers to meditate
on her life.

This was a time of trouble in the land, and people prayed
for leadership. One day a young and charming prince came to
the queen's land and he, seeing Snow White in her coffin, was
deeply moved by her beauty and youth. Raising the crystal lid,
he unknotted the black silk scarf, loosened the red leather belt,
and raised the dead woman's lips to his own. Imagine his shock
when she sat up straight, opened her lovely dark eyes, and
looked at him! "I have returned," she said, "and now I will be
queen, and you may be my prince and consort."

The old queen, hearing a noise of rejoicing, inquired and was told that Snow White had returned from death. Now she knew that her time was ended, and that she must prepare for her own journey to death. On went the white wool robe, on went the red leather belt and the black silk scarf, and on her feet she placed red shoes, in which she would dance her final dance and sing her final song, of power, of all she knew, of all she had done. This dance and this song would be remembered so long as people lived in the queen's land.

The old queen summoned her subjects, and, in the presence of the new young queen, the prince, and all her people, she danced until the earth opened beneath her, then she danced her way down into the very bowels of the earth, where Death waited to receive her.

You may think this is the end of the story. And many people think that was the end. But I know another version. The old queen, on meeting Death, decided that her time to leave the earth's surface had not yet come. She still had things to do, books to read and write, trees to sit under, seeds to plant and tend in her garden, thoughts to think and feelings to feel. And, although she had danced her final dance and sung her final song, she still had something to say. In short, she was an old woman but still very much alive!

So, thanking Death for her time, the old queen returned to the surface of the earth, but not to her old home, where a new queen reigned. She went instead to another country, to the home of an old friend and companion, a woman her own age, who welcomed her, and there she lived out the rest of her days, not quietly, but with great enjoyment. As she had gained so much wisdom from her experiences of life and death, she was much sought out, but she only made herself available for a short time each day, and the rest of her time was spent as she pleased.

If we think of the story of Snow White, old or new, as a story of the cycle of nature, as the three-part Goddess is herself an archetype of Mother Nature, then the overlay of morality falls away, good and evil are no longer so interesting. The more compelling and dynamic dialogue is the one between change and stasis, the need for the old to give way to the new, for a phase of ruling to give way to a phase of retreat and meditation, which in turn may give way to more connection with the world. The role of youthful beauty falls away before the more complex roles of age.

We don't always make these changes easily, without wild feelings. By just reacting, smashing her mirror, the aging queen discards her former visual standards and her link to the outside world. Now she will have to find her own guidance. As one who ignores her dreams and hasn't herself descended into the underworld, she will first act unwisely, guided by her wild emotions rather than by her own wisdom. But in a world where the female principle is honored, the queen will gradually come to an understanding of her transformation. She will work with rather than against the natural process.

It is autumn as I write this, and the unpicked roses in my yard wither on the bush as it goes dormant for the winter. A good friend is dying of AIDS, and I plan an autumn casserole to take to his lover. Change is constant around us. But we hesitate to apply it to our own lives. Like the old queen in my story, we ignore our dreams and act as if we were immortal, shunning the counsel of death until we are forced to acknowledge it. We ignore the wisdom of Sun Pu-erh, and remain immersed in the pursuit of an illusion. At the last minute we change, under duress, but not many of us leave this life dancing. Fewer return from the encounter with death.

"Snow White" is a tale from the North, where skin color is indigenously light, and in the above version that image remains. But here is another version.

EBONY BLACK AND LITTLE WHITE HAIR

Once there was a queen who was wise and compassionate, and very much loved by her subjects. She was a magnificent woman, the finest dancer among a people who, honoring dance as a sacred art, chose the most skillful dancer as their leader. This queen was tall and large, with skin as smooth and black as ebony, lips red as blood, dazzling white teeth, and hair as black as jet, braided in many braids. This queen loved to look into her magic mirror, and she beheld there not only herself but all that went on in her land. She had one great weakness: she was afraid of growing old, and would not tolerate anyone who was old around her.

One day, when the queen had undone her braids and was combing her hair, she found a single white hair among the jet black. She plucked out the white hair and threw it into the fire. But from that day on white hairs appeared more and more frequently, and then one day the queen's mirror showed her that a whole patch of hair was white, far too many to pluck out. That same day the mirror showed a serious drought in the land, and much suffering among the people. The queen felt very tired, and wished, for the first time, that she had a daughter to carry on her tasks.

The queen's wish was granted, and she bore a healthy daughter with smooth black skin, lips as red as blood, and a head covered from birth with thick, curly white hair. Never had such a child been seen in the land, and the people were shocked. What did this mean? The drought had not abated, and many people were starving.

The queen, carrying her daughter on her back, walked the width and breadth of her land, visiting her people and helping them as she could, but despair walked with her, and the people complained openly. Perhaps the white-haired child was to blame. Her deformity, her white hair, her ugliness, as they now called it, was the cause of their suffering. (They forgot she had been born after the drought had already taken its first toll.) The child, fearful because of the fear she inspired, never spoke, and this further estranged her from her people. After seven years of drought, the people demanded that the queen sacrifice her child so that the drought would end.

The queen, who was a true mother and loved her little girl more than herself, offered to die in her daughter's place. But the people were immovable in their demand. Desperate, the queen took her daughter into a desert place, saying she would kill the child and bring back her heart. When the two were alone, the queen held little White Hair to her breast, and rocked her, and prayed aloud for help. Just then a strange old woman walked out of the desert with her herd of goats. Taking the woman's appearance as a response to her prayer, the queen begged her to take the child, and to give one of her goats to the queen, which she would sacrifice and take its heart back to her people. The old woman agreed, and the queen sorrowfully took leave of her white-haired daughter in the desert. When she returned to her people, they saw with amazement that her hair too had become completely white. But that day it rained for the first time in seven years. The long drought was ended. The people rejoiced and honored the queen for her sacrifice. They made statues of the white-haired girl, and created a dance to celebrate her as their savior.

Her mother, knowing from her mirror that the girl lived and was well, was content, although she missed her daughter sorely. Each time she combed and braided her long white hair she thought of her child, and imagined that it was her daughter's hair she was combing and braiding, instead of her own.

Meanwhile little White Hair was living with the strange old woman in the desert. She had no human friends, and the strange woman, although kind, hardly spoke to her. But she had seven goats. These were the playmates of the little girl, who grew up sure-footed and nimble and willful as any goat.

One day, years after her mother had left her in the desert, White Hair was out as usual with her goats when a young man came looking for directions. He came from another country, where his father was king. The young man had been sent to find a wife, and he had looked everywhere for someone who could match his own spirit of adventure, his love of silence, and his kind heart. Hiding behind a rock, he watched the white-haired girl dancing with her goats, and his heart went out to her.

And so the story continues. Perhaps White Hair will want nothing to do with the king's son, or perhaps she will fall in

—— love with him. She will certainly face great challenges, even death itself. Eventually, White Hair will return to her mother and her people. Will she return in triumph, or in crisis, turning to her mother's wisdom and guidance? We will see her at some moment reunited with her mother, dancing, in the fullness of her power, for this is a story of woman's leadership.

Blackness in this story is associated with fertility and growth, riches and wisdom. Whiteness is the dazzling whiteness of teeth and the time-bleached whiteness of age. Fearing age as a precursor of death, the queen is unaware of the consolations of age. But one role of woman cannot be disavowed without affecting the others. The white-haired child is seen as ugly and dreaded by the people, as the white hair of her own age is shunned by the queen. The people and the land reflect the psyche of the queen, just as her mirror reflects the totality, for she and they are really one in this story. Like all fairy tales, in which wholeness is the goal, this is a hopeful story of a culture in which nature is still miraculous and sacred, where beauty is an adornment, a celebration, an art of expression, a reflection of nature rather than an opposition to nature.

These stories can and should be written and rewritten, as fairy tales have been told and retold, for so long as a story is true to any woman's psyche it will be a true story for all of us. So long as we continue to tell our stories and to ponder for ourselves their meanings in our lives, we retain the ability to shape and give meaning to our most difficult times.

Understanding the ways in which the concept of beauty functions as a metaphor for many different things—for youth, power, goodness, wickedness, innocence, and experience—we may feel ourselves less as prisoners of the concept, more as shapers of our own destinies.

3

BEAUTY AND

DANGER

The Chinese says,
  "I would like you to tell me the truth, Madame, about
your daughter. Has your son hit her. . . . ?"
  Frightened, the mother gives a low whimper. But the
older brother hasn't heard. The mother hesitates, she gives
the Chinese a long look. She answers: "No, Monsieur, I did,
because I was afraid he would kill her."
          —Marguerite Duras, *The North Chinese Lover*

As soon as Snow White reached the age where her beauty surpassed her stepmother's, her life was in danger. As soon as Sun
Pu-erh's teacher looked at her, he saw that she was a beautiful
woman, and that therefore it would be dangerous for her to go
out into the world. One of the great paradoxes of patriarchal
culture is that beauty, praised and valued as it is, however it is

defined, is often dangerous to the woman thought to possess it. In order to survive not only immediate physical danger but the trauma of living constantly in a dangerous situation, women need extraordinary resources. The violence that surrounds women's lives is matched only by our powers of endurance.

The story of the woman who survives danger by means of her spiritual development and resourcefulness is as old as storytelling itself. It can be found as far back as the Sumerian story of Inanna, who returns from the realm of death and replaces herself in the underworld with her consort Dumuzi, whose cruel death she then laments. This is a story related to the cyclical death of the growing season and to the life cycle itself. The sacrifice of Dumuzi is eased when his sister, Geshtinanna, offers to share his time in the underworld, so that he will spend only half the year there, and she will spend the other half of the year in his place. This myth, involving sacrifice and cycles of death and resurrection, is the precursor of many later stories and religious traditions, including the story of Demeter and Persephone, and the story of Christ.

There is a motif of sacrifice in human mythology, related to the lunar myths that mark the monthly disappearance of the moon, the daily disappearance of the sun, and the annual disappearance of the crops, the barren period of the earth. Sacrifice also gives meaning to the endless cycle of human life, death, and birth, which assures the continuance of humanity while ensuring that no individual survives death.

The idea of human immortality is a challenge to the omnipotence of death. Even the immortality attained by the Taoist masters is a matter of only a thousand years, more or less, renewed only once by tasting the peach of immortality, which itself ripens every three thousand years. In other words, death is inevitable for all living beings, and all spiritual traditions recognize this, while some, like Christianity, offer immortality for the spirit.

Early cultures sacrificed the king, the consort of the Goddess, to ensure the continuance of the life cycles and the fertility of the land. The sacrificial victim was sacred, a god himself, often the lover-son of the Goddess, honored in a belief system that understood death as part of the life cycle. The blood of the victim was thought necessary to renew the blood of the Goddess, periodically shed in menstruation and childbirth. Perhaps the very first form of sacrifice was menstrual blood, offered without loss of human life, the most mysterious and awesome human phenomenon observed by early people.

The importance of blood in the earliest rituals is attested to by the presence of red ochre, found in abundance at the oldest archaeological sites. Later, male animals, the boar, the stag, the bull, were sacrificed in place of human victims as we see in the story of Snow White. The king, no longer a sacrificial victim, continued for thousands of years to derive his power from his association with the Goddess, understood to be his mother and his lover. Sexual union between a king and a priestess of the Goddess, a sacred temple prostitute, commonly marked a king's ascension to power.

In the shift to patriarchy, the meaning of the sacrificial victim was displaced, as many attributes of male and female were reversed. The offering of the woman to the service of the male god was explicitly sexual, the offering to a superior power of her womb, her fertility, and the beauty that came to signify her sexuality. This sacrifice is celebrated in the story of Mary, whose womb was impregnated by the God of the Hebrews, and whose son, like Inanna, harrowed hell and returned from the dead after three days, the same three-day period of the darkness of the moon.

The old idea of sacrifice is still celebrated when a nun takes vows of chastity and becomes the bride of Christ, often shaving her head to indicate her renunciation of beauty. Rather than being a celebration of the sacredness of the woman's offering, her offering is tainted by the shame attached by Christianity to her sex and to her beauty. The violent suppression of female power that stands as background to this sense of shame is described explicitly in the Babylonian myth of the great Goddess Tiamat, destroyed by her own descendant, Marduk.

The lord trod on the legs of Tiamat,
With his unsparing mace he crushed her skull,

When the arteries of her blood he had severed,
The North Wind bore it to places undisclosed.
On seeing this, his fathers were joyful and jubilant,
They brought gifts of homage to him. . . .

He heaped up a mountain over Tiamat's head,
Pierced her eyes to form the sources of the Tigris and the Euphrates,
And heaped similar mountains over her dugs,
Which he pierced to make the rivers
From the eastern mountains that flow into the Tigris.
Her tail he bent up into the sky to make the Milky Way,
And her crotch he used to support the sky.

The violent dismemberment of the dragon figure of Tiamat reappears centuries later in the Old English epic poem *Beowulf*, in which the hero destroys and dismembers the terrible mother of his opponent, Grendel. It persists as a motif in the archetype of the terrible mother-whore destroyed, which stands behind such figures as Snow White's wicked stepmother and other evil mothers in traditional stories. These terrible mothers are often depicted as beautiful women whose beauty signifies not goodness but evil. They are split-off aspects of the old Goddess figure, who embodied the principles of life and death, nurturance and destruction, all part of the life cycle.

Perhaps most disturbingly to us now, extreme violence against women appears as a recurrent theme in popular culture, for example, in the celebrated movies of Alfred Hitchcock, in which a succession of beautiful women are brutally murdered. Where the depiction of violence against women is considered entertainment, it is part of a larger pattern of a culture ruled by violence.

The simplest way to illustrate this is to walk through any sampling of movies in a modern shopping mall. More than half will show extreme violence and cruelty, increasingly directed at women and children, also including violence perpetrated by women and children, the ultimate horror movie. The theme of the beautiful woman in danger is so much of a standard in the Hollywood movie industry that it is referred to in shorthand as "womjeop," meaning "woman in jeopardy," and used as a basic criterion for measuring the potential box-office draw of a project. As media sexualization of children increases, they are shown alongside women as objects of violence.

Although in "real life" violence is directed at women and children without much concern for their appearance, in the movies the victims are routinely beautiful. It is their beauty that makes the violence against them interesting. It is the violence that makes their beauty interesting. No longer limited to hard-core pornography, this link between violence and beauty is regularly reflected in advertising images in magazines and on television.

This idea that a beautiful woman is in danger is so much a part of patriarchal culture that it has become virtually invisible. The sacredness of the eternally diminished feminine is honored in our culture, and the violence that keeps the older sacredness of female power in check is meant to be implicit, not noticed, a silent threat. Urban women tense ourselves, ready for attack, whenever we enter an elevator or a lonely street. If we make the connection between the vulnerability of feminine dress and shoe styles and the frequency of violent attack, we run the risk of being labeled abrasive, carping feminists.

In times of transition, like ours, the paradoxes become apparent. Women are simultaneously endangered and seen as dangerous. Protests against the unfair treatment of women proliferate, as do backlash swings against the protestors, seen in the continuing polarization over women's reproductive rights and the issue of abortion. But protests have not availed to diminish violence or mistreatment. We must therefore look to ourselves and to our oldest traditions for sources of strength and wisdom. The clearest of these sources are those derived from the spirit.

SUN PU-ERH

Sun Pu-erh's story, introduced on page 3, is in some ways typical of spiritual traditions concerning beautiful women. When her teacher looks at Sun Pu-erh and decides she cannot go off on her own to meditate because of the danger posed by her beauty, he is simply recognizing the weight of centuries of violence against women. When Sun Pu-erh takes matters into her own hands by burning her face with hot oil, she is taking over the role of the powerful molester, and using it for her own purposes of spiritual growth. This is what makes her so unusual in patriarchal culture, unusual but not unique.

A beautiful woman who seeks spiritual growth is hampered by the violent possessiveness and lust of men—fathers, husbands, brothers, strangers. Tibetan Buddhist traditions contain several stories of women who were beaten and mistreated and yet managed to survive and become adepts in their spiritual practice. Nangsa Obum was beaten by her father-in-law and died of a broken heart when her infant son was taken from her, but she returned to life and became a yogini, a great teacher. Beautiful women in the Bible are constantly at risk, like Susanna in her bath, gazed on lustfully by the village elders.

From early church times into the present day, Christian women have been molested by priests and monks as well as by laymen and non-Christians. Sometimes, to avoid men's advances, Christian mystics have mutilated themselves and been canonized for so doing. Fairy-tale heroines are often subject to the jealous violence of husbands and strangers as well as sisters and stepmothers. The more beautiful the woman, the greater her danger, and often the greater her endurance and resourcefulness.

What remains disturbing for me in all of these stories is the acceptance by so many different cultures of violence toward women, especially by members of a woman's own family. Such violence is considered normal, and the acceptance of violence by the women themselves is also considered normal. What is unusual is resistance, and it is precisely resistance that is necessary for spiritual development. But the resistance, in these traditional stories, seldom takes the form of active violence in self-defense. Self-mutilation is more common, along with endurance, and, most usual, escape. What is also common is the refusal of the woman to place any value on her own appearance.

Sun Pu-erh's decision to disfigure her face is matched by
the fasts and self-sacrifices of Christian mystical women, with
a difference—she acts entirely out of a practical need to make
herself unattractive to would-be molesters, whereas the Christian tradition contains more hatred of the body, especially the
female body. This misogyny carries over into the present, when
women are still faced with the double bind that pressures us to
be sexually attractive and punishes us with harassment, assault,
and discrimination when we are sexually attractive.

Sun Pu-erh, in going against the cultural dictates of her
time, was a woman of extraordinary determination and courage.
She was also a woman with the support of her husband and her
teacher to follow her own spiritual path. Even so, in order to
leave her home she had to disguise herself, even to her husband,
and pretend to be mad. Sun Pu-erh's husband, also a student
of the Tao, complained to their teacher that his wife had gone
mad. The teacher replied, "If she is not mad, how can she become an immortal?" The husband did not understand. From a
spiritual viewpoint, the teacher was saying that sanity is a matter of human, not divine, consensus. The cultural consensus that
requires a woman to be obedient and conventionally beautiful
prevents her from achieving the spiritual wholeness that will
lead her to immortality.

> Sun Pu-erh looked at her face in the mirror. Scars and pock-
> marks dotted her face. Since she had not combed her hair for
> a month, she was no longer the beautiful wife of a wealthy
> merchant. Sun Pu-erh was delighted. She was now ready to
> make the journey to Loyang. With a piece of charcoal she
> smeared her face and her clothing. Looking like a mad beg-
> gar-woman, she ran out into the living room, laughed wildly,
> and rushed out the front door. A servant tried to stop her,
> but she bit the girl in the arm.

DIALOGUES WITH MADWOMEN

From a modern perspective, it is a psychiatric commonplace
that neglect of appearance is an early symptom of mental illness

in women. Feminists writing about this phenomenon link it with the pressures experienced by women who try to live up to the impossible standards set for them, but whose development tends in a different direction. Unfortunately, there is often no leeway for a woman to develop against the grain of her culture. The same feminist literature documents the punitive and often violent nature of methods used to contain mental patients.

More elusive are the connections between the violence expressed by some madwomen, the violence they experience from others, and the standards for feminine appearance and behavior that deny the existence of violence and suppress normal reactions to violence, such as anger or self-defense.

Academy Award–winning director and writer Allie Light, whose documentary film *Dialogues with Madwomen* began from and includes her own experience as a patient self-committed for depression to the Langley-Porter psychiatric ward in San Francisco, told me of "help" offered to women in her ward:

A consultant was brought in to teach the women patients how to take care of their appearance. As they put books on their heads and walked around to improve their posture, Allie asked the head nurse, "Why should I do this?" Thirty years later, she still remembers the nurse's reply: "It will make you feel that you don't have to worry about how you look. It will take your attention off yourself, and you can focus on other people." Allie remembers that in her depression she was "utterly indifferent" to her own appearance, and wondered to herself, "What does this have to do with anything?"

While doing research for her film, Allie looked at an old British newsreel, which showed women mental patients being taken to a beauty school, while a man's voice-over explains that this is part of their treatment. She also found footage taken at Bellevue Hospital in New York, which showed a woman being dragged into the ward by two attendants, then given shock treatment, then, a week later, dressed up and wearing makeup, shaking hands, smiling, and being released. Thinking about these stories together, Allie and I wondered at the belief system that assumes that if the outside is acceptable the inside must therefore be fine. This system is used to constrain women from protesting the façade of "appropriate" appearance and behavior.

There are several different ways of understanding the appearance and behavior of women diagnosed as mentally ill. One is the shift from external to internal vision, which sometimes characterizes the experience of people who are caught in extreme states without the ability to communicate clearly about what is happening to them. In such cases a woman may simply be unaware of her outward appearance, and indifferent to it, a state of mind not considered acceptable for women.

Another possibility is resistance, that a woman may be challenging the standards of appearance she has suffered from in the past, but doing so in ways she is not able to comment on, or she is not listened to by those around her. She may be reaching out in ways that form incomplete communication, with actions or gestures that are not fully understood. Such a woman may need support and validation for her perception of the limiting and restricting effect of social standards of appearance.

Still another possibility for understanding "mad" behavior is to think that the story of Sun Pu-erh has archetypal value, is a metaphor for many women's experience. We could then suppose that a woman in the midst of a big crisis might damage her own appearance for spiritual reasons, which seem quite clear to her, but which, again, she is unable or unwilling to communicate to others. A remarkable example of fictional insight into this situation is *Wide Sargasso Sea*, Jean Rhys's twentieth-century telling of the story of Rochester's mad wife from Charlotte Brontë's nineteenth-century novel *Jane Eyre*. By filling in the life story of the infamous madwoman in the wealthy Mr. Rochester's attic, who so terrifies poor Jane Eyre, Rhys brings her readers to a very different perspective, the madwoman's own, beginning with her childhood in Jamaica, leading to her captivity in a strange house in a strange country. Appearing to others to be a monster, she feels herself to be a poor prisoner, but she has lost the ability to communicate her terror in words.

This sense of the importance and inaccessibility of words to those trapped in their own extreme states is described by one of the women in the film *Dialogues with Madwomen*, who says that being able to speak about her experience is an ability she has not always had. This woman once cut herself severely in an attempt to indicate her need for attention and help. She said, "There was finally something nobody could argue with. . . . You could say, 'Oh, maybe you don't feel like that,' but you can't tell me that I'm not sitting here with blood all over my arms now, can you?" The same woman, describing the therapy that finally helped her out of psychosis, said the best thing about her therapy was that "I learned to talk about what was going on."

This difficulty in saying what is happening is frequently experienced by people in extreme states, both women and men. But it is a particular problem for women, who have been defined since infancy, not by their ideas and actions, but by their appearance, which marks them as other, as victim, as target. They are not expected to speak clearly—on the contrary, they have learned to be silent.

Behind these practical ideas I have mentioned, there is an approach to the extreme states of mental illness that suggests that such states may contain valuable information for all of us, like the old concepts of the holy fool and the wisdom-speaking oracle. By simply pathologizing the undeniable suffering of those caught in extreme states, we lose sight of the original sacrificial meaning of madness. Once "lunatic" meant one who was possessed by the spirit of the moon. Everyday, consensual experience of reality was offered up by those who became possessed by a spirit of revelation. As for centuries past the value of madwomen's experience, like the meaning of their reactions to abuse, is routinely ignored by modern psychiatry.

THE PERILS OF PATRIARCHY

What is true across the board is that a woman walks in peril regardless of her choices about appearance. Sun Pu-erh transcended her peril by means of her strong foundation, her single-hearted determination, and the skills and support given by her teacher, and even then she needed the intervention of heaven for protection from would-be molesters. It took a hailstorm and severe injuries as well as the repeated warnings of his companion that it was bad luck to interfere with a madwoman before the sleazy character who wanted to rape Sun Pu-erh finally decided he should leave her alone.

When Sun Pu-erh attained enlightenment, she expressed her gratitude to the people of the nearby village who had fed her and allowed her to take shelter near them for so long, but she did so in a way peculiar to herself and her own creativity. She made two figures of branches, one resembling her, one resembling a man. Goddesslike, she breathed life into them, then sent them into the village to outrage the local people with their overt sensuality and affection for each other. The villagers responded by deciding to burn the two "people" in the abandoned house where Sun Pu-erh had lived, an indication of how threatening open sexuality was in traditional China. As the smoke from the bonfire rose, Sun Pu-erh appeared in the sky, flanked by the two figures, and spoke to the astounded villagers of her enlightenment, promising them that these figures she had created would be guardians of the village for the next five years. She transformed the figures back into branches, which she threw down to the villagers, then she ascended to the sky. The villagers created a shrine in honor of Sun Pu-erh and the two figures, and they did indeed enjoy unheard-of prosperity for the next five years. Sun Pu-erh returned to earth to help her former husband on his path before she joined the immortals to share in tasting the peach of immortality.

Sun Pu-erh, as the only woman among them, was also the only one of the seven Taoist masters whose enlightenment was first hampered by her beauty, then associated with fertility.

This aspect of *Seven Taoist Masters*, along with the fact that the entire story-line revolves around the ripening of the immortal peach in the Queen of Heaven's garden, suggests the influence of a prepatriarchal Goddess-centered tradition on this tale. In fact the roots of Taoism lay in shamanic practices that date back to Goddess worship in ancient China.

Whereas the Goddess religions ritualized death as part of the life cycle, this story offers the possibility of transcending death by becoming immortal. The Taoist masters, as they grew in spiritual capacity, became ruddy-cheeked and healthy, youthful in appearance. When their teacher, Wang Ch'ung-yang, decided to get rid of the students who were not sufficiently dedicated to attain the Tao, his solution was to break out in boils and rashes and die, emitting noxious odors from his corpse whenever crowds of people came around. Only his most devoted disciples remained to carry his body to its final burial place, as he had instructed them.

In his enlightened state, bodily appearance, health, and life itself had become illusory roles, which he was able to assume and discard as needed. Similarly, when Sun Pu-erh returned to visit her husband, Ma Tan-yang, she showed him how she was able to sit in a bath of boiling water undisturbed, and perform seemingly impossible feats. She was no ghost, but she had achieved mastery over her body by her years of disciplined practice. Her example inspired Ma Tan-yang to leave his comfortable home and to complete his training as an immortal.

Sun Pu-erh's astonishingly provocative, outrageously creative behavior may serve as a challenging model to contemporary women, for if ever a woman has redefined female appearance and the limitations of the female role to suit her own need for growth, it is this Taoist woman, who lived nine hundred years ago in China.

In challenging her entire culture, even her respected teacher, Sun Pu-erh is a paradoxical model for us now, a woman who deliberately took on the roles of ugliness and madness in which so many women suffer involuntarily. She did so because this was her quickest, perhaps her only, path to enlightenment. The important distinction between her and women who abuse their bodies unconsciously is that for Sun Pu-erh ugliness and madness were only temporary roles, just as beauty, wealth, comfort, sanity itself were roles she was able to assume and discard at will.

Not all women have such fluidity as Sun Pu-erh, nor do all traditions value fluidity. Some traditions value rigid adherence to specific codes of ethics. Sun Pu-erh lived in a culture where some pursued the Tao, but where the dominant culture was very conventional and very repressive. The response of the villagers to the two figures created by Sun Pu-erh was indignation and then the decision to burn them. And yet in that same culture there were brothels in every city.

After Sun Pu-erh's teacher, Wang Ch'ung-yang, died, his other disciples went their own ways. One of them, Liu Ch'ang-sheng, found a brothel in which to study and overcome his obsession with beautiful women. He said to his colleagues who tried to talk him out of going to the brothel:

> . . . the methods of cultivation that you speak of are only appropriate to those who have strong foundations. I am afraid I would not be able to change my attitude by will. I need to expose myself to the activities in the brothels, so that I can see through the illusions of sexual attractions and desire.

The proprietress of the brothel introduced Liu Ch'ang-sheng to Madam Yu, saying that she "excels in dancing, music, poetry, painting, and chess, and she is beautiful and gentle."

> Madam Yu looked at Liu Ch'ang-sheng and saw that he was not only handsome but had a regal bearing that set him apart from her other customers. Whereas her other customers desired her body and often made violent sexual approaches to her, this man respected her and spoke to her gently, treating her not as a sexual object but as a friend. Liu Ch'ang-sheng conducted himself according to what Wang Ch'ung-yang had taught him: "View everything before you with calmness. True stillness is when a landslide passes before you and you are

not disturbed." Thus, Liu Ch'ang-sheng treated the beautiful woman before him as an empty form. . . . Liu Ch'ang-sheng and Madam Yu enjoyed each other's company as friends. They ate together. They played music together, and they even slept together in the same bed, but as far as Liu Ch'ang-sheng was concerned he was sleeping beside a plank of wood. All this time Liu Ch'ang-sheng told his eyes to look but not see Madam Yu's beauty; his ears to listen but not hear her seductive voice. Anybody looking at their actions would see two people playing with each other like children.

When the other women in the brothel heard about these strange goings-on, they were curious and wanted to know more. The proprietress was tolerant because of the gold pieces that Liu Ch'ang-sheng produced magically.

Thus Liu Ch'ang-sheng was often accompanied by five or six ladies who were continually amused by his lack of sexual interest toward them and the friendly and understanding way in which he treated them, not as objects for pleasure but as intelligent human beings.

I am inspired by Liu Ch'ang-sheng's unconventional decision to study his attachment to women's beauty. At the same time, I am painfully struck by the calm and precise way the storyteller describes the way the women in the brothel were accustomed to be treated, and what a relief it was for them to be treated as "intelligent human beings." This situation in a novel written almost five hundred years ago still applies to the condition of many women today.

Seven Taoist Masters makes no distinction between the beauties of women, or indeed between any appearances, except as they become an obstacle to development. While noting that many men behave violently toward women who are not under the protection of their families, the Taoist author of this book sees such behavior as foolish and undeveloped, a mark of those who do not seek enlightenment. However, it is not the task of the Taoist to correct such foolish activity, only to behave differently, in accordance with one's own original nature, the nature one is born with and strives, through spiritual practice, to regain. By finding original nature, one lives in harmony with the Tao.

The concept of original nature is so profound and so useful that it may overshadow a question that haunts many of us: what does this attitude of toleration say about widespread violence toward women?

In patriarchal religions, there is a long-standing identification of women, our appearance and our sexuality, with temptation, uncleanliness, and evil. Implicit in this is toleration or even advocacy of violence against women today. For if women are seen as evil temptresses, men's violence can be justified.

Male violence toward women is inextricably connected with issues of sexuality and beauty. Because beauty is often equated with goodness, and goodness with chastity, women have often been identified as beautiful virgins. They have suffered from assaults on that important identity. First encouraged to be beautiful and to seclude themselves in preparation for marriage, Muslim women, when raped in war, as they have been in this century in Bangladesh, Iraq, and Bosnia, must then cope with the outrage of their families as well as the trauma of violent rape. Under patriarchy, a woman's virginity is the property of her family and then of her husband.

Men who are taught to believe that women are beautiful and good virgins, but beautiful and bad whores, with no middle ground, have no healthy way to express their sexuality without denigrating women. Repressed sexuality has a way of gaining expression through violence. In cultures in which men are traditionally more powerful than women, men commit most of the violence and women are mostly victims of violence.

NANGSA OBUM

The Tibetan Buddhist story of Nangsa Obum approaches these intertwined issues of violence, women, and appearance from still another perspective. Sun Pu-erh mutilated herself in order to pursue her spiritual path. Great violence was used against Nangsa Obum, but it didn't prevent her spiritual development. Both women, because they were beautiful, had to deal with violence evoked by their appearance.

> *The beautiful bodies of the gods*
> *Are like borrowed jewels.*
> —Song of Nangsa Obum

Nangsa Obum was born in Tibet to a humble but pious family. She was unusual from birth, an exceptionally beautiful child, who spoke, according to legend, with her first milk. She developed rapidly into a woman whose beauty reflected her goodness, her ability to meditate and also to do "worldly work." Seeing this, her parents kept her at home, although she had many suitors. This was fine with Nangsa Obum, who loved to meditate, until one day she was spotted by a "harsh nobleman," Dragchen Samdrub, at a village gathering. Seeing her beauty from afar, he sent his servant after her. This servant "pounced on Nangsa like an eagle attacking a rabbit, or like a falcon falling upon a small bird." Against her protests, Dragchen informed her that she would marry his son, Dragpa Samdrub, and so it happened. Her parents agreed to the marriage, admonishing Nangsa to be a good wife, to put herself last and her husband and his family first.

Nangsa was admired and loved by all for her beauty and goodness, especially by her husband, who scarcely allowed her out of his sight. But her husband's aunt, Dragchen's ugly sister, Ani Nyemo, was jealous of the power the family wished to give Nangsa and plotted against her. She treated Nangsa badly, called her a "peacock," and accused her of flirting with other men. Seeing the aunt's jealousy, Nangsa analyzed her own situation, realizing that her beauty, her child, and her family's love were all obstacles to her spiritual development, but that the jealous aunt was a guru, who would force Nangsa to grow.

Ani Nyemo's lies and the possessive jealousy of Nangsa's husband led him to beat her, although she had done nothing to merit a beating. He beat her severely, breaking three ribs, and stopped only when Nangsa's servants came running in response to her screams.

A guru in a nearby monastery realized in his omniscience how special Nangsa was, and that she would become a guide to others. To speed up the inevitable process of suffering he foresaw for her he disguised himself as a handsome beggar. As the beggar, the guru went to Nangsa's window and sang a song that she recognized as spiritually profound, so she invited him up to her room. Finding them there, her father-in-law beat her again, more severely than his son had, and took her infant son away.

Nangsa died in the night of a broken heart, and her family was advised, by a diviner, to place her body, under guard, on an eastern hill. Sure enough, after going into the realms of death and being blessed by Avalokitesvara, the King of Compassion, Nangsa was returned to her body, a *delog*, or wise soul, who has returned from death.

Although Nangsa's husband and father-in-law were impressed with her return from death, they were still not spiritually awakened. They persuaded her to come home with them, but they didn't listen to her teachings. So she returned to her parents' home, but they also failed to understand her, and thought she was being a disobedient wife. Her mother threw her out, and would have beaten her but for the intervention of her friends.

Nangsa went to the monastery, where the guru, Sakya Gyaltsen, lived, and he accepted her as a student. There she cut her hair, gave away her precious hair ornaments, and dressed plainly, as a yogini. She was happy in her meditation practice. But her father-in-law and husband gathered an army to bring her back. They captured the guru and, when they saw Nangsa "without ornaments looking like a yogini," they cursed Sakya Gyaltsen, comparing Nangsa to a series of animals, and Dragchen, in his worldly power, to the sun:

> *You are an old donkey living in a dirty stable.*
> *Why did you rape our beautiful wild horse?*
> *Why did you cut off her mane?*

They moved to attack the guru, but he "reached out and grabbed the mountain on one side and moved it to the other side," whereupon all the monks who had been injured in the army's attack were healed, and the guru flew up into the sky, singing and urging Nangsa to show her powers, "so they will become devoted to you."

Nangsa used her shawl for wings, flew into the sky and sang to the astonished crowd below, reversing, one by one, the curses of the men, and concluding:

> You tried to saddle the wild mule who lives in the forest,
> That is why I ran away.
> Now I am showing you my power.
> You tried to make the delog Nangsa Obum into a wife,
> But . . . you cannot hold me.

Impressed by the sight of these beings flying in the air, Dragchen and Dragpa and their army prostrated themselves before the guru and yogini, and Sakya Gyaltsen and Nangsa prayed for them, explaining the impermanence of the precious human body, which is to be used in devoted spiritual practice. All were converted, even the dreadful aunt, Ani Nyemo, the harsh father-in-law, Dragchen, and the jealous husband, Dragpa, who devoted the remainder of their lives to the Dharma, the teachings of the Buddha. "Nangsa stayed in the mountains and not only flew, but left her thighprint and footprint in many places as though stone were butter."

The story of Nangsa Obum, like the story of Sun Pu-erh, operates on several levels, using beauty as a metaphor for spiritual development, and at the same time demonstrating graphically the danger and extreme violence suffered by women because of their beauty, and the ways in which beauty is an obstacle to spiritual growth. Nangsa Obum's beauty as a young woman is described in detail in the story:

> Her face was like a shining moon. Her hair was silky like
> new shoots of rice. Her hair had been dressed by her parents

and ornamented. She had on earrings and necklaces of the highest quality. Nothing was missing in her costume.

The Tibetan culture in which Nangsa grew up placed great value on physical beauty and wealth, but these values existed within a spiritual context, which saw the illusoriness of material things, and even saw the beauty of the gods as an illusion. In *The Tibetan Book of the Dead*, freedom, or enlightenment, is understood as detachment from all illusion, whether of beauty or ugliness, whether pleasing or disturbing.

But in order to arrive at such a place of detachment, ordinary human beings must first understand the illusions around them. Therefore, Nangsa Obum and her guru used simple, clear language to describe their spiritual practice. They took the curses of Dragchen and Dragpa and reversed them, showing that the use of women as ornamental objects of pleasure is an illusion like any other, that comparing women to animals can be a double-edged sword, for animals, like humans, seek freedom—especially wild animals. But above all, they demonstrated the power of their practice, for if they were only to be victims, the army would not be changed by seeing their example. Therefore, they flew through the air as they taught, just as Sun Pu-erh appeared in the sky above the astounded villagers when she had achieved enlightenment.

The paradox embedded in the story of Nangsa Obum is the central paradox of the myths concerning women's appearance under patriarchy. We are expected to be beautiful, worshiped for being beautiful, endangered by our beauty, and it is seen as an obstacle to our spiritual development. If we become attached to our own beauty, it is certainly an obstacle to our development, but even if we remain unattached, we must still contend with the jealousy and lust of others. And yet, if we are ugly, our ugliness is read as an outer sign of something wrong inside.

Nangsa Obum and Sun Pu-erh were each able to transform their internal energies by means of spiritual traditions based on internal alchemy, transformational meditative practices rooted in ancient shamanic traditions. Understanding the obsession with material things and superficial appearance of those around her, each turned that obsession inside out by means of her un-swerving, single-minded devotion to spiritual practice. Their lives were challenging and provocative examples of the need for each of us to cultivate our most extraordinary powers.

I find that these stories from old Asia challenge and provoke me to go a step further, thinking of my own contemporary context. While Sun Pu-erh and Nangsa Obum may seem re-mote and entirely exceptional, we are each faced with situations comparable to theirs in our daily lives, and we are each capable of single-minded courage and focus, as they were.

Because of cultural attitudes toward women, beauty, and sexuality, especially the idea that women are objects for the sexual pleasure of men, women are constantly placed in physical danger, danger of rape, of assault, of abuse, of battery, and of insult as well as injury. Another area of danger is psychological, the danger posed to a woman's inner sense of self when she realizes that her beauty makes her attractive to men in ways that are uncomfortable, even frightening to her.

We need not disfigure ourselves like Sun Pu-erh, nor suffer the violence endured by Nangsa Obum. But we will do well to examine the demands made on us to look a certain way and to behave a certain way. If these demands are stifling our own inner growth and spiritual development, then we may need to take decisive action. For this, whether it is a matter of deciding to leave an abusive relationship or an abusive work situation, or simply refusing to comply with restrictive demands, great courage and clarity are required. The basis of these is belief in our own integrity.

SHAME AND FEAR

Because sex is so problematic, at once repressed and exploited by patriarchal culture, it is unusual for a woman to be com-fortable with her own sexuality, and she often lacks cultural support to develop a sense of comfort and security.

Since the time when Inanna leaned against an apple tree and admired her wondrous vulva, women have lost touch with self-

love, not overnight, but as a result of long repression and bru-
tality. Sexuality has become a source of shame, rather than
delight, for many women, who feel inadequate whatever they
do or don't do, not because of any inherent inadequacy, but
because women's sexuality is viewed ambivalently in most cultures. Sexual pleasure is shameful, and lack of responsiveness is
shameful. Even to speak of sex is shameful, and to be ashamed
to speak of sex is also shameful. Sun Pu-erh's delightful joke
on the villagers has its bleak side, as they react so violently to
the playful and affectionate behavior of her lifelike stick figures.

Because of the shame and fear widely associated with sexuality, sexually attractive appearance, while sought after, also
has a shameful side. Women who have been sexually assaulted
are still asked what they might have done to encourage assault—how they dressed, were their movements provocative,
and so forth. Susan Brownmiller followed her classic study of
rape in the United States, *Against Our Will*, with an analysis of
the phenomenon of femininity, as constructed and upheld by
patriarchal culture. In *Femininity*, Brownmiller concludes that
"extreme" femininity is harmful to women because it consists
in "self-imposed masochism (restraint, inhibition, self-denial, a
wasteful use of thought and time) that is deliberately mistaken
for 'true nature.' "

Sun Pu-erh was able, through her own personal power, to
transcend the limiting roles of beauty and ugliness that threaten
so many women. This may not seem possible to an abused
woman or child who believes she is being punished because of
her beauty or her ugliness, or her essential nature. The abused
woman is trapped in the role of victim, often without support
or help to understand her role, much less to transcend it. If
abused as a child, she has no way of defending herself against
the physical or emotional abuse of those who are older and
stronger. But she must react somehow. She may react as Sun
Pu-erh did, by assuming a disguise, but she often does so unconsciously, making herself unattractive by gaining or losing
weight, ruining her complexion with food or overexposure to
the sun, wearing concealing clothing, even cutting or otherwise

hurting herself; or alternatively, she may depend entirely on her appearance to appease men. The disguise itself becomes a danger, threatening to destroy health and self-esteem.

Healing the psychological wounds of abuse depends on a woman's ability to change her relationship to the inner critical voice or presence that determines that she is unacceptable as she is. This may be a long process, requiring strong and sustained emotional support. Such healing may need to take place before a woman can effectively challenge the restrictive cultural consensus, or challenging the culture may be an important aspect of the healing process.

Individual women growing up with memories of childhood incest suffer, not only from their own individual traumas, but from the collective situation in which women and children are raped routinely. And still the first question often asked about a woman who is raped is "What was she wearing?" In other words, "Did she ask for it?" Mothers still blame their own daughters for being raped or molested. Mothers still blame themselves for having been molested.

Only in the past decade have women and men been speaking out in public about the abuse they experienced as children, and how this was invisible and inaudible for so long. At the same time a debate in psychoanalytic and therapeutic literature has raged over Freud's famous decision that stories of childhood abuse were common fantasies of women with little or no grounding in reality.

> When Sigmund Freud's female clients told him they had been sexually abused in childhood, he said these were fantasies. Why didn't you believe us?
> —Allie Light, *Dialogues with Madwomen*

Increasingly, women are turning to accounts of childhood abuse written by women, both fictional and journalistic, to gain an understanding based in women's own experience.

How shocked we all are by the stories of child abuse that we hear and read. Then we probe into our own memories, often to find things we ourselves have forgotten, repressed, but not lost. We act out of the fear we felt as tiny children, the fear that caused us, so many of us, to forget what happened, so that we are afraid of everything without even knowing it.

When the adults we looked to for sustenance and support became objects of fear, the world was no longer a safe place, and nothing could be trusted. It is this fear, the frequent, normal response to omnipresent danger, that itself becomes a new danger, the danger that we will constrict ourselves, limit our own growth, give in to fear and despair. In women, this fear is connected with our sense that our bodies, our appearance, the very beauty we are expected to cultivate, are somehow shameful and dangerous.

Such fear cannot be reasoned away, as its roots are experiential, lodged in the body and in old memory. It can only be explored with great caution and respect, with the understanding that the woman who is the explorer is not alone in her fear and shame, that there is a great network of women who share these with her. Beneath the fear and shame there are desire and longing for all that has been repressed and denied. It is while finding these long-buried longings that the healing begins.

FEAR OF EVERYTHING: MARGUERITE DURAS

> I often think of the image only I can see now, and of which
> I've never spoken. It's always there, in the same silence,
> amazing. It's the only image of myself I like, the only one
> in which I recognize myself, in which I delight.
> —Marguerite Duras, *The Lover*

For many years I have read the work of Marguerite Duras, French novelist, playwright, filmmaker. There has always been a feeling for me of something hidden, something important that informs all her work but remains beneath or behind it. More than any other writer I know, Duras depicts the spirit of longing that stands behind our contemporary fascination with ap-

—— pearance, and also the obstacles that stand in the way of our longing.

A sense of love, desire, fear, and despair permeates her work. There is also, even in her earliest writing, a sense of profound detachment in the midst of great turmoil and violence. In her writing about suffering, pain, and despair, Duras transcends despair. *The North China Lover* (1992) is a new telling of the story of *The Lover* (1985), which in turn reflects back on *The Sea Wall* (1950), Duras's third novel. These stories provide a commentary on Duras's adolescence in French Indochina, now Vietnam, her love affair with a wealthy Chinese man, the poverty of her family, and her love and shame for them, especially for her mother, who had periods of insanity. The story is set within the greater context of the forests and plains of Vietnam, the poverty of the peasants, and the effect upon them of colonial culture. The young girl who is at the center of the story is depicted as precociously seductive, aware of her young glamour and the momentary power over men's hearts and wallets that she wields. On the cover of *The Lover*, there is a photo of the young Duras, the image she describes in the opening of the novel. She was fifteen and a half years old. Duras describes in detail her premature aging process, how she "grew old at eighteen." Her focus is on the passing moment of youthful beauty.

Details of this story, peripheral characters, were to appear in novel after novel, all concerned with the themes of impossible love affairs, beauty, desire, despair, poverty, madness, and fear. Every now and then the mention of someone being beaten passes through the text.

The silence of women pervades Duras's work, writing that sings with a command of language transcending the obstacles of translation. *The North China Lover* clarifies something that was described first in *The Sea Wall*. In that early novel there is a scene in which the mother, literally beside herself with anxiety and guilt, beats her daughter for an entire evening. The occasion of the beating is the gift of a large diamond from the daughter's wealthy admirer, a man besotted with the young girl's beauty.

The reactions of the daughter to the beating are mentioned only minimally, described with a near-clinical detachment, although it is clear that the beating is severe.

In *The North China Lover*, written forty years later, about events that occurred nearly sixty years earlier, there is a conversation between the girl's Chinese lover and her mother. The lover asks the mother if she allowed her older son to beat her daughter. The mother replies that she did it herself, so that her son would not kill her daughter. She asks if the girl had spoken about the beatings to the lover. He says never, that he guessed it from her fear of everything.

I have seen this fear in so many women who have been abused as children. Most are also very creative women, and most do not initially connect their fearfulness with their histories of abuse. The tendency is to seek distance. Duras, so talented, so strong with her language, her vision, her passion to tell and retell her stories, has circled, among other things, around the mystery of her own fear, which goes back to early childhood, to the cruelty of her older brother and her mother's insanity.

In *The North Chinese Lover*, the mother says that her son insisted his sister must be broken, like a horse, otherwise she would be lost, going off with any man who approached her. The primitive story of male ownership of a woman's sexuality, that story which underlies so much cruelty, despair, and fear, so much of the world's violence, is here laid bare once more.

In this late novel, the remoteness of narrative description, no doubt necessary for the young author's first telling of a story so laden with the weight of painful memory, has changed utterly. Here the Chinese lover takes on the feelings of despair, grief, and horror that the girl cannot allow herself to experience, and his feelings are in turn taken on and expressed more fully by the author. Her detachment has become more profound as her willingness to explore her own past has led her into her deepest memories.

The girl was not broken, only wounded. She retained her spirit, her sexuality, her desire, above all her will to write.

Duras, who survived the Second World War in occupied Paris as a member of the French Resistance, who witnessed the aftermath of the concentration camps and wrote about the aftermath of Hiroshima, celebrates love, not violence, the human spirit and the landscape in which it survives.

She also recognizes and documents the violence, jealousy, and vengefulness in each of us, the danger we pose to ourselves, the double nature of human beings struggling with their own shadows. The detachment with which she embraces all these aspects of experience is a transformation of the early remoteness, which, for her as for so many women was an essential protective device. In many of her earlier novels, Duras used a male narrator, whose existence further distances the reader from the unbearable experience of the female protagonist. His understanding provides the bridge of communication from the silent woman at the center of the fiction to the reader. But in the later work the silence, and its multiple meanings, are communicated directly by the author.

Above all, Marguerite Duras writes of desire, the opposite of fear, desire of the body and of the heart, both superficial and profound, desire for wholeness, which challenges danger, encompassing beauty, ugliness, violence, and fear. In so doing she offers another way to detachment, similar to the way chosen by the Taoist master who went to live in the brothel. Duras's way is to study her own desire, the desire of a woman who has always refused to be limited by cultural confinement and who has finally broken through the barriers of her deepest fears.

Duras's writing, and the writing and films of other women who continue to depict the abuse of girls and women, serves to validate, to affirm, to make real experiences that have long been denied. As an alternative to, or in conjunction with, therapy, such artistic validation goes a long way toward bridging the fearful gap in communication between women who have been hurt and those around them.

There is a stillness at the heart of Duras's writing, but that stillness is not identical with the terrible silence of women who do not speak of their own pain, yet who feel it deeply. Her

stillness is eloquent, a transformative force, akin to the stillness
that the Taoists cultivate.

*True stillness is when a mountain crashes in front of you and
you are not afraid. It is when a pretty woman or handsome
man stands in front of you and your desires are not roused. In
stillness a parent can patiently teach a wayward child. In stillness
an elder sibling can instruct the younger. In stillness husband
and wife can live in harmony. . . . Thus, stillness is the center
of activity, yet in activity there is stillness.*
　　　　　　　　　　—Wang Ch'ung-yang, *Seven Taoist Masters*

4

BEAUTY AS

OBSTACLE

Everybody hates to hear how hard it is to be beautiful, but I can tell you that because of the way I look, I know people are watching my lips move and aren't hearing what I'm saying. It makes you understand prejudice.
—Cybill Shepherd, *The Advocate*

Sun Pu-erh's beauty is an obstacle to her development only for a moment. As soon as she hears that her teacher will not let her go to Loyang because of the danger posed by her beauty, she solves the problem by getting rid of her beauty. For her colleague Liu Ch'ang-sheng and others like him, women's beauty is an enduring obstacle because of his attachment to it and the sexual craving it inspires in him.

Whether it is perceived as a source of danger or privilege, beauty is an obstacle to spiritual and psychological growth so long as it is viewed as a possession to be attained and hoarded, rather than as a role to be occupied temporarily, by anyone, as the occasion arises. This chapter focuses on the ways that beauty functions as an obstacle to women's spiritual development, and suggests some ways that we can work with this obstacle, becoming more flexible in the process.

Lacking a secure sense of identity, which allows us to respond to the needs of the moment, we women are often caught between dangerous old standards of who we are and dangerous new standards of how we should look. In order to effect change, we must start by acknowledging the implicit assumptions that keep us from wanting or daring to change. Many of these have to do with appearance and with the all-important question, Who is looking?

WORKING WITH THE INTERNAL CRITIC

Women who feel overwhelmed by the expectations of others usually carry around a fierce internal critic, who watches and condemns everything about the way they look. For such women, experiencing themselves in ways other than the visual can be a transformative experience. Speaking with a woman who dances and does movement therapy, I asked her how she experiences herself while dancing: does she see herself, feel herself, or what? She said she feels her movement first in her own body and then in relation to the space around her, at which point her awareness tends to shift from the body to a more visual sense of shapes and light and shadows. Dancers often work in rooms with large mirrors on every wall. As a teacher, she usually covers any mirrors in the room where she is working, because she finds that paying attention to the mirror distracts her and her students from their own feelings and from a sense of their movement based on body sensations.

For these dancers as for many women, the internal critic is projected onto the mirror and reflects back a viciously constructed image. Similar feelings are often expressed by dancers working with video as a study guide. They must first work with the hopelessness of seeing themselves through the lens of their own internalized critics, deadly enemies out to stifle self-esteem and creativity. This hopelessness is partially based on the acceptance of a purely visual standard of value.

But there is also a built-in paradox, based on our ambivalence toward women's strength. A dancer or a figure skater needs great strength and endurance in order to perform the leaps and stretches required of her. But she is expected to look fragile, like a snowflake or a flower. She must have muscles in her legs and arms, but these muscles must not show. An American television commentator describing the Olympic gold-medallist in figure skating, sixteen-year-old Oksana Baiul from Russia, admired her "nerves of steel on the inside, and on the outside, limbs that seem soft and light as a feather." Physical and emotional strength is paired with visual fragility. What we want to see is different from what we know.

The power of a mirror is only visual and reflective—it can't show inner reality. In the story of Snow White, by descending into apparent death Snow White escapes the judgment of the mirror and the persecution of her jealous stepmother. Sun Pu-erh's mirror tells her what the world will see, an ugly madwoman, not what she is in the process of becoming, an enlightened immortal. In both of these stories, the visual standard is challenged. It is not the sole measure of a woman's value.

By shifting awareness from visual to tactile perceptions of feeling and movement in space, my dancer friend dances right around her visual critic, and gives herself a chance to work out her creative impulses. This is a sensory-grounded way of working with issues of identity and with roles of beauty and ugliness.

When I teach classes on this subject, I spend a lot of time helping students to explore different ways of perceiving their own bodies and others', experimenting with roles, identity, and channels of perception (sensory-grounded ways of perceiving, for instance, seeing, hearing, feeling, and moving).

Recently I've started using paper bags as teaching tools: they are cheap, easily obtained, and recyclable. In my classes and workshops we wear our paper bags and we change them, cutting out eye, ear, mouth openings, decorating them to represent the roles we identify with, those we long for, those that repel us. Two women wearing paper bags on their heads relate to each other very differently from two women looking with anxious, jealous, or critical eyes at each other. Wearing my paper bag, I feel more related to my own inner experience, freer to experiment with movement and sound, to explore different ways of being in the world. I can be someone else. I can leave, momentarily, my own small identity, become a monster or a movie star, or someone very silly.

As I broaden my sense of who I am to include much more than the way I look to others, I move from the idea that my experience is determined by a visual critic to a wider awareness of myself as someone who feels, who moves, who hears and speaks, who is actively related to others and to my environment. I feel more powerful, more comfortable with myself, and paradoxically, less concerned with myself—more able to think of others when I am less concerned with what they think of me.

The visual critic is often aided and abetted by words, words first heard in a parental tone of voice, which suggest that the hapless woman at whom they are directed is doomed whatever she does, doomed by obesity, awkwardness, "bad" skin or hair or teeth, the "wrong" shape of some part of her body, some "mistaken" something about her, or even doomed by her own attractiveness. Such an internal critic is often mistaken for an inner guide, and acts as a forbidding figure, blocking creativity, self-esteem, even adequate functioning in the world. It is easily awakened by the slightest criticism from outside, and a woman who has consciously worked on her self-image for years may be devastated in a moment by a critical remark by her partner or coworker, or even by a passing stranger.

CHANGING ROLES

So long as we are stuck in the role of the one who is watched and criticized for our appearance, we are victims of the critic, and the ideal of beauty remains an obstacle to our development. The only way out is to switch roles, changing identities or changing channels of perception. Although the idea of deliberately changing identity is a very old one, found especially in Eastern religions but also in fairy tales all over the world, there is little cultural support in the West for actually doing it, and it remains an intense challenge.

Some people seem to be endowed from birth with the ability to change roles according to the moment. They may become actors or politicians, or, if their tendencies are more internalized, writers of fiction. For others, like me, identity seems fixed and rigid. We are what we think we are, and we may not even realize that we feel trapped in our limited identities. In my case, it has taken a lot to shift me from my single, stubborn identity, something like a young Joan of Arc, crusading for justice against impossible odds. Probably the most helpful forces for change have been my own aging process and the awareness tools provided by my studies in Taoism and process work. You, dear reader, may have a much easier time experimenting with new identities.

I remember a time in my life when death forced me to change my usual identity and take on a new role.

In 1982 my father died suddenly on an operating table. He was seventy-two. Although my sister and I both rushed to New York as soon as we could, he died before we could say goodbye. I had to go to the morgue to identify my father's body, a legal requirement so that his body could be released for the funeral. Seeing the look I read as fear on my father's dead face was a terrible and forceful experience for me. I think that was the first time I began to act as an adult without thought or undue concern for how I might appear to others.

As we planned the funeral with a rabbi, one of my uncles announced that he would speak about my father. Very well, I said, surprising myself with my forcefulness, but I must speak also, as my mother doesn't wish to. The rabbi was not delighted (he was of the old school that still believes women should be seen but not heard), but I prevailed, much to the relief of my mother and sister. Stunned by their own grief, they were happy to be represented by me.

I spoke at his funeral about my father's love of gardening and fishing, about how little I had valued my father in his lifetime, and how much I missed him once he was gone. My voice was rough, like a boy's breaking voice, and in that moment I became the son my father had longed for. I was thirty-nine and a mother; I had no idea what I looked like and I didn't care. I had spoken before in public many times, as a teacher and as a filmmaker, someone with an image to uphold. This was the first time I spoke of my own feelings, difficult ones, in a way that contradicted the usual image I strove for as someone cool, competent, in control.

MY FATHER'S LEGACY

My father's legacy to me was a surprise, having to do with failure. My father cared little or nothing about his appearance, but loved beauty outside of himself, in nature, in the roses he passionately tended, in my mother's eyes, which first attracted him to her, in the ocean where he fished for long hours. He would have been an artist, but for his sense of obligation, first to his mother and sisters, later to my mother and to us, his two daughters, and so he worked for many years as a postal supervisor. My father believed you could not make a living following your passion. He was, as my mother frequently reminded him, a failure. He followed his passion anyway, in his spare time, on his days off, in the mornings before he left for work, gardening, fishing, roaming the docks, looking at fishing boats with wistful eyes, building and fixing things, reading, humming odd tunes to himself.

Although he died suddenly, unready for death, my father left a legacy of spirit that appears in every rose on my rosebushes, in every word I write, every time I find myself gazing at the ocean, or hammering a nail, or failing at something and realizing I will go on anyway. When I put on my oldest, shabbiest clothes and head out to the garden, I am my father. This was his legacy to me, an occasional, rare freedom from concern about appearance, and my hard-won willingness to risk, even to experience, failure.

Some women have the experience of changing roles or taking on an unfamiliar role much earlier in life than I did. Others come to it only near the end of their lives. We have so many different roles in our psyches, roles that turn up in our dreams and experiences, and beg to be lived by us. But the visual standard is a limiting, binding rule, which holds us back until something much stronger pushes us over the edge.

FLORINDA

Just such a push was experienced by a woman who calls herself Florinda Donner-Grau, a member of an unusual group of anthropologists/shamans led by Carlos Castaneda. In *Being-in-Dreaming,* Donner-Grau recounts her *Alice in Wonderland*-like experiences with a group of Mexican Indian shamans. Time contracts and expands; she finds herself tossed through the air, conversing with a donkey, perched on a treetop. More overwhelming than the physical disorientation is her emotional state, as she swings from euphoria to fear to fury. In the course of these experiences, she learned that her "identity" as a young, white, middle-class female student was only one role among many available to her, and that by remaining tied to that one identity she was enslaved by it. She could, if she chose, move fluidly from role to role, without being trapped in any one. Beauty and privilege, she learned, are snares that hinder women and men from development.

These lessons are not easy to learn, and Florinda, whose name was given her by one of her mentors, was introduced to many altered states of consciousness, so that she could shake loose some of the fixed preconceptions she had been taught since birth. In some of these states she encountered one of her teachers as an old woman, a young woman, and an old/young man, and she was deeply disturbed by the shifts from her normal ways of identifying people. The women in the shamanic group all appeared to her in radically different guises, and one of them explained to her that playing with appearance was one of the challenges they had taken on among themselves.

The young Florinda was initially unaware of the roles in which she cast other people as well as herself, unaware of the limitations imposed by these roles on the people who identify with them. So, for instance, her blond hair and fair skin helped to identify her as someone who was beautiful and privileged, but she carried this role with no awareness, not identifying herself as either beautiful or privileged. At one point she is told,

> Privilege based merely on having blond hair and blue eyes is the dumbest privilege there is.

Being-in-Dreaming offers hints and guidelines for personal development through nonordinary states of awareness. Florinda's story acts on our imagination like a fairy tale. Now more accessible than ever before to our contemporary culture, shamanic traditions from all over the world offer possibilities for our dreaming imaginations to work with the situations in which we find ourselves. The key is our willingness to let go, even briefly, of the single-belief system we have inherited from our culture, in order to entertain the possibility that there are other ways of perceiving reality and realities other than those we have imagined.

The group to which Donner-Grau belongs emerged after years of seclusion to offer lectures and seminars based on their shamanic experiences, apparently for no personal gain. All over the world, indigenous shamans and teachers of ancient wisdom traditions have been making their teachings available to those who are interested on a scale unheard of before. Some are clearly seeking profit; many others are working from other motives. Our dominant belief systems, which emphasize individuals and neglect the whole, have proved too destructive to our planet's ecology. And so many teachers from alternative traditions are emerging from the shadows. You may seek out such a teacher, or you may discover your own inner teacher, who is capable of recognizing and working with the obstacles to your development.

As soon as we approach the subject of beauty as an obstacle to spiritual development, the work of understanding the obstacle has begun. This work has a special urgency when it is understood as a recognition of and preparation for death.

SUSAN — THE WOUNDED HEALER

Susan Barton was an attractive blond woman of twenty when she hurtled through the windshield of her car in an accident that disfigured her and led to two operations by a plastic surgeon. At the age of forty-four she was diagnosed with breast cancer and had a mastectomy. She is now a striking blond woman of forty-six with one breast and a distinctive scar on her face. Thinking back over these events, she says that having the mastectomy seemed minor compared with the original trauma of having her face scarred, even though the face injuries were not life-threatening, and the breast cancer was.

Having a raw, scarred face, as she healed from plastic surgery following her accident, made Susan as a young woman feel "like an intrusion on other people." Unless you live in a culture where women are veiled, it is impossible to disguise the face (and even in a veiled culture the veil comes off at home). Having stayed in a kind of retreat for many years, holding back her desire for more education, working in temporary, low-paying jobs, Susan is just now, in her forties, beginning to take on consciously the personal power required of her first by her accident and then by her illness. She is a woman of considerable presence, and others are drawn to her for some reason they can't always define. I see Susan as unusually able to focus on whatever is happening in the moment, an ability that seems to give her quite a lot of energy.

When we spoke about her accident, I was struck by the part it played in her life, for had she not been scarred, Susan would very likely have married early and taken on a traditional feminine role to which she was not at all inclined. She imagines that she might, in reaction, have pushed herself out in the world in ways that might also have been wrong for her. From one perspective, her suffering was a meaningless tragedy. From another perspective, the years of retreat following the accident gave Susan a deep humility that serves her very well in the work she is just beginning to take on.

Susan is learning, in her work and in her life, to dance the dance of the wounded woman, the scarred woman, the one-breasted woman, stepping toward the role of the wounded healer, the shaman who can use her own experience to help others. It is a pleasure to watch her emerge into this new identity, as she begins to bring her private experience into the public domain, teaching, leading workshops, consulting with organizations.

I sent the first draft of my description of Susan to her for her consent and feedback, as I do with all my writing about individual women, along with some photos I had taken of her. This was her response:

> I must tell you that what you have sent me, both the photos and then the writing, shocked me. I took one look at the photo of me unobscured by hair or crazy facial expression, the full-faced one, gasped and dropped it. I could not believe that I could be that ugly! Then I put it away and didn't look at it again for two weeks. I took it out, having done some inner work by now, and put it on a bookshelf for all to see. There it remains. Facing the reality of that photo has helped me, after all these years of aging and consciousness raising, to begin to free myself of this myth about beauty.
>
> I've been no freer of the need to be seen as beautiful in society's terms than most women. I've been fighting it for a long time, as a "new age" woman trying to embody deeper values based on spirit and consciousness, but it's been a hard struggle made more present by aging and illness.
>
> My relationship with [her Finnish partner] has helped immensely. He seems to see beauty in far broader terms than any American man I've known. He thought the photo was beautiful for its strength and wildness. Shortly after I met him

he told me he wishes his face looked like mine. I think it took me a while to realize that his vision of me has begun to free me from the fear and obsessive thoughts I've harbored about my fading beauty and attractiveness.

This freedom is immense. It allows just what you speak of about moving between identities, choosing rather than being victim of a single identity. I am feeling proud these days of my changing, changeable face and body. I love the fierceness that comes through as I take new stands for myself and others, as we bring forth our feminine expressions of power. I like being "ugly" sometimes. And I like knowing that the beauty I sometimes feel in my heart when I am most connected to spirit comes through on my face as well. . . .

I believe my accident may have been the trigger to turn inside more, to accept the superficiality of most of the relationships and choices I had made thus far. It also gave me the inner strength I needed. I think my lack of self-confidence in the world stemmed from the lessons of my family of origin. Every one of us kids lacked a deep sense of worth, scars or no scars. Though my parents encouraged academic excellence in me, I somehow never overcame the family/social belief about the hopelessness of a woman's attempts to be a success in the world.

It was only for a short time after the operations that I felt very self-conscious, but after a while, I found I was still attractive to men. . . . Many, many people over the years have commented that they haven't noticed the scars until I mentioned them in talking about my past history.

I feel I am a "normal" woman, and yet what is happening to me now, this shamanic opening that one might expect from someone who has undergone a true descent to the underworld, doesn't fit our usual pictures of "normal." I believe the cancer—having a life-threatening illness—has given me the permission I have craved all my life to feel worthy of the spirit's presence in me. And, consequently, to feel that my life as a woman is worthwhile. My body is my guide, more and more, as the spirit moves through it free, at least some of the time, of my limited self.

Susan's story is in many ways my story, and the story of many women. I see in myself and in other women Susan's struggles: to accept herself as she is; her need to reassure herself that she is still attractive; her sense of being drawn to the inner life; and her sense of being distracted by her own appearance.

We are women groping to find our fullest selves in a changing and contradictory social context, moved, at least some of the time, by the spirit. This search and struggle to become whole intensifies as death comes closer to our everyday lives. As I see its effects on those whom death touches, I realize what mystics have known through the ages, what is really the lesson underlying our interest in passing appearances. That is the importance for each of us to live constantly with the awareness of our own death, because in this way we realize the value of each moment.

RENÉE: BEING IN THE UNKNOWN

That death is a functional reminder of the brevity of life was brought home to me as I spoke with Renée Howell, a thirty-four-year-old woman who had advanced ovarian cancer.

Renée had chemotherapy and lost her hair, something that had happened to her twice before. When I first met Renée, she had shining brown hair, beautifully cut and carefully brushed. Later I saw her bald or wearing an embroidered cap, looking very thin and pale. Always, she had an extraordinarily sweet smile. But this time she wore a blond wig, bobbed, with bangs, and a white ribbon tied around it in a way that reminded me of a fairy-tale heroine.

She said, "I just got this wig. I've been running around bald for about a month and I'm getting sick of it. Everyone says you look so beautiful bald, but I notice that they don't shave their heads. They could be beautiful like this too!" She continued, "Outside, with people I don't know, they either stare at you or they would like to stare but don't. Baldness is not my true identity. I wouldn't choose to be bald. It's a statement I don't want to make, of being somehow radical, above appear-

ance, on some spiritual trip, or being a cancer patient on chemotherapy. I don't want to be identified with any of those
things."

Renée, like many young women, had a fairy-tale fantasy of
being carried off by a wonderful man and living happily ever
after. She said she gave up on that fantasy when the cancer was
diagnosed. "Who the hell would want to get involved with me
now," she said, laughing, "A crazy man . . ." and then tears
came to her eyes.

Seeing Renée in her blond wig, I thought of the golden-
haired heroines of European fairy tales, whose hair represents
spiritual treasure. Renée was so happy to hear this, so relieved
to be direct about the issue of appearance.

On the advice of her doctor, Renée decided to stop her
chemotherapy treatments, as they didn't seem to be working.
She tried alternative treatment, working with diet, psychotherapy, and prayer, asking her friends to pray for her and join a
healing circle with her. She spoke a little about what it would
mean for her to live, to be creative, write a book, be a therapist,
be a teacher. Knowing she could die very soon was "really
being in the unknown." Living her life like a fairy-tale heroine,
as her disease advanced, her willingness to take outrageous
chances increased.

Renée told me about her first two chemotherapy experiences and the resulting effect on her hair. I found this fascinating because of my own obsession with hair, dating back to
childhood traumas of bad haircuts and home perms, and because of the huge emphasis placed on women's hair in our culture. Losing her hair the first time, Renée says, was traumatic.
Her hair was long, and she was very proud of it. She said that
her hair was a big part of her identity as a woman, that she
believed she would feel really ugly without it.

When Renée was a child, her mother insisted that she and
her sisters wear short pixie haircuts, which they hated. At night
in their beds they fantasized about how they would grow their
hair long when they were adults. "Mine will grow out of the
house," one would say. "Mine will grow down the street,"
another would elaborate.

Renée had heard of women in chemotherapy shaving their
heads so they would not feel themselves victims of their loss of
hair. By doing it themselves before it happened to them, they
felt more powerful. But Renée didn't feel ready to shave her
head. She cut her hair shorter and shorter as it thinned out,
finally wore a hat to cover the bald spot on top of her head.
For about a week she wore a wig, then her hair started to grow
back.

The second time Renée had chemotherapy her hair fell out
much more slowly, and she never had a bald spot. She kept it
shoulder-length and, to make it seem thicker, she had a red-
tinted cellophane wrap. When her hair started to get thick again
after the treatment, she had it cut short, enjoying the feeling of
having short, thick hair. She liked the different stages of her
hair, liked having her own color back, brown with blond high-
lights. I noticed that, although I was deeply concerned about
the seriousness of her condition, I felt very comfortable having
this discussion about hair with Renée, a discussion similar to
many I have had over the years with girlfriends and women
friends. It seemed somehow just the right discussion for us to
be having.

Renée was prepared to shave her head the second time she
had chemo, and was a little disappointed when she didn't have
to. So this third time, when her hair fell out very quickly, she
decided to shave it. She felt that shaving her head was a ritual,
like a monk's entrance to a spiritual path. I thought that her
resistance to having people regard her bald head as a statement
was perhaps a resistance to her emerging identity as a spiritual
teacher.

She thought about the advantages of losing her attachment
to how she looked, the freedom from concern for others' reactions, but still she felt embarrassed about going out in public
with her bald head. She mentioned that with this third treatment her eyelashes had started to fall out, and also her eyebrows. "It is a relief," she said, "to have this whole issue come
up, so that it isn't just a dark, unconscious thing."

It took courage for Renée to speak about these concerns.
Although we women are expected to concern ourselves with

appearance, we are also expected to be silent about it, to be beautiful without effort or worry. According to this way of thinking, a woman near death is not supposed to be thinking of how she looks. Beauty, after all our emphasis on it, is in the end just a matter of appearance, an obstacle to spiritual growth. We are not meant to dwell on it. And yet how can we ignore something that demands so much of our attention?

A few months after our first discussion, Renée had lost a lot of weight and her tumors had grown. She was very ill, and yet she insisted on doing as much as she possibly could. She decided to move back to California, to a cabin in the redwoods, an amazing decision, given her weakness. I thought again of how she lived her life like a fairy tale, setting off on an impossible adventure, from which she might not return. Once again, Renée's appearance changed drastically. Her hair grew back and was once again short and thick; she was very pale, and her thinness was extreme. Her pants and shirt were loose, and she tended to shuffle a bit as she walked. She looked very eccentric, more like a witch woman in the woods than a young heroine.

She was still very determined to heal her illness, and she became quite feisty, somehow organizing all her friends in Oregon to pack her up and help her move, and all her friends in California to help on the other end. Her courage and determination were extraordinary, but she was very, very tired. Somehow she found the energy in the midst of preparing to move to tell me how much our conversations meant to her, and how important this whole issue of appearance was in her life.

After moving to California, Renée, having obtained financial help from many friends, and accompanied by her mother, went to Germany for further treatment. She experienced a period of renewed energy and well-being, and traveled to Paris, a long-deferred dream. She returned home feeling hopeful about her healing process, and began to paint. On March 9, 1994, Renée died suddenly at her home in California.

Women carry so much of the unconscious, hidden longing of our culture for beauty, for the many things beauty stands for, among them sensitivity, goodness, spiritual wholeness.

Merely to reject beauty is to reject the longing. Merely to carry the longing, unconsciously, is to suffer and to be victims, as we have been for so long. If we can unravel the meaning of our longing, like Susan and Renée, live conscious of our varied effects on the world and on our own inner worlds, we would transform a heavy burden into something very light and wonderful, a gift, like the branches Taoist Immortal Sun Pu-erh threw down to the villagers to ensure the fertility of their fields.

5

MATERIAL

GIRLS

I am having a fight with myself. It goes something like this:

ME: *You keep saying beauty is a role; beauty is dangerous; beauty is an obstacle to spiritual growth. And yet you're just as obsessed with beauty as ever; furthermore, you still haven't defined it.*

I: *How can I define it? It's a role, a matter of cultural consensus, mass hypnosis. There's no such thing as beauty.*

ME: *Then how come you stare at some women and not at others? How come Audrey Hepburn, Marlene Dietrich, Greta Garbo reach out of the movie screen and grab you by the heart? How come even in* Seven Taoist Masters *Wang Ch'ung Yang looks at Sun Pu-erh and says, "Men will desire your beauty." He doesn't say, "Men will desire the illusion of your beauty!" She's beautiful!*

I: That's what he means, though. Her beauty is an illusion—
he's just being realistic about the power of illusions.
ME: Then you'd better go further in exploring your fascination
with beauty, or you'll never get free of it.

BEAUTY QUEENS

In my prefeminist adolescent days I always cried when Miss America paraded down the runway. In my secret heart of hearts I wished that in some miraculous transformation I would someday find myself on that runway, my arms filled with roses, a crown on my head, tears in my eyes, and enormous pride in my heart. I cried when the Queen of England was crowned, and I cried when my best friends won an Oscar for their documentary film.

These tears, like the tears I shed when I hear a union song, or a civil-rights song, or "Amazing Grace," are tears of recognition of a part of myself I seldom acknowledge. There is in me, as there is in many women, a queen, a leader of people, a royal presence, a sacred prostitute, a lover of kings, a representative of the Goddess on earth. This sense of womanly royalty, of leadership, is an archetypal part of human nature, a role that was well represented in the earliest religions and governments, a role that was gradually removed entirely from the major religions and governments of the world, removed, disavowed, repressed. Remnants of this archetype can be traced in the Tarot deck, with its images of the Empress, of Courage shown as a woman, and in the stylized Queens of the modern card deck, which descended from the Tarot. Images of powerful women, not men with breasts added like Michelangelo's women but women distinctly female and distinctly powerful, are characteristic of artifacts dating to four thousand years before the Common Era and earlier, and can also be found up to the present among some indigenous cultures.

Once there was no contradiction between ideas of womanhood and ideas of power. This image of the powerful woman appears in women's dreams and art. It never disappeared entirely from mainstream culture, but was distorted by the negativity attached to the idea of a powerful woman—she had to be represented as a witch, a shrew, a harpy, a nagging bitch, ambitious, the power behind the throne. When she has been the actual power on the throne, like Queen Elizabeth I, her life has been surrounded by stories casting aspersion on her true womanhood.

While it is clearly the spirit of female power that inspires my emotions about crowns and trophies, I have many questions about the implications of beauty pageants and competitions to find out who is the most beautiful, successful, or artistic. This chapter is about women's beauty as a material commodity, its value measured by the responses of judges and audiences, and what that means for our psychology and self-image.

As I write this chapter, it is summer here in Portland, which is famed for its rose gardens. The Rose Festival is imminent. Rose courts have been elected from the various schools, and pictures of senior and junior rose princesses glow from the newspapers. I think of all the battles that have raged in the past twenty years over beauty pageants and beauty queens, the fury of feminists and the defensive fury of contestants and pageant organizers. The posters showing a naked woman sectioned off like a piece of meat at the butcher's, the demonstrations and pickets and writings from all perspectives.

In the full-color newspaper picture of the junior Rose Court, all smiling girls in pink, I see several dark faces, several Asian faces, not yet a full rainbow but the beginnings of one, a tremendous change from the beauty courts I remember as a child. The pictures of the senior Rose Court are even more impressive. There is ethnic diversity and there are a number of pictures of young women dressed unconventionally, excitingly, some wearing baseball caps and sweatshirts. The copy alongside their pictures speaks of their many accomplishments in and outside of school. Another inner conflict breaks out in me.

The logical and also furious feminist in me says, "This is just perpetuating the beauty myth, just widening the scope and pushing the early boundaries of women's obsession with appearance."

But someone else in me says, "If young African American girls and Native American girls and Asian American girls and other young girls who differ from the mass-media standard of beauty will look at this picture and think, 'I look like that. I'm also beautiful,' then we must have beauty courts, and they must resemble rainbows more each year."

But then the feminist, who is very persistent, replies, "Over all these years of white beauty queens, how many young white girls have looked at the pictures and said, 'I look like that. I am beautiful'?"

And the other in me argues, "First, let us deal with this intolerable prejudice, which causes young girls to think themselves ugly solely on the basis of their ethnic background."

"But what about young girls who think themselves ugly because of their size or their weight or their blemished skin or their physical handicaps or scars or because they've been sexually abused for being too beautiful or just because they are girls?"

As I take one side and then the other, I realize I am recapitulating, in my mind, an argument that has gone around and around and around. And then I remember the religious fundamentalists who stand outside of these arguments between women and shout, "Back to the Bible/the Koran/the Torah! Back to traditional (meaning patriarchal) family values! Vanity, thy name is Woman!"

None of these arguments, feminist or fundamentalist, seem to impinge on the young faces glowing from the newspaper pictures. These young women were born after the seventies' protests against beauty pageants. I suspect that women have been protesting beauty contests for hundreds, perhaps thousands, of years. Perhaps women protested the contest in which Esther was selected as queen to Ahasuerus.

I am now an older witness, not a young participant in the ongoing debates. My older inner voice mellows: "Whatever we older ones think or say, young women will dress up or down and compete to be beauty queens and princesses, and other young women will scorn them, and young men will take the entire range of roles for, against, and indifferent, and in favor of similar competitions for themselves, and hopefully all will be recognized and all will be free to stand up for their momentary roles and change their minds and identities as time goes by. Best if we older ones stay out of the fray, for the young ones, left to themselves, will deepen the colors of the rainbow and invent the most wonderful and wacky alternatives to the whole procedure."

In spite of all the commercial pressures and patriarchal double binds about the true nature of women's beauty, these beauty contests celebrate something important. This is the same motivation that makes young Wodaabe men and women primp and preen themselves at their annual festival of erotic pleasure —the urge to adorn oneself, to attract a partner. Adornment is not at all a bad thing, especially when it is expressed freely by both sexes. But when repressed, these normal impulses of adornment and sexual attraction are driven underground, and may emerge in distorted and violent forms.

One of the commonest forms of rebellion among adolescents in our "advanced" culture is manifested in appearance, in punk or gangster or grunge or militant dress, hair, and demeanor. Male youth are traditionally contained in hierarchical societies by being put into uniform and trained in military discipline. Female youth are contained in all societies by the more subtle pressure to look and act in ways considered "feminine." Such containment goes side by side with apparently unrelated outbursts, of madness, of gang violence, of institutionalized repression. A most orderly society, which valued physical beauty highly, was Hitler's Third Reich.

There is a difference between the spontaneous, natural urge of young people to adorn themselves for each other and themselves, and what is done with those urges by commerce and culture. The most hopeful thing I notice about some contemporary beauty contests is the way some of the young women who participate insist, outrageously and creatively, on defining their own standards of appearance.

MOVIE STARS—MARILYN AND MADONNA

Although I have always been fascinated by beautiful women, my criteria for beauty has shifted considerably over time. Marilyn Monroe was threatening rather than beautiful to me when I was a young girl because she seemed to represent all I didn't want to be. Although she was called a sex goddess, she wasn't powerful in her own right, only by virtue of her ability to attract and manipulate men. Using the word "goddess" to describe Marilyn was like using "queen" as a title for the winner of a beauty pageant—the context demeaned the terms.

As a young woman I was embarrassed by my own large breasts and wanted nothing to do with Marilyn. I wanted to be elegant and slender, like Audrey Hepburn. It never occurred to me that all the movie stars were white.

Marilyn, I thought, was a sleazy woman. I didn't think of her consciously as a prostitute, but I was repelled by the way she flaunted her sexuality. Now, when I look at her image through middle-aged eyes, I am impressed with her youth and freshness, with the abundance of her sexual appeal, her curves, her glowing flesh. Her clothes still seem sleazy to me, but they set off her face and body to great advantage. But was she, in effect, a prostitute? Are movie stars who sell their sexual attractiveness the same as prostitutes? Or is selling one's image different in some crucial way from selling the act of sexual intercourse?

As a young woman I was following the primary message of my culture: sex was shameful and prostitution was dirty. Why then, I might have asked, noticing a less conscious tendency, one not so much discussed as promoted, was sex omnipresent, and what about the men whose business made prostitution so profitable? With the impetus of the feminist movement of the seventies, many of us did finally ask those questions. We found out, in great contrast to modern conditions, about the ancient history of prostitution as a sacred act performed by priestesses who represented the goddess. When sex was sacred, prostitution was an act of celebration. Priestesses adorned themselves in the name of the Goddess and the royal men who visited them adorned themselves also, in the name of the Goddess.

In that time, the sexuality of women was worshiped, as it was later feared and then despised. Surely the precursor to penis envy was male envy of the orgasmic, procreative, and nurturing powers of women.

Long before the time when Liu Ch'ang-sheng visited the women in the Chinese brothel, prostitutes had degenerated in public opinion. They were seen as shameful necessities for men who could not conquer their sexual desires. This denigration of sexuality applied also to the way prostitutes adorned themselves. For centuries, a woman's appearance has been categorized according to whether or not it marks a woman as a prostitute. As several writers on the history of fashion have pointed out, the moral standards for women's appearance have varied widely. At one time merely to expose an ankle was considered immoral, while low-cut bodices revealed bosoms that, at another time, were cautiously covered.

Standards for women's appearance and also for our behavior are arbitrarily linked with morality. As feminists have often remarked, it is hard to distinguish, on moral grounds, between a woman who sells her sexuality for marriage and economic security and a woman who rents her sexuality on a nightly basis. In both cases, a woman's sexuality is a commodity, and her value is closely linked with her appearance. Traditionally, however, prostitutes have been more open about the commercial value of their appearance than "respectable" women.

Knowing of the glorious past of prostitution changes my perspective on modern prostitutes. When I look at Marilyn Monroe's movies now, I find her call-girl image fascinating, and sometimes quite beautiful, although never the object of my own hungry gaze the way that Audrey Hepburn, Dietrich, and Garbo have been. Perhaps because of the detachment I feel from it, Monroe's projected image in movies helps me to reflect on the role of the beautiful white woman as commodity.

GENTLEMEN PREFER BLONDES

Gentlemen Prefer Blondes (1953), starring Marilyn Monroe and Jane Russell, offers an impressively witty analysis of the economic value of a woman's appearance, based on Anita Loos's zany 1926 novel about the adventures of two New York call girls.

Howard Hawks, the irreverent director of *Gentlemen*, had a genius for challenging cultural premises in his screwball comedies, and he was aided here by Marilyn Monroe's comic talents. Her showgirl performance of "Diamonds Are a Girl's Best Friend" is in itself a rich and ironic commentary on the connections between beauty, sex, and money, taken a step further in the movie by Jane Russell's imitation of Monroe singing a passage from the same song in a French courtroom, and turned through another round three decades later by rock star Madonna's extension of Monroe's persona in the music video *Material Girl*.

When I was younger, what disturbed me most about Monroe, and what is brought to the surface more and more specifically by Madonna, is the undercurrent of violence that swirls around her image. The same undercurrent seems connected with business in America, suggesting interconnections between violence, commerce, and sexuality. Francis Ford Coppola has built a brilliant career on his *Godfather* series of movies exploring those connections.

Marilyn Monroe was the opposite aspect of the Maiden to Audrey Hepburn, representing, as she did, open sexuality. Reflecting her society's ambivalence about sex, she was frequently portrayed in the midst of danger, real or imaginary. There is a mystery that still clings to her death, with rumors that she was murdered because of her relationship with the Kennedys.

In *Gentlemen Prefer Blondes*, I find Hawks's variations on the standard Hollywood themes of women, beauty, sex, and violence more complex and interesting than the unconscious formula found in too many contemporary movies. In the staging and presentation of the song "Diamonds Are a Girl's Best

—— Friend," we can find a microcosm of the film's approach to the
materiality and transience of sexual appeal.

The "Diamonds" sequence in *Gentlemen Prefer Blondes*
begins with a shot of women in long pink tutus, with flowers
in their hair, waltzing with men in black evening wear under
a huge chandelier. A closeup of the chandelier shows that it
is alive, made of women dressed in skimpy black who are attached to a frame by their arms and legs, an image of bondage.
The camera pans from the women on the chandelier across the
dancing couples to discover Monroe sitting, her back turned
to the camera, in a strapless, low-cut, slinky, hot-pink gown
with elbow-high hot-pink gloves. When she turns around, surrounded by suitors holding pink hearts, she taps them with her
black fan and says, petulantly, "No!" She is then rushed around
the stage by men in black, holding her arms, who present her
to other men holding up pink hearts to her while she sings
an aria of No's, followed by the song "Diamonds Are a Girl's
Best Friend." She is surrounded by an adoring bevy of flower-
garlanded women in pink tutus, to whom she imparts musical advice, saying quite directly that men's affections are as
transient as women's youthful charms; that therefore women
should rely on the permanent security offered by diamonds.

In a world where power and wealth belong primarily to
men, and women's main, and fleeting, assets are their looks,
women cannot afford the luxury of romance without keeping
a crafty eye on the stock market. I remember very well my
mother, disappointed in her expectations of my father's earning
power, telling me over and over that I could just as easily fall
in love with a rich man as a poor man. Irritated by her tone,
which was only half joking, I didn't recognize the line as Marilyn's in *Gentleman Prefer Blondes*. I wanted to believe that I
could be independent, that love was a matter of romance, not
connected to material concerns.

Money and the independence it promises are the primary,
identified focus of the musical sequence in *Gentlemen*. But the
images of danger, bondage, and violence form a disturbing,
more secondary motif, and comment on the basic victimization

of women who are not sufficiently cunning or alert. Women attempting to use their appearance to bankroll a secure future run the risk of being victimized by their intended prey.

The screwball comedy of Hawks's movie, supported by the strong teamwork of Russell and Monroe, goes further than Anita Loos's satiric novel in its use of powerful and disturbing imagery and in its biting commentary on the economic context of relations between the sexes. This is the movie dialogue for the scene between Lorelei Lee (Monroe) and her fiancé's wealthy father (Taylor Holmes):

FATHER: *You don't fool me one bit*
LORELEI: *I'm not trying to, but I bet I could.*
F: *Do you have the nerve to stand there and pretend that you don't want to marry my son for his money?*
L: *It's true. I don't.*
F: *Then what do you want to marry him for?*
L: *I want to marry him for your money.*

L: *Don't you know that a man being rich is like a girl being pretty? You might not marry a girl just because she's pretty, but goodness, doesn't it help? And if you had a daughter, wouldn't you rather she didn't marry a poor man? You'd want her to have the most wonderful things in the world and to be very happy, so why is it wrong for me to have them?*
F: *Wait a minute, they told me you were stupid, but you don't sound stupid to me.*
L: *I can be smart when it's important, but most men don't like it, except for Gus, he's always been interested in my brains.*
F: *No, that much of a fool he's not.*

The chameleonlike star Madonna used the persona of Marilyn Monroe outrageously and successfully to exaggerate the myth of the material girl. She also experiments with different images, perhaps keeping in mind that Monroe, after all, died young. Andy Warhol's *Interview* magazine (summer, 1993) carried a photographic essay on Madonna by Herb Ritts, designed by Madonna, in which her appearance is modeled on Marlene Dietrich at her most glamorous. Dietrich was remarkable for her ability to retain a sexy and glamorous persona well into old age, using a shrewd mixture of camouflage, exposure, and sheer chutzpah, and avoiding camera closeups.

Madonna is not alone in her witty and disturbing ability to satirize while imitating the role of the sex goddess in American culture. Janis Joplin, Laurie Anderson, Whoopi Goldberg (who appeared dressed as a Southern belle for her part in the 1993 Academy Awards), and others have played iconoclastic roles comparable to Madonna's. Marilyn Monroe was herself a walking self-parody.

But Madonna seems to raise more hackles than any woman doing similar work, and I wonder if this is because the gap between her persona and her personality is less evident than in the case of, say, Whoopi Goldberg, who flaunts her acting ability, especially her strengths as a mimic and caricaturist, more than her sex appeal. Or is it simply, as a hostile newspaper journalist suggested, that Madonna is getting too old for her role?

Madonna's predilection for sado-masochism, a taste applauded by another iconoclast, Camille Paglia, is deeply frowned on by many feminists for its perpetuation of the image of woman as victim. Her success in marketing her own image is probably much more disturbing to proponents of patriarchal power. Madonna's images, which just as often show her in the dominatrix role as in the role of bound victim, revive the *film noir* focus of the forties on the *femme fatale*, as in *Double Indemnity* and *The Maltese Falcon*, but in her case, the creative, conceptive role is her own, not a male director's. This *femme fatale* figure, who is responsible for the downfall of unwary men, echoes the dark side of the Goddess, her destructive, death-dealing force. As such she has enormous mythic resonance. The force she echoes is seldom a real attribute of modern women, who rarely wield such power in the world. It is therefore, as Madonna says in her book *Sex*, "a fantasy."

Looking at the many aspects of beauty in modern and post-modern times, it seems clear that beauty poses serious problems for women in the ways it functions as danger, as obstacle, and as morally denigrated commodity. Only if we look at the spirit behind the concept, at its mythic, archetypal roots, can we understand the deep hold this problematic idea has on our hearts and minds. The most paradoxical illustration of this is the "sex goddess."

The sex goddess of modern popular culture, whatever her other qualifications, and these change with the blowing wind, must look young, and, as the song "Diamonds" remarks, "we all lose our charms in the end." A Taoist immortal might retain her youth, but, judging from the story of Sun Pu-erh, she would have to dispose of her physical beauty in order to attain immortality, and then she would be, not a sex goddess in the modern sense, but a Goddess of fertility and creation, like the enlightened Sun Pu-erh.

Once again, the paradox of old strengths behind modern liabilities emerges. Just as the fragile rose has been used by generations of poets to symbolize the transience of life and the ideal of evanescent human beauty, so perhaps we can use the momentary glow of youth, which characterizes the sex goddess, as an object for meditation. We may conclude, from such a meditation, that the youthful spirit of women's beauty is, like the Maiden aspect of the Goddess, one face of a complex reality.

UGLINESS

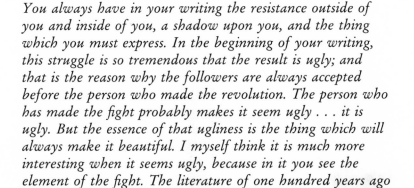

You always have in your writing the resistance outside of you and inside of you, a shadow upon you, and the thing which you must express. In the beginning of your writing, this struggle is so tremendous that the result is ugly; and that is the reason why the followers are always accepted before the person who made the revolution. The person who has made the fight probably makes it seem ugly . . . it is ugly. But the essence of that ugliness is the thing which will always make it beautiful. I myself think it is much more interesting when it seems ugly, because in it you see the element of the fight. The literature of one hundred years ago is perfectly easy to see, because the sediment of ugliness has settled down and you get the solemnity of its beauty. But to a person of my temperament, it is much more amusing when it has the vitality of the struggle.
—Gertrude Stein, *How Writing Is Written*, 1935

6

THE MAGICAL

POWER OF

UGLINESS

A DREAM

Recently, in a dream, I went to my bathroom mirror and saw a metal band on my neck, which I removed. Immediately a breastlike growth sprouted. Then I saw, to my horror, many breastlike growths, all with nipples, hanging all around my neck. I had never noticed these, and I wondered if now I had become ugly. When I woke up and thought about my dream, I remembered a picture I had seen recently of the statue known as Artemis of Ephesus, her torso completely covered with breasts, one of the many images associated with the Great Mother.

I thought about this image of myself sprouting breastlike growths, and thereby becoming ugly, or wondering if I would be ugly. From horror at the change in my appearance, I began to see these images of growth and nurturance in terms of my hesitation to be all that I can be. The growths sprouted from my neck, the site of voice, of communication with the world. I realized what a transition it is for me to be writing this book, reexamining myself and my assumptions about beauty, about ugliness. The part of me that looks at new growth and fears its ugliness is a timid, conventional part, but the new growth is insistent, is what it is. It nurtures, like the breast it appears to be, offering an anodyne to fear as I enter a new phase of creativity.

I am approaching menopause and with it the third age of my woman's life, in which I expect to bring my creativity to full power. This is a time for courage and freedom, for releasing the new growth, which was fettered by metal bands, for welcoming and celebrating the new appearance even as I mourn the passing of the old. That this is a transitional time between the Mother and Crone phases of biological womanhood has large significance in terms of how I see myself and how I am seen.

Now ugliness is expected of me, although no one ever says so. I am expected to hide the ugly signs of age, but that they are ugly is generally agreed. It is clear to me, as I am complimented for looking young, that we reserve judgment of beauty for youth and only very exceptionally for age. One part of my developmental task, then, is to come to terms with this new ugliness in my life, without wholly identifying with it. There is something of value in this ugliness.

THE POWER OF UGLINESS

"Beauty" can function as an obstacle and a danger for women or its power can be transformed or redirected for creative use. "Ugliness" is a concept of great power, which we tend to split off and disavow, but which offers treasures for growth and development, provided we are willing to explore the meanings and experiences of ugliness in ourselves and in those we love.

The exploration of beauty leads inexorably to ugliness. While beauty is usually an ambivalent concept, symbolizing both good and evil, innocence and experience, appearance and reality, ugliness almost always symbolizes badness or evil. In rigid systems, where bad is bad and good is good, ugliness doesn't usually transform into anything else. But our human tendency toward change appears in traditional stories, such as the story of Sun Pu-erh, the fairy tale "Beauty and the Beast," and the English tale of "Gawain and the Lady Ragnell."

In these stories ugliness is understood to be a phase of identity, a temporary disguise to be dropped when the spirit is able to manifest itself. This understanding is essential to the attainment of fluidity, the ability to encompass more than one role in a moment or in a lifetime. To gain such an understanding requires the courage to explore the unexpected depths of ugliness, and examine the various powers associated with looking ugly.

Some deities of Tibetan Buddhism and other Eastern and indigenous religions display their ugliness as an aspect of their power, which is horrifying and destructive, no more or less important to the scheme of things than creative beauty. The blood-drinking demons of Tibet, male and female, with their necklaces of fresh human skulls, who dance on the prostrate bodies of their victims, are objects of meditation for Buddhists, who believe in the importance of death as giving perspective and meaning to our short lives.

Without the barren, deathlike time of winter, the fallow time, there is no spring, no regrowth, no life. Death and life are completely intertwined, but traditionally young life is pictured as beautiful, and old age and death are associated with ugliness.

THE STUDY OF UGLINESS

Until its recent development as an area of intense interest to scientists and philosophers, "chaos" was considered a term of opprobrium, something to avoid, something that was not worthy of serious discussion. Like chaos, ugliness is an aspect of experience, which is interesting in its own right, and from which there is much to learn. Just as the scientists studying chaos needed to find a deep, underlying order in chaos to justify their studies, so the study of ugliness requires a sense that somewhere beauty will emerge. But because the usual attitude toward ugliness (as, until recently, toward chaos) is that it is something to avoid, to get rid of, to overcome, the learning doesn't come easily.

A man who suffers from chronic schizophrenia told me, when I said I was writing a book about appearance, that he thinks the most beautiful thing is the love of two ugly people for each other, because they must love each other for what they really are, not just what they seem to be. His remark gave me an insight into my writing, but also into his illness, which coexists with remarkable sensitivity and intelligence, not always seen by others.

If all else is equal, ugly men and ugly women are not treated equally in society. The ugly white man is free to be brilliant, accomplished, rich, even a movie star or television anchor. One great literary exception to this double standard is Cyrano de Bergerac, who suffered torments on account of his enormous nose, believing he was not desirable to the woman he loved. The character and story of Shakespeare's Othello are an eloquent example of the effects of racism. But the standard is set in Madame de La Fayette's *The Princess of Clèves (1678)*, said to herald the modern novel. Describing the players in this account of intrigue at the royal court, the author mentions the powerful Prince de Condé, who, "small and ugly but possessed of a proud and haughty soul, charmed with his engaging wit the most beautiful women." Basically, since appearance is not considered a defining characteristic for a man, provided (huge proviso!) that he is white, ethnically acceptable, and can afford to dress respectably, an ugly man is not considered to be any less a man.

The ugly woman, even if she too is brilliant, accomplished, and rich, must still deal with a relentless standard, almost always internalized, which tells her she is inferior as a woman because of her ugliness. The best-known American example is

Eleanor Roosevelt. The French term *jolie laide*, used to describe a homely woman who is nevertheless attractive (Colette and Edith Piaf are the most famous examples), underlines the importance of appearance for women.

Women may take on ugliness, especially in the sense of the *jolie laide*, as a challenge to assert power. In Woody Allen's film *Manhattan Murder Mystery* (1993), Anjelica Huston in the role of a famous writer remarks to Woody Allen, her editor, that she is not beautiful but that she has sex appeal, as well as talent, success, and great skill at poker. The catch is the implicit requirement that she dress and care for her hair and makeup with devastating skill in order to reinforce her position of ugly but sexy beauty. The fact of her successful authorship is not enough to qualify her for male interest. Woody Allen, on the other hand, dresses and presents himself with his usual nonchalance, relying on his wit, talent, and the convention of rumpled (male) genius as sufficient social assets.

In Maggie Greenwald's film *The Ballad of Little Jo* (1993), based on a historical figure, a young upper-class American woman decides to pass as a man in order to live independently once she has been cast out by her family. She buys men's clothing, cuts her long hair, and cuts her face with a razor. The resulting scar attracts attention, but doesn't prevent young women from being attracted to the young man they believe she is. On the other hand, when she considers reverting to her woman's identity, a Chinese man she rescued from a lynch mob, and who became her secret lover, says angrily, "What man would want you? Half your face is destroyed with that ugly scar." His Asian appearance and her scar function, in their racist, sexist environment, as parallel handicaps.

To change this centuries-old prejudice, women would have to set very different standards for our appearance, standards based on internal experience, allowing us to decide for ourselves that we are beautiful, ugly, or simply in a phase of being indifferent to the way we look. This is terribly difficult, as, coming from long generations of conditioning, we find it so hard to identify with being beautiful or ugly, or to allow ourselves the luxury of indifference. In order to set different standards, we must first become aware of the nature of the standards imposed upon us, and then ask, What is it we are not supposed to be? Why is ugliness forbidden to us?

Let us explore the role of ugliness as a possible source of strength. A South African story, "Mulha," which I read in Ethel Johnson Phelps's collection *The Maid of the North*, offers an unusual example of a young woman who is forced to take on ugliness as a role and discovers its unexpected advantages. This is my brief retelling of the story.

MULHA

Mulha was fourteen, a pretty young girl, when she had her encounter with ogres, the fierce Inzimu and his sister, Imbula. These ogres were ugly monsters who liked to eat children.

One day her parents were out in the field and Mulha was looking after her two younger sisters. Bored and hungry, she decided to open the storage pot, which was forbidden to the children, to see if there was something special to eat. When she opened it a small, fanged animal jumped out and grew into a huge ogre before her eyes. Mulha knew it was Inzimu because of his long tail.

By trickery and swiftness, Mulha saved herself and her little sisters from the Inzimu. First she hid her sisters, then she swam across the river, knowing the Inzimu could not cross water. Happy that their children were safe, Mulha's parents feared the Inzimu's return. They packed up and went to relatives in the valley, and sent Mulha off to a married sister in a distant village.

Mulha persuaded her parents she could make the day's trip alone, and she promised her mother to remember not to eat anything on the way. But she saw some ripe, juicy fruit on a tree, and she couldn't resist climbing it. When Mulha came down, out of the tree trunk came a big ugly Imbula woman, with a huge snout and a hairy red pelt all over her body. The crafty Imbula forced Mulha to exchange her brightly patterned skirt for the hairy pelt. As soon as Mulha put on the pelt, she looked just like the ugly Imbula, and the Imbula looked just like Mulha, except for her tail, which she wrapped around her waist and hid under Mulha's skirt.

The two went together to Mulha's sister's village, where the Imbula was received as Mulha and praised for her prettiness, while poor Mulha, who looked ugly and strange, was sent to live in a poor hut with an old woman.

Mulha soon discovered the magic power in her ugly red pelt. All she had to do was ask for food and it was hers. She shared her food secretly with the old woman, and they lived comfortably in their hut.

When Mulha went each day to the river to bathe, she discovered that the ugly pelt slipped off while she was in the water, and she resumed her human shape. When she came out of the water the pelt adhered again, and she was an ugly monster.

One day Mulha's sister saw her in the river. She went to ask the chief's wise old sister for help. The two women followed the monster to the river, and witnessed her transformation. They confronted her, demanding an explanation. Mulha told them her story. Then, hurt by her sister's doubt of her, she said she was happy and needed nothing from them. But the chief's sister believed her and decided to set a trap for the Imbula, who was, with her taste for eating children, a great danger to the village.

Knowing the greediness of the Imbula, the chief's sister set out a bowl of milk on the ground, and said that all the maidens of the village must walk around it. The Imbula pleaded shyness, but the villagers insisted that she walk. Her greedy tail slithered out to suck up the milk, for no Imbula can keep her tail under control when milk is around. Once revealed, the Imbula was killed by the villagers, and at that moment Mulha was restored to her own form.

Mulha married the chief's son, whose family paid a bride price of one hundred cows to Mulha's father, and so both families lived in comfort.

This is a story of initiation into womanhood. Mulha is fourteen when she meets and outwits both ogres, and the story ends with her marriage and the payment of a bride price. It is a story of a culture in which a woman's ability to feed herself and her family is highly prized and ritually valued with the payment of a bride price at the time of marriage. Young Mulha is hungry when she opens the storage pot, and hungry when she climbs the tree to pick fruit.

No one blames Mulha for being hungry and opening the forbidden storage pot, they just warn her of the consequences of her actions. If she can outwit the ogres, so much the better for her. The ogres, for their part, are hungry monsters known to devour children. That's what brings the Inzimu into the hut in the first place. Later, it is the greed of the Imbula that betrays her. Hunger, which gets people and ogres into trouble, is a natural inclination, no more to be condemned than any other natural process.

Mulha escapes the Inzimu by swimming across a river, knowing ogres can't cross water. Whenever a woman jumps into the flowing river of her own transformation, no ogres can follow. The initiation rites have begun. And Mulha must go on alone. Of course she promises not to eat anything on the way, and of course she breaks her promise. The fruit she can't resist is the fruit of experience, fruit that feeds her growth. Like Eve in the Garden of Eden, Mulha is an innocent who can't resist forbidden fruit, and who thereby gets more knowledge than she thinks she wants. Unlike Eve, Mulha belongs to a supportive culture, which accepts that a hungry woman seeks food, and doesn't punish her for doing so. She gets herself in and out of trouble by her own resilience, and with the help of the villagers.

When Mulha eats the fruit, the female ogre appears. In this story of a young woman's initiation the main players are all female. The Imbula goes after Mulha's appearance, her identity as a pretty girl. Mulha is considered by her parents to be the prettiest maid in Swaziland, but her beauty is not the key to her growth in this story. Rather, growth is marked by her ordeal of enforced ugliness, when she is made to wear the ugly red pelt and becomes an ugly monster. Mulha quickly discovers the power of her disguise, for the pelt enables her to command food at will, the most valuable thing she could have. But this state of affairs is only temporary. Like water, all must change.

Twice, water appears in the story as a place where the power of the ogres can't reach. First, the Inzimu can't follow Mulha across the river. Later, while Mulha is bathing in the river, the pelt slips off, and she becomes her own self, a pretty young woman. Mulha will return to this role, but she returns with the fluid awareness of what it is to occupy another role, another perspective on reality.

True to the archetypal pattern of initiation or quest stories, Mulha's adventure ends with her return to her true self, and her sharing of the gift or secret she has found. The Imbula's magic pelt, kept secret, is a privilege hoarded by Mulha and the old woman. It gives Mulha self-sufficiency, a great gift for a woman, but it keeps her isolated from her people and from her social role as wife and mother.

The chief's wise old sister is a very important figure in this story, for it is she who thinks of the welfare of the whole, of the village and of Mulha, and who sets a trap for the Imbula. In her cunning she is similar to other figures of older women in fairy tales, and in her wisdom and care for the whole she is a kind of fairy godmother, but an unusual one, for she is a character in the world of the story, the chief's sister, not a magical figure from outside that world. Unlike the poor old woman who is happy to share food with Mulha and keep her secret, the chief's sister thinks of the needs of others. She is an initiatory figure for Mulha, a model for wise elder womanhood.

The magic of the pelt dies with the monster, but its function lives on. Mulha has become a woman whose family will be prosperous and have all the food they need. Now the ugly, greedy Imbula, who was a scary figure of her childhood, is someone the woman Mulha has been, and that is a memory of power.

The story of Mulha makes me wish that every young girl had the chance to become the ugly monster she harbors inside herself and fears. We all need access to that figure, as she is the source of power and nurturance. Untransformed, she is the demon of our nightmares and waking terrors, a shadow figure who carries all our unknown, rejected aspects, our violence, greed, jealousy, and hatred. But entering into her, wearing her pelt and discovering her power, is a very different experience from being terrified by her as an external threat. Once taken over, the monster's power can be transformed, but only with the help of wise eldership, personified by the chief's sister.

Women who have been abused as children by monsters in the form of fathers, brothers, or other shape-changers, have special need for access to their own inner monsters. Otherwise the inner monster, like the outer one, attacks the woman, continuing the childhood abuse.

I know several women who have been able to use their inner monsters creatively in their lives.

MARIANNE AND THE MONSTER

Marianne Pomeroy, a nurse and psychotherapist, is a very warm, nurturing woman, and, like many women, she has always been very adapted to the needs of others—friends, family, patients, clients. She was diagnosed with breast cancer twelve years ago, at the age of forty-seven, and had a mastectomy followed by chemotherapy and radiation. After a six-year remission, the cancer metastasized, appearing in a rib and her chest wall, requiring additional chemotherapy and radiation.

Over the years, Marianne has used her illness as a vehicle for growth and awareness. The first time she investigated her experience of the cancerous tumor in the context of a therapy session, she discovered, in connection with her symptoms, "a dream figure, a hairy monster who lived in the basement and ate rats. She was wonderful!" Marianne understood this figure to be related to her tumors, and she grew very fond of it. She explored how the monster looked, sounded, and moved, and even how it felt to be such a monster.

After that therapeutic work, Marianne said she was no longer afraid of what was inside of her, because she knew it was related to the hairy monster, which she describes as "extremely primitive—it had been kept in the dark all my life, all its life. Somehow that work cleared up any fear I had about what was inside of me. I knew that whatever I was scared of and wasn't able to bring into awareness would come from this hairy monster."

Marianne's monster is an undeveloped part of her, which she connects with her own repressed aggression and split-off pain. She traces this back to a traumatic experience she had in early infancy. So long as the monster is repressed, like all repressed parts of the psyche, it is terrifying and destructive. Once recognized as a principle of growth, it can transform into an ally of remarkable strength and power.

Living the monster, for Marianne, entails paying attention to her irrational feelings and needs, especially in relation to other people. This means doing things that are important to her but that may not make sense to others, leaving conventional appearances behind and following her own wild and unpredictable nature, impulses that go against the nurturing, responsible, mothering figure that has previously been her main identity. It means resting when she is tired, walking away from other people when she needs to, "just being one hundred percent behind myself doing that. Because there's also a message to hurry up. Hurry up and be alive!" She laughs, and continues, "Be alive to everything that you have."

This willingness to follow her own needs first has led to improved relationships with her family and friends.

The monster is only one part of Marianne's inner life. She speaks of an inner voice, male, very clear, that acts as a guide; of a maternal figure, "a good mother"; and of a more detached, observant "light self." Her sense of identity now changes from moment to moment, as she allows room for each of her many parts, knowing that her life, literally, depends on her ability to change. She describes herself as "moving from one identity to another," as she works with the pain in her body, feeling it, complaining about it, turning her complaint into a wail, a chant, a movement, even a dance, saying to me, "I think that's my dying work. That's what dying is. And I'm doing it without physically dying. . . . Maybe if I do it really well . . . my own death will be more familiar to me."

Marianne has outlived her original prognosis by several years. Despite the advanced metastasis of her cancer, she went to Zagreb for a month to lead peer counseling groups with Bosnian survivors of wartime rape, and returned filled with enthusiasm to continue her work in that area. She says that her life now is a matter of walking on a razor's edge, between her sense of fulfillment from being useful to others, and recognizing her own physical limitations and needs. I see her life as a transformation, from a woman terrified by hidden monsters to a wise elder like the chief's sister in "Mulha," thinking of the needs of the whole planet.

Inspired by Marianne, who loves her inner hairy monster, I think again of the Imbula, such a fascinating figure of cunning greed. It is the Imbula's tail, which she wraps around and around her waist and conceals under Mulha's skirt, that eventually betrays her by slithering down to suck up the milk. That tail, irrepressible, greedy, milk-loving, ancient appendage of the Devil, snakelike, always causes trouble for its owner, especially when she tries to hide it.

TAILS AND SCARS

I have a scar across my midsection, which, when it was new, was raised and colorful, and wrapped around me like the Imbula's tail. I was horrified. I had been told by the surgeon that I would have a tiny, hairline scar. Although a second surgeon, consulted for a backup opinion, had warned me that he would not perform such an operation, and that there was danger of a scar as well as complications, I didn't want to hear of any problems. Now my flat tummy and slender waist, the pride of my young womanhood, were gone. In their place were a bulging navel and a thick ropy scar, surrounded by stretch marks and sagging skin. This was the aftermath of childbirth and bungled surgery, undertaken in a frantic attempt to turn back a speeding clock.

I hated my scar and all that went with it. Looking in my mirror I thought I had aged twenty years in the one year since I had first become pregnant. This triggered a major depression.

I wish I could say that, like a fairy-tale heroine, I accepted my fate and made the best of it, or that I, like Marianne, learned to love the monster whose tail was wrapped around my middle. I wish that I, like Sun Pu-erh, could have entered immediately into my new role of ugliness with a sense of freedom. But I didn't. I complained, moped, raged, and then repressed my feelings. I made rash decisions affecting my life and my family's, without understanding what I was doing, or why. I acted unconsciously, and failed entirely to see that, by losing my identity as a conventionally attractive young woman, I had new possibilities to explore.

I did explore those new possibilities anyway, but I did so with an attitude that made difficulties for me and others. Now, twenty years later, I feel compassion for my young angry self. Like many other women of my generation I was caught in a time of shifting standards without the tools or understanding to adapt with fluidity. I didn't have the base of self-esteem or security to make the change in my primary identity easy, and I didn't have the tough single focus that some women have developed to survive difficult situations. What I did have was a wild imagination and a love of reading and movies, which gave me access to what other women have done and thought. That was when I discovered the writing of Dorothy Richardson and Virginia Woolf, the science fiction of Ursula K. Le Guin, culturally diverse writings of the new women's movement, the new blossoming of women film directors such as Marta Meszaros from Hungary and the work of writer-director Marguerite Duras. I dreamed and wrote myself through my difficulties, and my scar was the key to a new kind of dreaming, which connected me to experiences I had never before imagined.

I thought I might someday make a film or videotape about my scar and other women's scars. There are so many stories. Alice Walker describes, in the last chapter of *In Search of Our Mothers' Gardens*, how she was struck in one eye by a pellet from her brother's gun when she was eight, and how she prayed, not for sight in that eye, but for beauty, for release from the ugly scar that sat above her eye.

I've made other films and tapes, not yet that one, but the imagination of doing it, of turning my scar into an asset by using it creatively was a saving act for me. When I saw the poster of Deena Metzger with her tattooed mastectomy scar, I imagined myself having a tattoo, a garland of leaves and flowers winding in and out of my ropy scar. Once, in company with other women, I painted designs on my scar with body paints, and danced, flaunting my decorated scar. I've written a lot about my scar, both prose and poetry, and in one poem I compare it to a fault line in the earth, warning of impending changes.

I've imagined the operation itself, the time when I lay unconscious, opened by surgeons' knives. I've imagined that I, like the surgeons, have cutting power, power to lay things bare to the bone, to the guts, a truth-telling power I am learning to use so skillfully that I, unlike my surgeon, leave only the finest lines to commemorate the operation. In imagining, I've made that power accessible. I always had it, but it would tend to jump out in unconscious and unintended ways. I would make cutting remarks, without meaning to, and hurt people unintentionally. Of course I still do those things, but less often, and less hurtfully, I think, than in the past. And when I cut with intention, I really cut!

My scar is now a mark of initiation. I've shown it to women who've shared secret or visible scars with me, and we've talked about our feelings and experiences the way warriors talk over their battle memories. I notice that I have an incredible sensitivity in the whole region of my scar, which acts as a guide for me to changes in mood or atmosphere I might not otherwise notice. When I feel irritated or uncomfortable in my midsection, I know it's time to turn inward, to find out what's happening inside me and also around me. As a therapist's tool, my scar, with the experience surrounding it and the sensitivity it has engendered, has become a gift of great power, something like the Imbula's hairy pelt.

My scar was my first major, visible sign of being marred, marked by life, damaged, as I saw it. I still have problems with my image, naked, in the mirror and still look sometimes with envy at the smooth, bare midriffs of young women in summer. Once, though, I thought to myself about how the Aztecs used to sacrifice perfect, unmarked young women to their angry gods, how we value young, unmarked flesh in chickens and other animals slaughtered for food. What an abrupt reframing! The Aztec priests, it is said, cut the hearts from their living victims. My many marks and flaws suddenly took on a new, perverse value, the value of the survivor.

Because of my scar I'm extremely sensitive to scars on others. I was having lunch with my friend Beverly one day when I noticed a faint scar that traced a wiggly line from her upper lip to her nostril. When I asked her about it, a whole story unfolded.

Beverly, like Susan, was in a car accident as a young woman. As she describes it, the accident "cauliflowered" her face. At the time she had been feeling very depressed, even suicidal. She said that the damage to her face was a relief, because then, she felt, her outside matched her inside. She had been uncomfortable about feeling bad and looking good.

After the accident, Beverly worried briefly that her scars would ruin her appeal to men, but that didn't happen and she continued to have lovers. Her mother was more concerned about her appearance than she was, and was greatly relieved when, several years later, Beverly met a plastic surgeon who was able to correct the disfigurement, leaving only the small scar I noticed. I was struck in our conversation with how little Beverly seemed to have been affected by her scars. It was almost as if the accident had been an event she was waiting for and expecting, as if she felt relieved when it finally happened, because then she would no longer be mistaken for the pretty woman she resembled but with whom she felt no connection. For Beverly, a striking woman who is a great example of the *jolie laide*, ugliness, like beauty, is an outward expression of inner experience, and it is the use of that experience that is ultimately empowering.

FAWN

I've known Fawn for years, but it wasn't until we had a telephone conversation about my book that she told me about her scar. She has an extensive scar on her shoulder and arm, which she has always covered with long sleeves. The scar is from a burn she received at ten months, a horrifying story about her mother spilling hot porridge on her. The scar is on her left arm, on the shoulder, the inside of her elbow, and on her wrist. She's felt awkward about it since childhood, and suffered when her mother insisted she wear short-sleeved dresses for special occasions.

A filmmaker, Fawn is interested in style as a form of artistic expression, and has often experimented with clothing and makeup as a way of presenting herself artistically to the world. But for Fawn, concern about appearance has lessened as her sense of self-acceptance has increased. I find this is true for many women.

Over the last four years, since Fawn turned forty, she has felt a gradual shift in her attitude toward her scar. She says she's felt a lot more self-acceptance in her forties, and a sense of well-being, which she expects to increase in her fifties.

But when she was a child, she used to wish she'd wake up and find the scar gone. When, in her early thirties, Fawn was told she might have thyroid cancer and might need an operation, she became hysterical, not out of fear of the operation but in dread of having another scar on her body. This was a real turning point in her life, for at this time, Fawn says, she took responsibility for her own healing process. She chose alternative treatment—meditation, change of diet, a more spiritual approach to living. The thyroid condition cleared and no operation was necessary.

Now, musing about her dread of having a scar, Fawn thinks that it might have been hidden by the wrinkles in her neck. She laughs, and says she finds such wrinkles attractive in other women. I ask how she feels about double chins, and we both roar with self-conscious laughter as she admits she's not so fond of them. She tells me her body looks younger than her face, and I say that my body looks older than my face. We discuss our awareness, new to Fawn, of a disconnection between face and body, how this is an internal sense as well as a visual sense.

Recently Fawn's lover was stroking her arm, and didn't realize she was touching the scar until Fawn mentioned it. At her lover's touch, Fawn realized that she'd been exposing her arm more, especially in a movement class she takes, and the realization of the many years of hiding made her weep. She said she felt a great release from sadness with these tears. "You learn to dissociate," she said, "and that doesn't let you own your feeling. I think that's a graphic representation of how I'm dealing with my life—beginning to know myself, letting more sadness in."

I realize that Fawn's newfound happiness with herself must come, paradoxically, from acknowledging her more difficult feelings. The value of a supportive relationship for this deep healing work is immense.

Fawn and I seem to have entered a time of life when self-acceptance comes more easily. Perhaps we are taking on our own eldership, assuming responsibility for the role of the one who looks around her with compassionate eyes at all she sees, even her own scars, her own imperfections. One of the benefits of the invisibility that seems to come to women with middle age is precisely that freedom to look instead of being looked at, so that how we look is a matter of action rather than passive being.

Although I've learned to value the gifts of my own experience with scarring and my own encounter with ugliness, ugliness itself still remains mysterious to me. Like beauty, ugliness is entirely a subjective concept, which varies according to the eye of the beholder and the consensus of society, yet that consensus is so strong that we believe we are responding to objective fact. My exploration of the mystery of ugliness takes me to more fairy tales, where so much depends on beauty, and beauty depends on ugliness.

7

UGLINESS AS THE OTHER SIDE OF BEAUTY

> *She is a Gorgon, a Medusa . . . that craggy face belongs to*
> *some period other than ours. The large features. The wide*
> *mouth, like the mouth of some deep sea fish. An outsize*
> *mouth designed for the devouring of life. She is one who*
> *alters very little, who is beyond affectation, beyond*
> *coquetry, even. She is the most beautiful of the ugly women*
> *of her time.* —Marguerite Duras, "Callas"

"Mulha" is unusual as a story because the heroine comes to terms with ugliness in herself and comes to know its power. In most European traditions, the heroine or hero deals with ugliness in someone else. The fairy tale "Beauty and the Beast," which I retell here from Arthur Rackham's version, is a love story about the transformation of ugliness in which a beautiful young woman learns to love an ugly beast who is, apparently, neither bright nor talented, but who is kind and devoted to her. Rackham used a long French version of the tale, written by Madame de Villeneuve in 1740.

BEAUTY AND THE BEAST

Beauty is the youngest daughter of a rich merchant who falls into poverty. Unlike her older sisters, who are greedy, selfish, and lazy, Beauty works hard to support the family, as do her older brothers and her father. When her father hears that a ship of his goods has come into port, he prepares to go there, and he is besieged by his daughters with requests for dresses and jewelry. Only Beauty asks for nothing. When he asks what he should bring her, she replies, "A rose," thinking that is a simple request that won't burden her father.

The merchant's goods are contested by others, and he leaves the port as poor as ever. On the way home he is caught in a blizzard, and takes shelter in a strange palace, a magical place where no one appears, but a stable with oats and hay is ready for his horse, a dinner is freshly laid, and he finds a room with a bed made up for him. In the morning fresh clothes are ready, and breakfast is set out in a sunny room, where he sees that the grounds of the palace are blooming with flowers, although outside the palace grounds the blizzard rages. Remembering Beauty's request he picks some roses for her. At that moment the terrifying Beast, master of the palace, appears, roaring with displeasure, and saying that the merchant has violated his hospitality and must die.

The merchant begs forgiveness, but the Beast offers him a condition. If the merchant brings one of his daughters to die in his place, he can go free. Otherwise he must return in three months and submit to the Beast's decision. Meanwhile, he may take with him a chest filled with whatever he chooses, and he chooses gold, which he finds lying about in his room.

Of course the merchant intends to return by himself, having said good-bye to his children. But Beauty insists on going back with him to die in his place. That night she dreams of a lady who tells her not to be afraid, and says Beauty will be rewarded for her loyalty to her father. Although her father and brothers try to dissuade her from doing this, Beauty is adamant.

When they arrive at the palace, although terrified when she sees the Beast, she is surprised by his courtesy to her. He insists that the father leave, but shows no intention of harming Beauty. Instead he shows her to a splendid apartment filled with books and music, called "Beauty's Room," and does all he can to make her comfortable and welcome. Apologizing for his lack of sense or wit, he charms her with his kindness, but when he asks her to marry him, which he does repeatedly, she refuses.

Among the many wonderful things in her apartment Beauty finds a looking glass, which shows her her father, back in her old home. As time goes by, Beauty grows very fond of the Beast, and would give in to his request to agree to stay with him, except that her mirror shows her father dying of grief for Beauty. She begs the Beast to let her visit him, and promises she will return in a week.

Once at home with her father, Beauty is snared by the evil plans of her two jealous sisters, who envy her good fortune with the Beast and think that by delaying her return they will provoke the Beast into devouring her. Instead, thinking she will not return, the Beast decides to starve himself. Meanwhile Beauty, missing her Beast, dreams that he lies dying in the garden, and decides she must rush back to him. She gets back to find him dying just as she had dreamed. She begins to weep and tells him that she loves him and will marry him. This breaks the spell he has been under, and instead of a beast, Beauty sees before her a handsome young prince. A wicked fairy condemned him to be a beast until a beautiful woman agreed to marry him. Beauty alone judged him by his heart, not by his looks or his talents, and so he offers her his heart and all he owns.

Like "Little Snow White," this fairy tale also ends with a wedding and with retribution. Beauty's jealous sisters are turned into statues by a fairy godmother, the same lady who appeared in Beauty's dream. She warns that the sisters will re-

main statues at the door of Beauty's palace until they repent ——
their sins and change.

Just as Snow White needed to take on the power of the wicked
stepmother by entering the realm of death, so Beauty must explore ugliness, of which she is initially ignorant. Judging by
superficial appearance, she believes that her sisters love her, and
she fails at first to see the inner beauty of the Beast. Only by
following her dreams and her heart is Beauty able to realize her
love for the Beast. The riches they both enjoy are material manifestations of spiritual richness, just as their beauty, unlike the
beauty of the evil sisters, is beauty from within, reflecting loving spirits.

"Beauty and the Beast" is a story about appearance and
reality, and, like most fairy tales, it is deceptively simple, holding within itself the complexity and ambivalence of European
culture's attitude toward physical appearance and material
riches. Beauty is a merchant's daughter, not a king's daughter,
and so the story is about living in the world of transactions, of
value and exchange.

Madame de Villeneuve's story goes into great detail about
the ambitions of the two older sisters—how, when their father
is rich and they are courted by many men, they refuse all who
propose because they plan to marry upward into the nobility.
Beauty refuses her suitors because she feels she is too young to
leave her father; then, when the family is poor and men still
offer to marry her for her kindness and good heart as well as
her beauty, she refuses because she feels her father needs her at
home. The love of Beauty for her father and her lack of a
mother are elements of the story that ask for psychological
readings. The mother element is represented by the lady of
Beauty's dream, who appears at the end of the story to distrib-
ute justice, but Beauty herself really embodies the maternal or
nurturing principle, in her care for all around her. The merchant
father is the worldly man who loses all his wealth and so paves
the way for gaining spiritual riches, but only by following a
demanding spiritual path.

The Beast, while terrifying in appearance, lives in a magnificent palace, not a poor hovel. Beauty has already passed the test of living in poverty at home, and she is not required by the moral system of the story to do so any longer. Her greedy sisters reflect the crass side of materialism, uninformed by love or understanding. Beauty and her Beast represent a curious ideal, which goes back beyond Plato, of beauty and wealth as physical manifestations of spiritual riches. The simple rose, for instance, which Beauty requests as a token from her father, turns out to be the one thing the Beast is unwilling to let go from his palace, for the rose, unlike the wealth the sisters covet, is living beauty, a mortal symbol chosen more often than any other to represent immortal beauty and the human soul.

By demonstrating her lack of concern for material wealth, Beauty shows her fitness to share the wealth of the Beast. But she is put off by the Beast's appearance. His ugliness, which has no apparent cause except for the unprovoked malice of a wicked fairy, is the unknown element of the fairy tale. Like the period of time in which Snow White lies dead in her coffin, the ugliness of the Beast, his Beasthood, is a mystery that contains the power and growth of the story.

The Disney animated film *Beauty and the Beast* makes a great departure from Madame de Villeneuve's version of the story. In the film the focus is on the development of the Beast, a young, handsome, but arrogant prince under the spell of a sorceress, whom he spurns when she appears as an ugly old woman, offering him a rose. His lack of courtesy is what gets him into trouble and sets the stage for the story: the ugly old woman turns into a beautiful sorceress who curses the prince to be monstrous forever, unless, by the time the rose loses its last petal, he can win the love of a beautiful woman. The magical rose remains fresh for a long time, and its last petal falls as Beauty declares her love for the dying Beast. But first the prince, as the Beast, must learn gentleness from Beauty, a quality he sorely lacks at the outset. In this case the Beast's ugliness is an external manifestation of the inner lack of grace he betrayed to the sorceress in her crone form.

One clue to the power of the Beast's ugliness is to be found in the magic looking glass, which Beauty finds in her room. Like the looking glass in the story of Snow White, this one also shows faraway things. Unlike the other glass, this one is not concerned with beautiful appearance but rather with showing faraway loved ones. The glass is a gift from the Beast, who understands Beauty's concern for her father. Like the sign on her door, "Beauty's Room," an entirely magical sign that the Beast somehow knew and prepared for her coming, the magical glass is a sign of the Beast's power. The power of the Beast, in men and in women, is very strong, is a source of knowledge, is an inner monster, self-destructive when unacknowledged, and enormously creative when integrated.

In this story the image of the mirror, which appears so frequently in fairy tales and also in movies, is an image of knowledge and magical vision. Mirrors reflect, they are visual tools; this all mirrors have in common. But what they reflect and what they symbolize are a vast subject. Like appearance, like beauty and ugliness, the mirror is a chameleonlike concept, which shifts its meaning according to context.

The greatest mystery of our fairy tale is the conjunction of Beauty and the Beast, the need of the prince to be released from his spell by the love of a beautiful woman, and the need of Beauty to find the power of the Beast. Without this power, beauty is dangerous and an obstacle to the woman who possesses it, for she is subject to the desires and jealousy of others, and she has no will of her own. This theme is amplified in the Disney film version of the tale, in which Beauty is threatened by the fierce pursuit of another suitor, a rough, crude village oaf, who values her beauty as a possession he can claim, who has no respect or care for her love of reading or her gentle nature.

The story of Beauty and the Beast parallels the story of Sun Pu-erh, for Beauty's way of overcoming the obstacle to her growth represented by her physical beauty is to embrace the ugliness of the beast, not by scarring herself, but by loving a monster who is kind and caring.

Contemporary women in the position of Beauty are often models, wives of powerful men, actresses, or other women who seek to move beyond their roles as beautiful women to find recognition for their whole selves. Lacking the magical power of the Beast, such women are confined in the role of beautiful object, subject to the whims of men and the jealousy of other women. This, the role of the beautiful woman as commodified object, was the role projected onto Marilyn Monroe and satirized by Madonna, in images where the Beast is represented by the threat and fantasy of violence. This role continually re-emerges in popular culture because of its reflection of the needs of women who are trapped in beauty-defined roles.

The challenge of loving the Beast is more complicated when the Beast is internalized, when a woman grows up seeing herself as an ugly monster. The entirely subjective nature of this role is not apparent to the woman, who suffers until she finds a way out.

Because ugliness is so entirely subjective, its power is mysterious, partaking of the unknown. Like all mysteries, ugliness has an aspect of initiation, which is how it often appears in fairy tales, as it does in "Mulha" and in "Beauty and the Beast." In these tales, ugliness is imposed on someone against her will. It is quite different from the assumption of ugliness as a conscious disguise, which we see in the story of Sun Pu-erh.

Another variation on this theme of ugliness as mysterious, forced initiation appears in a lesser-known English medieval story that provides a mirror image to "Beauty and the Beast." "Gawain and the Lady Ragnell" is told by Ethel Johnston Phelps in her wonderful collection of feminist folk tales, *The Maid of the North*. In this tale, which I retell here in an abbreviated version, the woman plays the mysterious role of the all-knowing, ugly stranger, and it is the man who is initiated.

GAWAIN AND THE LADY RAGNELL

Gawain was the devoted nephew and knight of King Arthur of Britain. It was his devotion to his king that led to his betrothal to the loathsome Lady Ragnell. King Arthur encountered Rag-

nell's stepbrother, the terrible Sir Gromer, while hunting in the
woods one day, unarmed and separated from his men. Gromer
had Arthur in his power, and threatened to kill him unless he
could answer the riddle Gromer posed: "What is it that women
most desire?" Arthur promised to meet Gromer in one year, at
the same place, unarmed, and either give him the answer or die.

When Gawain heard about Arthur's promise, he swore to
help Arthur find the answer, and they scoured the kingdom,
but although they collected many answers, none seemed to have
"the ring of truth." And then one day, shortly before the year's
end, Arthur encountered "a grotesque woman. She was almost
as wide as she was high, her skin was mottled green, and spikes
of weedlike hair covered her head. Her face seemed more animal than human."

The woman tells Arthur she is Lady Ragnell, stepsister to
Sir Gromer. She tells him she knows the answer to the question,
but she will give it to him only if Gawain agrees to become her
husband. Arthur is enraged, and thinks he will not even mention the incident to Gawain, but Gawain, seeing his distress,
persuades Arthur to tell what has happened. Gawain then insists that he will marry the woman, provided her answer saves
Arthur's life. The answer, supplied after several false tries, in a
whimsical manner similar to the climax of the story of Rum-
pelstiltskin, infuriates the terrible Sir Gromer. Just as Gromer
is raising his sword to lop off Arthur's head, Arthur cries,

"Wait . . . I have one more answer. What a woman desires,
above all, is the power of sovereignty—the right to exercise
her own will."

With a loud oath the man dropped his sword. "You did
not find that answer by yourself," he shouted. "My cursed
stepsister, Ragnell, gave it to you. Bold, interfering hussy!
I'll run her through with my sword. . . . I'll lop off her
head. . . ." Turning, he plunged into the forest, a string of
horrible curses echoing behind him.

Now Gawain must keep his promise and marry the loathsome Lady Ragnell, which he does, courteously and without

complaint, although everyone else pities him and is horrified by her. At their wedding feast Lady Ragnell is the only one to enjoy her food and her surroundings.

At last alone in their bedchamber, Ragnell demands that Gawain kiss her. He does so without hesitation, and she is transformed into "a slender young woman with gray eyes and a serene smiling face." The sorcery unnerves Gawain, and he is for the first time thrown off balance by the unknown. Lady Ragnell explains that her loathsome form was a curse laid upon her by her stepbrother, who said she must stay that way until the greatest knight in Britain would choose her for his bride. Gromer hated her because she defied his commands concerning her property and herself.

Gawain is thrilled, but Ragnell has more to ask of him. She tells Gawain he must make a choice, will he have her fair by day and loathsome at night in their bedchamber, or fair at night and loathsome by day. But Gawain responds quickly that he cannot make that choice because it concerns her. He says he will abide by her choice, whatever it is.

This is the final test, and Gawain passes it brilliantly. For when Gromer cursed his stepsister, he said that if she could persuade the greatest knight in Britain to marry her, and that knight then gave her the power to exercise her own free will, the curse would be broken forever.

> Thus, in wonder and in joy, began the marriage of Gawain and the lady Ragnell.

This story of Gawain belongs to a body of literature written down in the fourteenth and fifteenth centuries from an older oral tradition, centering on King Arthur and his court. The figure of Gawain goes far back in Irish mythology, and is linked with many stories concerning women in the tradition of Goddess worship, which persisted in Celtic cultures until at least the seventeenth century. In the fourteenth century the Goddess was still actively worshiped, and the church was beginning its fiercest period of persecution of witches and any others who opposed its strict patriarchal doctrines. Witches were not burned in England, they were hanged, but it was argued that their bodies should be burned for fear they would rise again and seek revenge, no doubt for the great injustice done them. Therefore the issue of free will for women was, literally, a burning issue.

The idea that the curse of loathsomeness, imposed on Lady Ragnell as punishment for the terrible crime of wanting her own way, can only be lifted by the action of Britain's greatest knight is a very interesting one. Here (male) perfection is married to utter (female) ugliness, a concept Gromer found so improbable that he predicted it would never happen. Yet, as in "Beauty and the Beast," one extreme contains the seed of its polar opposite. What is so unusual in this story is that perfection is the attribute of the hero, and that the heroine, who is also an antiheroine, is not at all perfect. She is, however, an impeccable spiritual warrior who is capable of keeping her equanimity in any role.

As in the story of Mulha, beauty is not perceived as problematic in the case of Lady Ragnell. It is her insistence on her own way, her rebelliousness, which dates back to the rebellion of the ancient goddesses against the gods who usurped their power, that is seen as problematic by her brother. In reaction, he imposes the curse of ugliness upon her, but leaves the way open for her to be redeemed through the action of a man. In this way he prepares for Gawain, hero of the age of chivalry, which offered a hope of change for women whose real lives were utterly circumscribed by patriarchal law and custom.

I wonder if the story of Gawain and Lady Ragnell has remained obscure, while the story of Beauty and the Beast is widely known, because it is so much more radical, against dominant traditions, that a man should be required to marry an ugly woman than that a beautiful woman should be paired with an ugly beast.

Perhaps it is because of its radical nature that the narrative of Gawain and Ragnell has a light, ironic tone to it, a tone common to medieval and modern stories of women who insist on having their way. Other examples are "The Wife of Bath's Tale" in Chaucer's *Canterbury Tales*, a slightly different version of the story of Gawain and Ragnell, as told by the bawdy Wife; Shakespeare's *Taming of the Shrew*; the Romanian fairy tale "The Girl Who Pretended to Be a Boy"; Grimms' "The Frog Princess"; and the movie *The African Queen*. Modern examples of women who claim their right to self-determination at the expense of their beautiful image are to be found in popular culture, such as television series from *I Love Lucy* to *Murphy Brown*, and can arguably be found in the sleazy slut fashions pioneered by Madonna.

In both "Beauty and the Beast" and "Gawain and Lady Ragnell," the protagonist, male or female, is challenged to come to terms with ugliness, associated with monstrousness and bestiality, to look beyond appearance to find the nature of the individual. This individual nature turns out to be surprisingly different from the prevailing stereotype of male or female behavior. The prince in "Beauty and the Beast" is unfailingly gentle and self-sacrificing, while Lady Ragnell is uncompromising in her will to preserve her freedom.

The story of Gromer's curse on Ragnell is a metaphor for the historical vilification of women. It recalls the horrors of the centuries-old church persecution of witches, when, according to contemporary witnesses and the records of the Inquisition, any woman who was old, poor, deformed, or in any way threatened male autonomy, was accused and summarily convicted of witchcraft. But the story of Gawain's courtesy to Lady Ragnell, and the miracle of their marriage, while part of a tradition of courtly love, goes back to a more ancient belief in the power of all the aspects of woman as nature.

In her ugly incarnation, the Lady Ragnell is green, with weedlike hair, and her face seems more animal than human. That is, she resembles plants and animals; she is green like the Green Knight, who is Gawain's nemesis and stern teacher in another Arthurian tale; she is another aspect of the fertility goddess with whose worship Gawain was continually associated in his search for the Grail, the former cauldron of goddess worship, appropriated by the church as a Christian symbol. Again, ugliness is associated with something sacred and powerful. As an archetypal figure this green woman merits our attention, for she provides images of healing and regeneration, which can be very powerful for contemporary women. I have observed just such a healing image in therapeutic work with women who have had breast cancer.

MARI AND THE GREEN, MOSSY SPIRIT

I first met Mari at a process work seminar held semiannually on the Oregon coast, where participants explore psychosomatic aspects of serious illnesses with the help of trained therapists. She is a massage therapist, a mother, a strikingly attractive woman, who has been diagnosed with breast cancer and who has chosen to work in alternative ways with her illness, using diet, exercise, meditation, and psychological and spiritual methods.

I was present when, asked by Dr. Arnold Mindell to describe her experience of her cancer, Mari said she imagined that the tumor in her breast was a green, damp, mossy thing, a creature from another world, which was repulsive to her. Encouraged by Mindell to find out more about this image, she began to move like the green, mossy creature, and her movements became a sort of dance, very powerful and fascinating. As Mari danced, she realized that she too was fascinated by the creature, which no longer disgusted her but had become a source of wonder.

The green, mossy creature brought to my mind the story of Gawain and Ragnell, and also another story, "Mossycoat," about the transformation of a young woman with the aid of her mother's sorcery. In this story, which has parallels to "Cinderella," a young Gypsy woman receives from her mother a magical coat, woven of green moss and gold, that enables her to travel anywhere and to perform acts of magic. The young woman's beauty, her basic attribute, draws attention from her upper-class employer and violent retribution from the other servants in the household where she finds employment. Her beauty is hidden under the grease of the kitchen where she works as a scullery maid, and where jealous servants hit her on the head with the skimmer, constantly telling her she is ugly and stupid. Only with the aid of her magical mossycoat is she able to emerge and triumph over her enemies.

Moss, which is damp and green, is an emblem of the vegetable world, related metaphorically to the human vegetative nervous system. The appearance of an image such as Mari's green, mossy creature, which transforms from something loathsome to something mysterious and wonderful as she enters into it and becomes more familiar with it, has great healing possibilities.

Mari told me that growing up perceived as a beautiful girl and later as a beautiful woman was very difficult for her. She believed that being attractive to men made her into a sexual object, and she felt great ambivalence about her appearance. What was beautiful to others was often ugly in her mind. She wrote to me about a teenage memory:

> I had returned from a basketball game feeling like the belle of the ball surrounded by adoring young men and was shocked when I got home and looked in the mirror. I looked like hell: wild-haired, big bags under my eyes, face splotchy with zits and unknown reds. I couldn't understand why anybody had even talked to me. I was completely unaware that my perception had been honed to be cruelly harsh towards my own image. Now, via my teenage sons, I have young women in my life again, and I hear them complain woefully about their hair, their noses, their fat, etc. How I wish they knew how gloriously, uniquely beautiful they ALL are.

Mari, like many women, has suffered from her culture's ambivalence about women's bodies, beauty, and power. Her archetypal image of a green, mossy creature, disgusting to her when it first appears, offers the possibility of an alternative force in her life, the force of nature, which is neither beautiful

nor ugly in itself, but which reflects the attitudes projected
upon it by humans.

Mari may, like many women, experience the ugliness of her
cancer as a trial imposed upon her, hoping for a transformative
miracle, much as she suffered the role of beauty. She may also,
at some point in her own life and work as a healer, take on the
role of the miracle maker, the force of nature itself, green,
damp, mossy, with its insistent, vegetative power.

By invoking the terrible powers of nature, Mari's story and
the stories of Gawain and Ragnell and Beauty and the Beast
evoke earlier, mythic stories of humans who interacted with
gods disguised as aspects of nature, as swans, bears, horses,
snakes, even lightning bolts. Their ugliness is the ugliness of
nature the creator and destroyer, to be feared and respected
rather than maligned. At one time fear and respect were given
to the ugliness of human beings, ugliness due to disease or old
age, believed to give its owner magical or shamanic powers of
knowledge and healing. In the Middle Ages the Christian
church declared such powers evil, and used physical appearance
(both beauty and ugliness) as evidence for the presence of evil.
But the magical power of ugliness persists as a force in human
belief, driven underground in mainstream Western culture, but
still respected by Tibetan Buddhism and some African-based
religions.

8

UGLINESS
AND CULTURAL
STEREOTYPES

*My girlfriends and I imagined ourselves as the porcelain pink prin-
cesses: Snow White, Cinderella and, the fairest of them all, Barbie.
    What a sweet toy for a little Black girl, a rubber-headed,
relentlessly white woman with plastic torpedo titties, no hips,
no ass, who needed a kickstand up her butt to stand because
she was permanently poised on the balls of her feet. My
graceless arches were flat next to hers. Barbie's hair never had
to be straightened. She had no burn scars on her tiny pink ears.
I liked to pull her head off, spike it on a pencil, or poke out her
Barbie blues with a straight pin. Mama was amused at what
she considered my precociously feminist instincts.
    ... We are still "girls" together, she with her chemically
straightened hair, me with my dread-locked Rapunzel dreams,
making believe that all that "political stuff" is behind us
because they make Black Barbies now.*
                        —Oni Faida Lampley, "The Wig and I," *Mirabella*

The role of ugliness is as much a social phenomenon as it is a psychological one. It depends only in part on the willingness of people to identify with their appearance over time. Ugliness, in the eye of the perceiver as in the heart of the one perceived, can be as much of an obstacle to spiritual growth and psychological wholeness as beauty. This chapter looks at some stereotyped ideas of ugliness in the context of women's lives, extending ideas discussed earlier about cultural standards of beauty.

Ugliness as a temporary role offers power to the woman who assumes it. Ugliness as a basic attribute is as much of a challenge as any other difference from mainstream values, such as racial or ethnic difference, poverty, physical handicaps, life-threatening illness, visible scars, extreme old age. More than any of these other values, which have certain sensory-grounded characteristics that can be described with some accuracy, ugliness is entirely a subjective judgment, based on a consensus by those who observe, whether they are external judges or internal. You might say that both ugliness and beauty are matters of mass hypnosis.

"THE UGLY JEW"

When my mother started looking for secretarial work after she graduated from high school, she was advised by friends to change her name, as it sounded too Jewish. With her fine, light brown hair and regular features she looked like a white Anglo-Saxon Protestant, not like an ugly Jew. Everyone in those days knew what an ugly Jew looked like, because caricatures were found everywhere. Shakespeare's evil moneylender Shylock was an example in "high" culture; popular cartoons and tales provided abundant examples, from which the Nazis drew for their anti-Semitic propaganda. Jews had beaked noses, frizzy hair, small eyes, thick lips. They were dirty as well as ugly, and smelled bad, exactly the same characteristics used to put down Africans, Asians, Hispanics, Gypsies in Europe, Native Americans in the U.S.

As a child, I looked more like my mother than my father, who had dark hair and olive skin. My mother seemed happy that I didn't look Jewish. But when I was in second grade I got my first pair of glasses. Then I was called Four-eyes. I had been an attractive child, but now I became not ugly, just plain. In my heart I feared ugliness as a curse that might be laid upon me. In my heart, I knew that I was "passing," that my "real self" would be considered ugly by many around me.

In fourth grade I met my nemesis. Barbara looked Jewish. She was the largest girl in our class, tall, plump, with crinkly black hair, which frizzed out in a bush. At a time when, according to my fashion-conscious mother, bright colors were used discreetly, as a "touch of color" in a scarf or belt, Barbara came to school in a too-long pink skirt with a dragging purple sash and a print blouse. Everything askew, sloppy. She was loud, and she picked her nose in class. Once she got into a fight after school with another girl, and the two of them rolled around on the ground, pulling each other's hair.

Barbara was the butt of jokes for my schoolgirl enclave. We were cruel in our hatred and fear of her. She was our image of ugliness. But because my last name was similar to hers, and because she and I were both Jewish, I knew in my heart of hearts that somehow we were kin. I still have our class picture from that year. I am somewhere in the middle, medium height and build, plain brown hair pulled behind my ears, glasses off, ordinary white blouse and dark skirt, lips pursed in a fake smile for the camera. Barbara, wearing the prescribed white blouse and dark skirt for the class picture, overshadows everyone. She is bigger, bolder, stands out as if she were wearing pinks and purples. How I wish I knew Barbara now! How I wish I could have allowed myself to know Barbara then, but I was too afraid. Of fighting with her? Yes, but more to the point, of becoming like her.

What would I have become if I had dared to be more like Barbara? Perhaps I would have followed my own creativity more closely, honored my Jewish background, suffered less from the visual standards I followed so blindly. Following Barbara's example now, I mix colors, dare to be sloppy, occasionally risk a fight with a friend, behave outrageously sometimes. I wonder what Barbara is doing in her middle age? Perhaps she is an account executive, wearing power suits and impeccable makeup. Or perhaps she is a mountain climber, or a freedom fighter, an artist, or a therapist, writer, teacher, like me.

As a young girl and as a teenager, I suffered from my sense of having to work all the time simply to look, if not beautiful, at least not ugly. I still put a lot of effort into my appearance. When my African American friends describe their teenage complications of dealing with bad hair, or finding makeup to match their complexions, they describe experiences similar to mine; I agonized as an adolescent over my hair's tendency to droop no matter how tightly I rolled it into curlers, wished I could cover those flaming pimples, and felt fat no matter how thin I was. But there is a difference between our experiences, a difference based on privilege. My knowledge and understanding of that difference came slowly.

It came to me in pieces. One piece fell into place when I first saw Whoopi Goldberg's one-woman stage show *Whoopi*, a show still available on videotape. Goldberg moves with startling fluidity from one character to another wildly different character, and is able to change her age, gender, accent, ethnic and racial background through movement, voice, and story. One of her characters is a young African American girl, who appears wearing a white shirt over her head, which she announces is her beautiful blond hair. With such hair, she tells us proudly, she can be like the beautiful blondes she sees on television, not just poor and powerless as she is in her everyday life. Goldberg, an adult African American woman, speaks and gestures precisely as a young girl, a child, would, so that she becomes, for the moment, that child. She also remains an adult who understands how the child projects her longing for beauty and privilege onto the snow white images she finds on her television.

The key word is privilege, the privilege associated with beauty and not with ugliness, the privilege of wealth, comfort, appreciation, love, high moral standing. Increasingly, as the global village predicted by Marshall McLuhan becomes a technological reality, we see images of privilege and beauty on the one hand, and oppression and ugliness on the other. These are polarized images of a world divided between those who have and those who have not. The polarity is real, in economic and political terms, and the extent of the injustice threatens to overturn our existing arrangements, an idea that brings terror to the privileged and relief to the oppressed.

The polarity is also psychological, and it exists in each of us. In each there is a greediness that denies whatever privilege we have, a critical element that denies our own particular beauty, that judges us as ugly, and a neediness that feels great sadness for our oppression.

And yet we sense our own beauty and privilege even as we deny these. Without pretending that the disease of racism is less virulent or widespread than it is, I think that those of us white folk who have trouble comprehending the seriousness of the disease might look first to the ways we split off and deny our own internal oppression, the ways we damage ourselves and others with judgments based on entirely arbitrary standards of beauty and ugliness.

''THE UGLY BLACK WOMAN''

Toni Morrison describes the Breedlove family in her novel *The Bluest Eye* in terms that indicate the changing nature of appearance:

> You looked at them and wondered why they were so ugly; you looked closely and could not find the source. Then you realized that it came from conviction, their conviction. It was as though some mysterious all-knowing master had given each one a cloak of ugliness to wear, and they had each accepted it without question. The master had said, "You are ugly people." They had looked about themselves and saw nothing to contradict that statement; saw, in fact, support for

it leaning at them from every billboard, every movie, every glance. "Yes," they had said, "you are right." And they took the ugliness in their hands, threw it as a mantle over them, and went about the world with it.

Morrison is speaking here of internal conviction supported by the world, which concurs in a poor African American family's judgment of their own ugliness.

In the context of racism, people learn as children to consider themselves ugly according to mainstream standards. Growing up surrounded by media images of whites can be a devastating experience if your skin is black, brown, coppery, or gold, if you have a "Jewish" nose or "bad" hair. Schools that use European culture as the basis for education ignore the pain and rage stirred in children of color by the omnipresent image of the white princess and her white Prince Charming.

There is an article in the Portland daily paper about an art program for homeless children, with a photo of a young white woman hugging a small black girl, who is showing her self-portrait to the teacher. The girl is smiling in the photo, but this is how the article describes her:

Ebony Baker, 7, has just completed a self-portrait—a grinning rendition of her wearing a bright red shirt and blue pants.

"I want to look like a boy," she says, though she can't say why.

Ebony isn't thrilled about the upcoming exhibit. "I don't want people to see my picture," she says. "It's ugly."

Ebony is one of many little girls who would rather look like, or be, boys, a tendency related to sexism in the world, but her self-identification as an ugly child is a problem rooted in racism. "Ugly" is a stock adjective commonly used to describe and put down girls in many communities of color where white standards of beauty prevail.

I think of the litany of color in the saying I hear from African American friends: "If you're white, you're all right; if you're yellow, you're mellow; if you're brown, stick around; but if you are black, go back!" The saying illustrates not only the discrimination against blackness, but the intense hierarchy of color, which exists in individual families as well as in communities. An African American woman emphasized to me the importance of understanding that not all families of color are supportive of their children's self-esteem. In some, light-skinned children are strongly favored over children with darker skin. Another woman told me of the saying, that if you are darker than "paper bag brown" (I think of the paper bags I use in my workshops) you are unacceptable.

A woman who is my age tells me that in her black college, sororities were based on skin color: light-skinned women belonged to one sorority; another was made up of women with medium-dark skin; another was for darker-skinned women. Women who were considered ugly were excluded from sorority membership, something I remember from my own white college experience. But for African American women, there is a double sting in being judged by white standards of appearance. Regina Turner, in an article for the journal *Black Male/Female Relationships*, called "The Sexual Ordeal of the 'Ugly' Black Woman," lists the following criteria for ugliness:

> *no curves (too skinny)*
> *big feet or flat feet*
> *overweight*
> *knocked-knees*
> *big eyes*
> *big lips (that get bigger when you get mad)*
> *imperfect teeth or gap(s)*
> *skin blemishes*
> *broad shoulders*
> *skinny legs*
> *too tall*
> *too short*
> *too dark (regardless of the temporary uplift of the Sixties)*

Some of these criteria apply to women of any color and some are specific concerns of black women.

According to Turner, the "ugly Black woman" is an outsider to her own culture, as "ugly" women everywhere are outsiders. She goes on to describe the situation of an "ugly Black woman":

Beyond the loneliness, there are a number of advantages of being placed in this predicament. If she survives, more than any person in this society the ugly Black woman is stripped of any illusions she might have concerning what constitutes the real essence of living. That is, there is no white male power or money, no white female "forbidden quality," no Black man's super macho, no Black beautiful woman's marketable assets. She has only her ugly self in whom few people believe. This means that beyond the strength she can muster from her family and loved ones—usually other Black women—no institution, no media will endorse her existence. Because the likelihood is greater that she'll be alone more, she has much time to think, probe, question and grow. In her growth, somehow she determines to do more, do it better, and make a difference. Being the very lowest on the totem, she develops more patience, more forgiveness, greater endurance, and more compassion. Why? Because she has to. If she is not careful, however, she could easily become a "monster" of insensitivity, strength and self reliance, becoming intolerant of and unable to understand weakness in others.

A fashion magazine called *Face*, aimed at Asian women, received a letter from a reader who describes herself as "an Asian American woman who has grown up believing she was ugly." These feelings, based on internalized racism, are widespread among women of African and Asian background in the U.S., who share the same feelings all women have about the importance of appearance. Across barriers of race and ethnicity, women are raised to demand beauty of themselves, but some women feel excluded from the start.

CATHERINE — "I'M NOT VERY TALL"

Catherine Hogue described to me some of the ways that she has been affected by judgments based on appearance. Catherine, who is an administrative assistant at a health-care center in Illinois, describes herself precisely, "I'm four foot eleven and three-quarter inches tall." Not short, tall. "I think I'm evenly proportioned, I weigh ninety-eight to one hundred and three pounds. I'm fifty-three. My complexion is . . . I guess I'd call myself brown-skinned, chocolate brown, milk chocolate." She wears her hair short and has a perm to straighten it every four or five months, but at one time she wore a huge Afro. She has five children, raised by herself, and nine grandchildren.

Catherine refers to her height much more frequently than she does to her skin color, but she has no illusions about the impact racism has had on her life. She speaks about being denied education, housing, and jobs, about having to struggle for promotion, even about being abused by her former husband for being both small and dark. The key for her is that her mother raised her to have "a good self-image." "You always, first and foremost, must feel good about yourself. Mother said, 'You remember who you are and what's important to you.' "

All her siblings have different skin tones. One sister is "high yellow," one is dark-skinned and larger than the others, one brother has the same skin color as Catherine. It was always understood that those with lighter skin suffered less from discrimination than those with darker skin. Catherine thinks that African American families encourage their children more often than white families do to focus on how they feel about themselves rather than on how they look. She thinks they also tend to have more tolerance for difference in height, size, shape, and skin color. "We're more tolerant of difference because there is so much difference in our families."

However, watching her granddaughters, Catherine sees them obsessed with their looks, with hair, clothes, makeup. One eleven-year-old "stays in the mirror—even if she walks past a window she has to look at herself." She attributes this obsession to the influence of television and to peer pressure. Catherine herself is quite clear about the importance of appearance for women in the world. "When I dress, I dress for success because I feel that I'm successful. At work, I wear suits, because I'm an administrator."

Catherine, like many women of color, has understood from childhood that beauty and ugliness are culturally determined, and that individual flexibility can go a long way toward survival and success. As we speak, I am struck with the resilient self-confidence of this woman, a longtime union organizer who has struggled all her life against discrimination and injustice. "I feel that I look very good," she says. "If anybody finds me unattractive, that's their problem—because I'm black, or because I'm not very tall, or because I don't weigh very much."

While being small can make it difficult for a woman to assert herself, not weighing very much is a great asset for women these days. Along with race and ethnicity, sexual orientation and physical ability, fat and age are aspects of appearance that are often used as grounds for discrimination.

"UGLY FAT, UGLY AGE"

Media consultant Freude Bartlett, a white, redheaded, freckle-faced, large-breasted, weighty woman of style, was visiting me in Portland and we were talking, of course, about appearance. Freude has limped since her childhood bout with polio. She told me about another woman who suffers from skin problems. This woman told Freude she thought skin problems were much worse than a limp. After thinking it over, Freude agreed with her, but she later sent me an article about the discrimination experienced by women in wheelchairs, which led me to think about the relativity of oppressions, and why it is we compare our troubles so judiciously. It must have something to do with the value of troubles, something we're loath to admit, but find surreptitiously in our gossip and speculation.

Then we talked about the magazine I had lying on my coffee table, *Harper's Bazaar*. Freude was outraged and at the same time perceptive about contemporary advertising images of thin young women. She said, "Large older women like me won't buy clothes they see modeled by a woman who's size twenty-four. We want to see models who are young and slim. Because there is no validation of age and wisdom to balance the premium placed on youthful beauty." Of course! Would a magazine that showed real women of all shapes and sizes and ages and colors, wearing real, affordable clothes, be able to obtain the advertising revenue it would need in order to survive? We agreed that it probably would not. The issue is ugliness—age and fat are categorically labeled as ugly, in advertisements and articles, in stories and in movies. But how extreme can the cult of youth and thinness get before it too is labeled ugly?

Several months later, *Harper's Bazaar* featured on its cover a model who is not only thin, she has hollow cheeks, mouth hanging slightly open, drooping eyelids, and a vacant stare. The caption says, "Beauty's New Debate: Anorexic versus Waif." Inside, in an article called "Body of Evidence, Eating Disorders and the Media: We Bite Back," editor Tina Gaudoin argued defensively that since they feature thin models who, she claimed, are naturally thin and not anorexic, the fashion world has no responsibility for the widespread phenomenon of eating disorders in women. "We're not endorsing eating disorders," she said. "What we are endorsing is change."

According to this article, the current vogue for waiflike thinness is a welcome reaction to "the pumped-up, aerobicized, silicone-breasted '80s." The argument is painfully specious and ahistorical. Models in the eighties were already several sizes smaller than models in the fifties. I remember the impact of an earlier waif, Twiggy, on the fashion scene of the sixties, and I wonder, with not much amazement, at the very narrow range of options for women's bodies the *Harper's* writer seems able to entertain.

But my wonder at her false logic fades before the images that accompany the article. Supposedly showcasing "natural thinness" and a realistic depiction of teenage waifhood, these photographs depict a very, very thin young woman wearing scanty white underwear and posed in a fetal position, staring up or at the camera with a vacant gaze. The same model, Kate Moss, is also photographed in close-up with fashionably full lips suggesting silicone implants, perched on a chair with her legs wrapped around each other, bare-buttocked, a sweater falling from her shoulders, looking to my skeptical eyes like a fashion model imitating an anorexic teenager, echoing, grimly, photographs from German concentration camps.

" 'Fashion,' " the article quotes a designer as saying, " 'is not about reality. It's about ideas and vision.' " The whole point of the article seems to be that because some women are naturally thin, and because photographers and fashion designers like thinness, fashion therefore celebrates nature. But what about women who are naturally large? Who celebrates that aspect of nature? What about older women? We do all age, but we drop out of fashion's sight as we get visibly old.

Four months after Tina Gaudoin's article, *Harper's Bazaar* ran a parody of her article under the heading "Move Over Waifs, the Bulge Look Is Here." The article describes the discovery of a new model by an unnamed *Bazaar* editor, a model named Wanderful, who had "arms three times the size of her wrists . . . was five foot seven and weighed 183 pounds—80 pounds more than the current fashion"; the article also describes a new "bulge trend," concluding with the following satiric blast: "What we are endorsing is revolution and change, which is what self-determination and liberation are all about. Besides, for the time being, bulge just looks better." In sharp contrast to the article on waifs, this article ran with no accompanying pictures.

People magazine, which devoted a cover article to the controversy over Kate Moss and the new wave of waifdom in fashion models, used, along with many photos of the fashionable Kate Moss, another model, Anna Nicole Smith, "the buxom Guess jeans girl," as an example of a "sexy and successful big girl." Smith, who is 5 feet 11 and weighs 155 pounds, is a lot bigger than Moss, 5 feet 7 and about 100 pounds. But Smith is still slim by many women's standards. The only thing really large about her is her bosom, the sexualized object that has been celebrated by men's magazines and mass media outside of the fashion world for many years.

The brilliance of the *People* cover is its juxtaposition of the high-fashion image of Moss with the country-and-western-style image of Smith. But what is it juxtaposing? Kate Moss, her face subtly made up, "natural" lipstick on her full lips, shown naked from the hips up with her arms crossed, concealing her breasts, looking available to the camera and to the spectator, is the image that dominates. In the bottom corner there is a small inset of Anna Smith, in a white shirt tied to reveal a bare midriff and ample cleavage, her bleached-blond hair glittering, wearing heavy eye makeup and bright lipstick. The text, in huge letters, reads, SKIN AND BONES, then in smaller script, "SUPERMODEL KATE MOSS is the ultrathin symbol of the underfed waif look. Is a dangerous message being sent to weight-obsessed teens?" Below, next to the inset picture of Smith, in even smaller script, "Big girls don't cry: Jeans model Anna Nicole Smith is sexy and successful—at 155 pounds." The message is complex: "Skin and bones" is high fashion and rates top billing; but the look is not sexy. Or is it? Whose sexual pleasure is being catered to?

The appeal of Anna Smith is fairly clear, aimed primarily at men and at women who want to attract men to their readily available, nurturing sexuality. She is a late-twentieth-century version of the decorative and male-oriented sex goddess as she has been depicted since the overthrow of the powerful Goddess of all nature.

But what exactly is the appeal of Kate Moss and the *faux*-anorexic look she so successfully embodies? What is there about the image of extreme youth, fragility, and helplessness, presented in the context of elegance and high fashion, that is so desirable, and what, exactly, is that desire for?

As I ponder my own fascination with the images in front of me, I realize that for me Kate Moss evokes my own maternal tenderness, and my own longing for maternal tenderness. I can identify with the waif and with the mother for whom the waif longs. It is her childlike quality that so fascinates me, and the adult context in which her childlike quality is set gives permission to indulge my own childlike dreams.

I imagine that her image becomes a blank screen for each of us to project our own complex relationship with childhood and the body of the child. That this is a sexualized relationship is clear, but the exact nature of the sexuality will vary according to the spectator. There is no trace of an intruding personality from Kate Moss to interfere with this freedom to project and dream as we gaze at her.

Because she provides such a blank screen, there is plenty of room for advocates of freedom of expression to argue in favor of such images, and for those concerned about the sexualization of early childhood to argue that such images are very dangerous indeed. The debate is important, and even more important is widespread public understanding of the connection between repression and explosion. Most violence against children seems to be perpetrated by adults who have themselves been exploited, abused, and above all, repressed as children.

The absolute neutrality of Kate Moss as the ultimate clotheshanger appears in the final image of the *People* article. Culminating a series of images of fashion models through four decades, which purport to show the changes in body image but which support a relentlessly thin ideal, with or without breasts, with or without body tone, the picture of Kate Moss in the nineties shows her in a wild costume designed by Chantal Thomass, her hair resembling the elaborate construction of an African tribeswoman, her lean body rigged in a mixture of stripes, gauze, glitter, and high heels. At this moment fashion imitates art. I can imagine a large woman similarly costumed, equally striking, although I don't imagine that a large woman would be featured as an example of high fashion.

I return to the *Harper's Bazaar* article on Kate Moss, and I turn the page. The next article is about Beryl Markham, the famous Englishwoman who lived as a colonialist in Kenya. Her new biography serves the magazine as a motif for a fashion safari to Africa, featuring lean, pale models in white or khaki surrounded by Masai warriors, whose dark bodies and colorful tartan robes are used as backdrops for the white models and the high fashions in which they are dressed.

The power of Beryl Markham's own writing about the Africa she loved is completely undercut by the relentlessly fashionable images of the article.

The whole issue of *Harper's* confirms bell hooks's writing about the racialized context of fashion, a context that intensifies and comments on the distortions of sexism. The ideas and visions in these pages reflect our twin cultural nightmares of starvation and colonization, used to sell high fashion to women who cannot enjoy the privileges gained at such great cost to the rest of the world because they are so busy trying to match an impossible and disempowering image of emaciated adolescence.

In strong contrast to this magazine "art," I remember some films Freude Bartlett made in the early seventies, short experimental films she put together on a reel, which she called *My Life in Art*. One showed a woman sweeping on the beach, sweeping and sweeping the sand into the sea. Another showed Freude's son, then an infant, sitting up and falling to one side. She made a loop of the film, so that we saw baby Adam falling over and over and over. These short films were among the first I saw to represent the sense of eternal repetition in the domestic lives of so many women. Freude, like other women artists of the time, was drawing attention to a few of the things women do and what that activity looks like to us, rather than to what we dream of looking like.

Freude and I met in the heady context of women's film festivals in the mid-seventies, when we and many other women thought that by studying the media and creating new, women-identified films, we would change something in the world, something oppressive and distortive, rooted in patriarchy.

Now Freude and I are both thinking about life and death as a series of mental constructs, appearances that point the way to enlightenment or to the endless wheel of life and fate. These pursuits haven't stopped us from noticing how we look. In fact, we are noticing how we go about looking at ourselves and at others in greater detail than ever before. A whole generation of women is looking in the mirror of self-reflection at a critical point in our aging process. We are looking back as well as forward, inward as well as outward.

As we look, we discover that the myths about appearance we grew up with don't match our experiences as we grow older. These myths concern ethnicity, youth, and size. We don't look ugly to ourselves, but if we consider the messages embedded in movies, television, and magazines, we have to admit that we are entering the realm of ugliness.

While we are expected to conceal sags and wrinkles by covering our bodies, we are judged as ridiculous if we apply too much makeup to our aging faces. Hairs that sprout on chins and upper lips at menopause are generally considered ugly, so are brown spots and moles, which increasingly mark our skin. Although we are told by doctors that women who are slightly overweight have less chance of developing osteoporosis, we are warned against gaining weight, and considered lazy if we do. Like my paternal grandmother, many of us dye our graying hair, diet obsessively, lie about our age, try to avoid the judgment of ugliness and worthlessness that we read between the lines of our youth-obsessed culture. But there is a limit to disguise where age is concerned. Eventually, despite cosmetic surgery, exercise, and careful diet, flesh withers and bones become brittle. Death stands at our shoulders—will we see her as ugly or as beautiful? is she an enemy or an ally?

From "The King Who Would Have a Beautiful Wife" (a Sicilian fairy tale in Andrew Lang's collection):

> . . . the king believed her words, and the marriage took place without the veil being once lifted. Afterwards, when they were alone, he raised the corner, and knew for the first time that he had wedded a wrinkled old woman. And, in a furious burst of anger, he dashed open the window and flung her out. But, luckily for her, her clothes caught on a nail in the wall, and kept her hanging between heaven and earth.
>
> [Four fairies happened to pass by and granted her "youth," "beauty," "wisdom," and "a tender heart."]

The next morning when the king looked from his window he saw this lovely creature hanging on the nail. "Ah! what have I done? Surely I must have been blind last night!"

And he ordered long ladders to be brought and the maiden to be rescued. Then he fell on his knees before her, and prayed her to forgive him, and a great feast was made in her honour.

"UGLY OLD AGE"

Think of all the adjectives that are most disrespectful in our society. They are all part of the ageist stereotyping of old women: pathetic, powerless, querulous, complaining, sick, weak, conservative, rigid, helpless, unproductive, wrinkled, asexual, ugly, unattractive, and so on, ad nauseam. There is, by the way, an exception to this, and that is the stereotype of the wise old woman. She, of course, never complains, is never sick, and although no one really would want to be with her, occasionally it might be fine to sit at her feet!
—Shevy Healy

The association of ugliness with old age is so prevalent that it is unconscious, except, of course, for the old, who are keenly aware of how their wrinkles, thinning hair, and otherwise aging bodies are regarded by the youth-obsessed culture around them. For centuries, fairy tales and folktales have depicted old women as easy targets for ridicule, based on their ugliness, which was simply taken for granted. In a startling aside in one of her Miss Marple mystery novels, the great detective writer Agatha Christie describes the moment when Miss Marple uncovers the foolishness of a young man who is about to be accused of a murder he didn't commit. Far from appreciating her rescuing intelligence, the young man says "fiercely, 'Be quiet, you old hag!' "

Now that old women such as Florida Maxwell-Davies, Barbara Macdonald, Baba Copper, and others are writing about their own experiences, we can see several sides of a complex situation. Old women are seen as ugly and often called ugly to their faces—by strangers and children on the street, by implication in the ageist remarks made constantly in the mass media, for example, in the many commercials that treat aging as a hazard to be avoided. How old women see themselves, however, may be a very different matter.

Here is Tish Sommers, the founder of the Older Women's League, quoted by her biographer:

> I look forward to the time when we can merchandise a cosmetic line to make youth seem older—a special crow's foot pencil, the silver bleaches, the stick to make those delicious brown spots on the hands, eyeline under the eye for that sexy mature look. Let the young ones eat their hearts out!

But of more interest to me, considering my own approaching old age, is the idea that old women may truly shift the emphasis in self-perception, having much less concern for how they look, and much more concern for what they do and experience. Baba Copper puts the basic issue, as she sees it, bluntly:

> The problem for old women is a problem of power. First, power over the circumstances and directions of our own lives and identity. Second, power as an influence upon the world we live in—the world we have served, in which we have such a large, unrecognized, vested interest.

So long as women are defined by appearance rather than by action, old women will be powerless in a world that sees them as ugly. This is a loss to the world as well as to the old women.

Ugliness is associated by mainstream culture with many aspects of blackness, with old age, and with fat. Of these, fat seems to be the great, adjustable variable. More than any other aspect of women's appearance today, fat is considered a moral issue, something bad, for which a woman is to blame. But one of the subtexts for our cultural hatred of fat is its association with power, the power of the large woman versus the apparent fragility of the very thin "feminine" woman.

WAYNELLE: A VERY AMBITIOUS PERSON

I first met Waynelle Wilder in 1987 at a conference where, asked to discuss the work we had just seen about a woman's memories of the Holocaust, I burst into wild crying and was comforted, held, and rocked by Waynelle. I thought she was the warmest, safest, biggest-hearted woman I had ever met, and it was no surprise to me to learn that she has a successful therapy practice. Over the years of our acquaintance, I have observed Waynelle's quietness in large groups, and also her ability to make extremely perceptive comments when asked to do so.

Waynelle has been many different sizes in her life, varying over one hundred pounds in weight as an adult. She remembers being thin as a small child, and very active, and says she started to gain weight when she started school, at the age of five. She was teased at school and at home, and remembers cruel children's taunts: "She can't get through the bathroom door, so she'll have to pee on the floor." Waynelle started believing there was something wrong with her. When she looks back now at photos of her childhood she sees that she was never obese, just round, a "beautiful, chubby child." When she says this I remember the chubby children I knew as a child. We children teased every one, unmercifully. Were we already under the influence of a deep-rooted cultural standard? There is a much greater acceptance of difference in size among traditional Polynesian cultures and some African cultures, but increasingly children raised in such cultures feel the pressure of Western media and culture.

Until she was ten, Waynelle was taller and bigger than the other children. She reached her present height of five feet two inches, slightly shorter than average for a white American woman, at the age of ten. She was aware of being both physically and intellectually different, way ahead of other children in school subjects. But once she got to junior high school she concealed her intelligence and starved herself to lose weight. She made herself small in every way, trying to match the image she believed was ideal for her age and sex. "I really sold out," she says now. "I wonder what I would have been like if I hadn't done that." She thinks she would have been more out in the world, a scholar, perhaps an English professor. I grin wryly, as one who did become an English professor and dropped the role rather early.

By junior high school Waynelle had an eating disorder. She typically would wait as long as possible before eating, skipping breakfast and lunch, then keeping dinner to a minimum. She says that her mother didn't seem to notice she wasn't eating, and was relieved that she was losing weight. No matter how much weight Waynelle lost, when she looked in the mirror all she saw was that she didn't match the thin fashion models in magazines.

Waynelle married a high school dropout before she graduated from high school. The marriage didn't last. At one time she thought she was pregnant, but in fact she was missing periods because she wasn't eating enough. In the late 1970s, when she weighed ninety-seven pounds, her husband told her that she should lose still another five pounds. By this time Waynelle was dreaming of pursuing men, dreams she interprets in terms of her need to develop her more "masculine," active side. In the midst of starving herself to conform to a "feminine" image, Waynelle was dreaming of a very different path.

When she was pregnant with her first child, Waynelle's doctor prescribed amphetamines to give her more energy. She became addicted to the pills, and lived on pills and a daily Fudgsicle during her pregnancy. Waynelle weighed 112 pounds when she gave birth to a premature son of 4½ pounds. She struggled with her prescription-drug addiction for nearly twenty years. The pills affected her metabolism, her moods, her sleeping and eating patterns, and her relationships.

As a single mother working at low-paying jobs, Waynelle took twenty years at night school to get her B.A. She entered therapy with a Jungian analyst, and went to graduate school to get a master's in literature. Having decided to become a therapist, she trained in Jungian psychology, also in process work, using her own eight-year Jungian analysis as the core of her training.

The mystery for me in Waynelle's story is how she got herself off pills and starvation and into school, therapy, and a rewarding intellectual life. How did she begin to realize her dreams? Somewhere in the late 1970s, she stopped taking the pills, started therapy, and by the early 1980s she joined Overeaters Anonymous, which she attended for five or six years. She says that in OA she learned to love people of all sizes, and this helped her to love herself at any size she happened to be.

Today Waynelle is a large woman, a therapist and a writer, happy with her unfashionable size and shape. She exercises daily, walking her dog for miles, and she has a good relationship with her partner. Where was her beginning impulse?

Waynelle says that she was intellectually starving, and that it was her drive to learn that got her back into school for all those years. "I am," Waynelle tells me, "a very ambitious person." She was still starving herself physically, and she still felt fat. Was it intellectual stimulation that led her to look for a solution to her tendency to starve herself?

My questions about Waynelle's story make me ask about myself also. I wonder about my own hunger, my own dissatisfaction with how I look and often with how I feel. But I also question the cultural context of our stories. The concern about weight as an issue haunting many women's lives is well known and increasingly well documented and analyzed. We do, as a culture, notice that we diet in the midst of world hunger, gaze at fashions on the same page with photos of victims of famine and war. We have been taking notice, at least with our more intellectual attention, for quite a while. And we find our incongruent behavior quite painful. Yet we don't, as a culture, seem to change. Or do we?

Is cultural change simply slower, larger, harder to observe than individual change? Roles persist over time. They change as they are occupied by different people in different circumstances. As roles change, even as archetypes slowly shift, individuals are able to take on new identities. Women obsessed with dieting cannot pay attention to issues of world hunger. Women who are afraid to go out into the streets cannot exercise wisdom and power in the world. Men obsessed with women cannot look at their own issues of repression and denial. No one who is obsessed with personal problems has much energy to think about world issues. And yet world issues influence and are influenced by our personal obsessions.

Our human cultures are interactive systems, and change is the only constant. The question is whether we will suffer the changes imposed upon us, or whether we will change consciously and creatively. One small beginning might be to consider why appearance is such an issue and what it is we deny when we deny all that is considered ugly. What is it, also, that fascinates us about ugliness?

The age-old fascination with ugliness appears vividly in movies and on television, where old metaphorical associations of beauty and ugliness with good and evil show up in the often stereotyped choice of actors or animated drawings. Here there is a wealth of possibility for showing transformation, possibility that isn't exploited to its fullest range, but that still tantalizes with the promise of freedom.

9

THE UGLY,

THE PLAIN, AND THE

BEAUTIFUL

FAIRY TALES AND MOVIE STARS

Fairy tales represent the folk culture of their time, the dreaming imagination of the people who tell these tales. As they are told and retold, what remains constant is the part of the story that represents something common to the culture but also unrecognized by it. Every fairy tale can be read as a story of the soul's journey through life. But it is also an account of its culture, of the group consciousness that created the tale and keeps it alive.

As the culture changes, the account of the soul's journey also changes. This is reflected in small and large ways, in the changing versions of fairy tales, which are still changing even now, retold, rewritten, made into movies and other narrative forms. The archetypal structure itself is slow to change, slow in human time, but that it too changes can be seen in the shift from the story of Inanna to the story of Esther, from prepatriarchal to patriarchal consciousness. We are, I believe, in the midst of another large shift, to a postpatriarchal consciousness that will eventually take on its own appropriate name.

Not so many of us read fairy tales anymore, and fewer tell them except to our small children. Instead of sitting around the fire and telling tales, our custom is to sit around the television and watch our favorite programs, or, more specially, we go out to the movies. But while our time is occupied with these entertainments, they do not always manage to fill the function of the fairy tale, to tell of the secret journey of the soul through life. Those that do something like that are cherished and remembered; they reappear in video stores and people rent or buy them, watch them over and over. This is the reason for the enduring popularity of such "classic" movies as *Casablanca*, *The Wizard of Oz*, and *Star Wars*.

Like fairy tales, these movies tell stories common to the secret culture of the audience. I use "secret" rather than "unconscious" or "hidden" because of the way we tell ourselves secret stories with which we don't identify openly, but which represent important aspects of ourselves and our longings, aspects that are cultural as well as personal. One of the strongest of these is our fascination, horror, and persistent interest in ugliness.

It is more usual to find an ugly man depicted in the movies than an ugly woman, as for instance in the recent *Man Without a Face* or *Elephant Man*, but the gangster films of the thirties provide some exceptions, like *Marked Woman* with its images of beautiful women disfigured, an image repeated in *Batman*, not only in the scarring of the Joker, but in the disfigurement he inflicts on his mistress. Such images of women disfigured are without exception treated as horrible. Ugliness in women in the movies is horrible.

Plainness, on the other hand, perceived as a neutral state somewhere between beauty and ugliness, is a topic of some interest, for plainness holds the promise of transformation to beauty. Plain women on the movie screen are usually foils for the beautiful actresses they appear with, but sometimes their transformation from plainness to beauty is the theme of the movie. In such cases, the original perception of their appearance is, like the perception of ugliness, that it is a liability, a drawback to their ability to live full and rewarding lives as women. The obvious attraction of such movies is the dream they offer to most of us, women and men leading plain, unglamorous lives, that somehow we too may be transformed, may become beautiful and blessed with prosperity like the stars on the screen. The theme is therefore perennial, cropping up every few years. It is rather difficult to execute, however, for we in the audience have fierce criteria for successful transformation. There is one film that set the standard for me, and that is *The Secret Garden* (1949).

THE SECRET GARDEN

This is how Frances Hodgson Burnett begins her novel *The Secret Garden*:

> When Mary Lennox was sent to Misselthwaite Manor to live with her uncle everyone said she was the most disagreeable-looking child ever seen. It was true, too. She had a little thin face and a little thin body, thin light hair and a sour expression. Her hair was yellow and her face was yellow because she had been born in India and had always been ill in some way or another. . . . Her mother had been a great beauty who cared only to go to parties and amuse herself with gay people. She had not wanted a little girl at all, and when Mary was born she was handed over to the care of an Ayah, who was made to understand that if she wished to please the Mem Sahib she must keep the child out of sight as much as possible. So when she was a sickly, fretful, ugly little baby she was kept out of the way, and when she became a sickly, fretful, toddling thing she was kept out of the way also. . . . [The servants] always obeyed her and gave her her own way in everything . . . by the time she was six years old she was as tyrannical and selfish a little pig as ever lived.

When her parents die of cholera, Mary is taken to live in Yorkshire on the great estate of her mysterious, moody, hunch-backed uncle. There, although she is labeled as plain and dis-agreeable by the housekeeper and most of the servants, she makes friends with Martha, a young Yorkshire servant, and with Martha's brother Dickon, an elflike child of the moors. Mary discovers the key to a secret, walled garden, locked and cursed by her uncle when his wife was killed there by a falling bough, and she also discovers her cousin Colin, born prema-turely as a result of the accident, and kept in bed, a presumed invalid, ever since.

Mary and Dickon restore the garden to its former splendor, they bring Colin there in a wheelchair, and there, inspired by the magic of the garden, he regains his health and learns to walk, even to run. Both Mary and Colin gain weight and color, and by the time Colin's father returns he finds the children and the garden miraculously transformed. In Burnett's novel, the focus of interest shifts from Mary to Colin, to a distinctly Christian mystic tone as the son takes on and then redeems the agony of the father.

The story of Burnett's Mary is a Victorian tale of transfor-mation from ugly, sickly, selfishness to beautiful, healthy, gen-erous girlhood. In this sense it is both like and unlike the fairy tales to which it is closely related. Both types, the ugly, selfish child and the generous, beautiful child are found often in fairy tales, but not in the same person. The ability of a person to develop from one role to its opposite is found in modern fic-tion, but seldom, if ever, in fairy tales, which split the human psyche into parts and keep them separate. Marriage is used as the symbol for the fusion of opposing parts, and disguise rather than psychological transformation indicates change.

The Secret Garden is the first movie I remember seeing. I was six in 1949 when it first appeared, starring Margaret O'Brien as Mary. It was based on and departed freely from the novel, keeping its focus on Mary as the central character. This movie had a formative effect on me, shaping and anchoring my beliefs about the importance of appearance, not just my own appearance, but my surroundings, especially in the hope it offered of miraculous transformation.

The opening section of the film, following Mary from the chaos of plague-stricken India to her nighttime arrival at the shadowy and mysterious mansion on the moors, is dark and foreboding. The film lightens with the cheerful morning entrance into Mary's room of the servant Martha, played by Elsa Lanchester, who is amazed to discover that Mary has never learned to dress herself, accustomed as she has been to being dressed by servants. Mary's first awkward attempt to button the endless buttons on her dress and shoes is rendered comic in the movie, set off by the appealing dignity of Margaret O'Brien's Mary.

When Mary is finally brought to meet her uncle (Herbert Marshall), he says several times in their first meeting, "I hoped you would be beautiful," a curious remark to make to a recently orphaned child. Mary's uncle is a man obsessed with appearance, still deeply in love with his dead wife, whose portrait hangs prominently in his study and who was a great beauty, a lively woman devoted to her walled garden. He is a hunchback, convinced that others shun him because of his appearance, and that his son will grow up afflicted with the same deformity. Mary is aware of being considered unattractive (what child would not be?), and her unusual response is to cultivate independence and a feisty, fighting spirit, in a manner similar to young Jane Eyre's in Charlotte Brontë's novel. She is fascinated with beauty outside of herself, with her dead aunt's portrait, and more especially with the living beauty of the garden, and her own ability to cultivate that beauty. Even when the gruff old gardener tells her she is just like him, pickle-faced, she is undeterred, and she simply persists in her determination to find her way into the secret garden.

Margaret O'Brien was a photogenic child with luminous features and considerable acting ability. Even at Mary's angriest, when those around her explicitly attack her for her appearance as well as her temper, her movie-star charisma is evident onscreen. Mary's dark, plain hair and regular features are contrasted with the blond curls and very feminine face and figure of her aunt and also of other little girls we see early in the film, but Margaret O'Brien's appearance as Mary was attractive to the film-viewing audience of the time.

By using appealing child stars as actors, the film understates the transformation of both children described in the book (Mary's cousin Colin is played by a young Dean Stockwell, whose glowing health is barely subdued in the movie's early scenes). The most unusual face in the film belongs to Brian Roper, whose Dickon has never, in my eyes, been equaled. But the real wonder of the film, which has stayed with me all these years, is the transformation of the garden. As spring comes to the bleak black-and-white filmscape of the Yorkshire moors the garden blazes into Technicolor, in a manner similar to *The Wizard of Oz* (1939). Unlike *Oz*, and unlike any subsequent film versions, the 1949 *Secret Garden* shifts back and forth between black-and-white and color scenes, a device that heightens the sense of magic in the children's private world of the garden.

The children bloom in the garden like new shoots of the beauty that was Colin's mother. Here again is a transformed echo of a fairy-tale motif, the one in which a beloved dead person reappears as a tree or a plant. Given the emphasis on beauty and ugliness in the story, the transformation of the garden becomes a metaphor for human transformation, and another in a great line of metaphors connecting women's beauty with cultivated nature, and women's ugliness with the wildness of nature left untended. More than the novel, which turns from Mary to Colin as hero and center of attention, the film emphasizes Mary's ability to become whom she will, to cultivate her appearance and behavior, if she chooses, as she cultivates the garden. What it does not show is a transformation in Mary's appearance, that magical transformation for which so many girls and women yearn.

The very fact that Mary's appearance doesn't change substantially in the movie was reassuring to me, a glimmer of hope that I, just as I was, could develop and become someone delightful, without any miracle other than the everyday miracle of nature and growth. Margaret O'Brien as Mary Lennox was one of my important early models, along with Lewis Carroll's Alice and Louisa May Alcott's Jo March. What they all had in common was independence of spirit, creativity, and great courage, and a notable lack of ordinary prettiness or reticence, qualities so often praised in little girls.

TRANSFORMATION, HOLLYWOOD STYLE

The visual specificity of film, combined with Hollywood idealism, produced several rather odd movies about appearance in which a supposedly ugly person is played by a conventionally beautiful movie star, whose glamour is never entirely extinguished by the role. An example is the 1945 movie *The Enchanted Cottage*, in which a homely young woman (Dorothy McGuire) and a handsome pilot (Robert Young), who was badly scarred in the war, meet and fall in love, thereby transforming each other, in their own eyes, into beauties. Although lighting and makeup are used to exceptional effect, and the film is quite powerful, there is still a considerable gap between the stars at their homeliest and what most of us would consider homeliness in life.

On the other hand, a still-famous transformation did take place in the film *Now, Voyager*, with Bette Davis as the neurotic daughter of a tyrannical, upper-class Boston matriarch. Davis's first appearance in the film is remarkable in Hollywood history. The first view of her is a closeup of her hand, holding a cigarette, the erotic symbol of the movie's unfulfilled romantic plot. Next we see her ankles and calves, thick and framed by a dragging hemline and heavy shoes. Davis is then shown full figure, a large young woman with heavy eyebrows, dressed like a schoolgirl. After being rescued from her awful mother by a fatherly psychiatrist(!), Davis, having spent a month in a sanatorium, is miraculously transformed. She is next seen descending the stairs on an ocean liner, dressed in the height of fashion, slim and fashionable, with plucked eyebrows and a new hairdo.

Now she is free to become an object of desire, also to exercise
her own desire, for a lover, a life, interests of her own.

The movie is complex in its allowances, and without a
Freudian fixation it is possible to understand the erotic desire
in this film as a longing for much more than sex. Even Davis
and Paul Henreid, her married lover, sucking on cigarettes
rather than each other, are shown in the process of building a
relationship with complex interactions around power, creativity, and generosity, focused on their shared love for Henreid's
young daughter.

One aspect of *Now, Voyager*'s enduring appeal, especially
to female viewers, is the motif of the abused daughter redeemed.
Bette Davis, having escaped from her own tyrannical mother,
helps her lover's daughter to escape from her mother, who dis-
likes her, offering support, both emotional and material, and
understanding. The child, who is not at all conventionally attractive, visibly blossoms under her substitute mother's lavish
care, providing another anchor for female fantasies of miraculous transformation.

Bette Davis is unusual among Hollywood stars for her willingness to appear in decidedly unstarlike roles, actually to alter
her appearance and to use her unglamorous aspects in the interest of a role. By the time she played Lillian Gish's cantan-
kerous sister in *The Whales of August*, her appearance as an
aged woman was authentic. She extended her early courage as
an actor by taking on the role of capricious, even tyrannical old
age, in effective contrast to Gish's industrious, helpful, and decidedly feminine old lady.

The Bette Davis character in *Now, Voyager* shows an independence popular in Hollywood wartime movie roles for
women. This supported national pressure on women to work
outside the home for the war effort. Eight years later, in another
Davis film, *All About Eve* (1950), the cultural climate had
changed. Davis played the very different part of Margo Channing, a celebrated but aging Broadway actress whose fame is
usurped by a young newcomer, Anne Baxter, the conniving Eve
of the film's title.

When Margo discovers the ambitious intentions of her all-too-helpful secretary Eve, she numbs herself with drink, then soddenly confesses to an old male friend that she has just turned forty, a confession she regrets as soon as she has made it. Davis, who was then forty-two, allowed herself to be photographed from angles that emphasized her sagging neck skin and aging features, a brave decision betrayed by the film's misogynist script, which banishes her from the stage and screen to invisibility in her mythical happy home as soon as she overcomes an understandable reluctance to marry her longtime lover, Bill. She says, "Now that I'm about to have a real life, I don't need to take roles that are too young for me." A few scenes earlier, still feisty, Margo demanded that her old friend, in whose many plays she had starred, write roles that suited her age, a demand he pooh-poohed, only to cast young Eve in his next play.

The movie plays curious reversals on fairy-tale motifs—Bette Davis as Margo is the proud and jealous stepmother redeemed in the eyes of her friends and the audience by the revealed deceptions of young Eve. Margo's jealous, drunken agony is mercifully brief—she is rescued by the devotion of her lover and her faithful friends. Having disappeared into the bliss of married life, Margo returns to the screen for one last devastating line. Congratulating Eve on her new award, she purrs: "You can put it where your heart ought to be."

All About Eve, like "Little Snow White," is a story about the struggles of women who change, told from the perspective of the aging woman, with the young usurper in the role of villain. In the movie's last scene, Eve retreats to her hotel suite to find it has been infiltrated by an even younger aspirant to the theatrical throne, a girl not yet out of high school, who, like Eve, would do anything to be a star. Truly Eve's days of glory are numbered. A film on the threshold of the misogynist fifties, *All About Eve* is redeemed by its intransigent look at the politics of youth and age, by the polished wit of its dialogue and staging, and by the magnificent appearance of Bette Davis, especially as she lurches to her feet in her great drunken scene and says, "Buckle your seat belts—this is going to be a bumpy ride." I keep imagining she will sail forth to devastate her young and puny opponent, but Davis weaves her unsteady way right past Anne Baxter, glittering as young Eve, and past the younger but already pungent Marilyn Monroe in a bit part. This rare combination of talent could have provided a wonderful moment in the history of female encounters; instead it stands as a silent reminder of how powerful the fear of aging can be for women whose identities depend on the appearance of youth. The film also stands as an example of ersatz transformation. Instead of taking on the power of her age, Margo Channing takes on a domestic role, which redeems her in the eyes of fifties morality, but which simultaneously erases her from professional visibility. Her "transformation" is to become invisible.

Women who feel and are seen as ugly, for whatever reason, often find that their "ugliness" renders them invisible, as people choose to ignore what they find difficult to contemplate. Like young Mary, relegated to her room in India and again in Yorkshire, like countless invalids and old people, those whom society finds no pleasure in contemplating are hidden away, to brew revenge or transformation, or simply to wither and die. Individuals die, but the role of the invisible, shunned Other grows in strength in proportion to its repression.

An understanding of ugliness is important for both personal and cultural growth. Often ugliness simply stands for the Other, or it may signify what Jung called the Shadow, the repressed, denied aspect of human nature. One approach to ugliness, which we have seen in fairy tales and movies, is to understand it as a temporary affliction, capable of being transformed to a state of acceptable beauty. Another approach is to imagine that the undesirable, shocking, repulsive qualities of ugliness are powerful, and contain some secrets of strength or magical ability worth having, even at the cost of forsaking the dream of beauty to pursue the power of ugliness. This is a more spiritual approach, found in mystical traditions all over the world. A third approach to ugliness is to understand it as the polar opposite of beauty, existing only in relationship to beauty, and

—
218

therefore containing within itself something of the spirit of beauty.

All of these approaches to the study and uses of ugliness are creative and transformative, assuming that ugliness is not a fixed state but a changing process, one that offers riches to be mined to those willing to challenge the social consensus concerning appearance.

CREATIVITY

Instead of counting your breaths or doing skikan-taza, it may be better for you to ponder a question like "What am I?" or "Where did I come from?" or "Buddhism teaches that we are all innately perfect; in what way am I perfect?" The technical Zen designation for such questions is Honrai no Memmoku, *"What was my Face before my parents were born?"*
—Yasutani-roshi, in Philip Kapleau,
The Three Pillars of Zen

10

PLAYING WITH APPEARANCES

Beauty and ugliness are temporary roles, defined by shifting cultural standards. These roles depend on agreement between those who play the roles and those who observe them. Still, it is difficult to detach ourselves from the belief that there is something that is true beauty, and something that is true ugliness.

In dreams and fairy tales, beauty and ugliness are attributes that may change, often by means of magic. To alter one's appearance is in some way to alter one's identity, or to prepare for a shift in identity. What does it mean when a woman disguises herself, or uses makeup, costumes, masks, props, artifice, or art? Is this the same for men as for women? Is the act of ritual masking the same as the act of applying makeup? Or is there a significant difference between, on one hand, following current standards of appearance to *make up* the inevitable gap between nature and culture, and, on the other hand, deliberately taking on the challenging aspects of nature as acknowledged parts of the self?

Little boys and girls are alike in their love of dressing up, costuming, making believe. Hidden behind a camera, I have watched many preschoolers reenact family history in their play. The child who takes on the role of storyteller or storymaster becomes the one who controls, rather than the one who witnesses and suffers. All things then become possible. Left to their own development, free to experiment with different roles, little boys will be fascinated by nail polish and makeup just as little girls are, and girls will don supercapes and swing from ropes along with boys.

But conditioning begins very early, and soon little girls are applying makeup in earnest imitation of their mothers, or the stars they see on television, while little boys are swaggering around with toy guns and scorning makeup as a girlish thing, to be despised. Since children's play is a reinterpretation of the adult world, it will reflect the biases of that world. So, if makeup is viewed as necessary enhancement for women only, as it is viewed by many, that view will be reflected in children's play with makeup.

My son was a child when the rock group Kiss was popular. His ninth birthday party was held in the playhouse at the university where his father headed the theater program. He persuaded some of the theater students to apply makeup to him and all his friends, mostly boys, in the style of Kiss, which, as I remember, meant that one-half of the face was white, the other black, with lightning slashes zigzagging across the cheeks, and other creative touches. The children had a great time, and I often think of that party when I see young people experimenting with purple hair, nose rings, or wild makeup. What a pleasure to tap into this deep source of human growth by pretending to be something so different from your normal identity.

The Kiss makeup was highly stylized and conventionalized, as is the makeup I see on the streets. It is extremely unusual to see anyone wearing makeup freely applied, as makeup itself is highly conventional, whether it is theatrical, ritual, or cosmetic. If the convention is not specifically androgynous, like Kiss, it is normally strictly based on gender and gender expectations. In mainstream Western culture, men wear makeup when they appear on television or in movies, either theatrically or as a cosmetic artfully designed to be invisible. Outside of the theater, men who wear visible makeup are automatically assumed to be in drag, "gender-benders," highly suspect to the cultural mainstream. Women's makeup is normally visible, even though the "natural look" is highly prized.

A woman is expected by the mainstream culture to be "naturally" beautiful, which means that she has maintained a specific body shape and tone, as well as "good" skin and hair, all criteria that shift according to time and place, but are considered universal in each time and place. The use of the moral terms "good" and "bad" when applied to skin and hair, especially when these terms are ethnically biased, reveals a lot about the antecedents and psychology of our cultural attitude toward appearance.

In media-influenced cultures, a certain amount of makeup that is clearly visible is considered a mark of good grooming for women. This makeup requirement can be successfully bypassed, provided the woman has "excellent" skin and hair and is very well dressed, according to shifting standards of dress, but the lack of makeup will then be read by many as a statement on the part of the woman, that is, that she is following a "natural" lifestyle, or perhaps that she is a lesbian.

These standards of appearance are used as criteria for hiring in business and in entertainment, and they help dictate who can be a television anchorwoman, an account executive, or a saleswoman, as well as an actress or restaurant hostess. The standards constantly change as fashion and cosmetic companies strive to increase consumer buying, but the enforcement of the standards by those at the top of the hierarchy is constant. Women may challenge particular standards of appearance and sometimes succeed in changing them. What is not tolerated is the refusal of women to pay attention to external standards, which are always gender-related. A businesswoman leading a seminar for executives finds she is treated with more respect when she wears a skirt as part of her business suit than when she wears trousers. If she does wear trousers, she is careful to soften the effect with feminine shoes and stockings, a designer scarf, the "right" jewelry. While other expectations apply to men that also restrict self-expression, they are quite different and tend to reinforce gender distinctions.

These criteria for appropriate or acceptable appearance can be viewed simply as tools of a trade; still, there is tremendous pressure in our culture to internalize the standards. Where there is pressure, there is counterpressure, and all sorts of rebellious acts are performed to counter cultural norms. Rebellion in dress is itself standardized by peer pressure, especially among adolescents. The "grunge look," like the hippie look and radical chic before it, has been coopted by the fashion industry in its ongoing attempt to make commercial profit from reactions against fashion.

The pervasiveness of concern for women's appearance is reflected in that remarkable modern art form, the comic strip. Cartoonist Cathy Guisewhite has kept her character Cathy out of explicit politics and in the dressing rooms of shopping malls, but she makes a running commentary on the conflict between the real bodies and lifestyles of professional working women and the dictates of the profit-oriented fashion industry. Cartoonist Nicole Hollander continues her more explicitly feminist critique of current world trends through her indefatigable character Sylvia and a cast of supplementary characters, including the Fashion Cop, who resembles the Good Witch Glinda in *The Wizard of Oz*. Neither of these strips has, to my knowledge, tackled the controversial subject of cross-dressing, which was briefly taken on by *Safe Havens*, a remarkable syndicated strip whose characters are black and white children, parents, and teachers. In one episode, Samantha, a sympathetic little black girl with great imagination and intelligence, decides that if she dresses in a man's trousers, shirt, necktie, and hat, which she pulls out of the school dress-up box, she will get more attention. The last frame shows one of the white women on the day-care staff saying to another, "Keep an eye on Samantha. She's cross-dressing." This strip is given added poignancy by the fact that Samantha is ignored both as a black child and as a girl.

CROSS-DRESSING

A form of rebellion with deep historical roots, cross-dressing is one of the oldest ways of countering pressure to conform.

The long history of cross-dressing—women dressing as men, men dressing as women—suggests that gender is not based on biology alone, that the male aspect of women and the female aspect of men is sometimes so strong that it demands expression, in one way or another.

In cultures with strong gender typing, the rebellious aspect of cross-dressing predominates. In the oldest goddess religions males were either castrated or dressed as women to celebrate the sacred rites. Remnants of such traditions persist in modern liturgical dress. Scholars suggest that such conventions reflect the replacement of female priests and bards by men in the long period of transition into patriarchy.

I once dreamed that I, a man, was in love with a woman, and then I realized that she was a goddess, and wouldn't love me as a human would. I often dream of myself as a man and as a woman in the same dream. Sometimes in my dreams others are men and women interchangeably. These parts of my psyche are parts also of the collective psyche, squashed into boxes and labels, which don't always fit our tendency to be fluid. My desire for fluidity comes out in dreaming, and sometimes I am able to bring it into my waking life.

My dreams reflect a collective tendency with ancient roots. In *On the Beauty of Women*, Agnolo Firenzuola has Celso, his central male character, paraphrase a story about the creation of humans as they now exist which was originally told by Aristophanes in Plato's *Symposium*. According to this story, humans were originally of three kinds, male, female, and androgynous. They were all double, round beings, having two sets of limbs and two faces on one round head. When they rebelled against the gods, Jove cut them all in half, and had Apollo craft them so that they functioned as half-beings. Those who had been androgynous were now heterosexual men and women, seeking their missing halves, admiring the beauty of the opposite sex, but those who had been from the double male or double female beings continued to seek their same sex, either "chastely" or "lasciviously," according to Celso. Men would admire and seek out other men, and women would have eyes only for the beauty and company of other women.

This story strives to account for the evident interest members of the same sex have in each other, as well as for the obvious attraction of opposites. I often notice how women's interest in appearance, while ostensibly directed at the attention of men, is in fact a means of bonding between women and between girls. Playing with makeup, dressing each other's hair, shopping and sewing and borrowing clothes are all traditional activities of girls and women, which cross sexual boundaries, as both lesbians and heterosexual women enjoy these things. Heterosexual men in mainstream culture tend to repress their interest in their own appearance, but gay men, like women, use appearance as a way of bonding with other men. Cross-dressers, however, because of the taboos associated with their activity, are often solitary, even secretive about their appearance.

There are many practical reasons for cross-dressing. During the centuries of male domination, women have often dressed as men in order to do things forbidden to them as women, to study, to fight as soldiers, to go about freely in the streets, to go out in company with the women they love. Men dress as women to express their own suppressed sexuality, their interest in costume and sensuousness, their fascination with all they categorize as the Other, sometimes to express their marginality, sometimes for reasons similar to the old tendency of white men to appear on stage in blackface, exploring and caricaturing Otherness from the safety of their own dominant position.

Although often associated in the popular imagination with

homosexuality, cross-dressing has historically been an independent phenomenon, practiced by heterosexual men and women as well as by gay men and lesbians. There is a Romanian fairy tale about this phenomenon, collected by Andrew Lang in his *Violet Fairy Book*, called "The Girl Who Pretended to Be a Boy." Lang's version is long and episodic—I have abbreviated it in my retelling.

FET-FRUNERS—
THE GIRL WHO PRETENDED TO BE A BOY

Once there were two emperors. One was a conqueror who ranged far and wide with his armies, and whenever he subdued a kingdom, he granted it peace, provided one of the king's sons came to give him ten years' service. The second emperor was a neighbor to the first. He sought no new land, but he prevailed in every battle with his conquering neighbor. Finally the peaceful emperor grew old and knew his neighbor would win against him. He was perplexed, for he had no sons to send into his neighbor's service, only three daughters.

The emperor's three daughters noticed his distress and begged to know the reason. He told them he wished one of them were a warrior, strong and able to deal death with his sword. The eldest daughter said she would go in place of a son and persuaded her doubtful father to let her try. Full of joy, she prepared to go off with trunkfuls of beautiful gowns and a spirited horse.

The old emperor decided to test his daughter's courage. Magician as well as emperor, he placed a copper bridge across a stream in her path, then turned himself into a huge gray wolf and sprang at his daughter. She was terrified, turned back her horse, and rode back ashamed to the palace.

Then the second daughter begged to try, and chose arms to defend herself, but was just as terrified by the huge wolf and rode home ashamed.

After a while spent doing women's things—embroidering, spinning, weaving, tending flowers—the youngest daughter asked to have her turn. Her father was reluctant, but agreed, saying he would have a good laugh when she returned with her head hanging from shame. "He laughs best who laughs last," said his daughter, and she proceeded to look for a trustworthy horse and a wise old counselor.

Searching her father's stables, the youngest princess came upon her father's retired warhorse. He spoke to her and told her how to feed and groom him, to bring back his health and vigor, so that she could take him with her as her horse and as her counselor.

Unlike her sisters, the youngest princess took with her only some boy's clothes, linen, food, and some money. She was undaunted by the huge wolf at the copper bridge, drawing her sword ready to cut its head off. The emperor placed a bridge of silver over the next stream, and disguised himself as a lion, who indeed frightened the princess. But she remembered her victory over the wolf and rushed with her sword at the lion, who retreated. Finally the emperor disguised himself as a dragon with twelve heads, waiting behind a golden bridge. This time the princess fought the dragon and managed to cut off one of its heads, at which point the dragon fell, and her father appeared and congratulated her on her courage and wisdom. He gave her his blessing and she went on.

Before the princess arrived at the court of the emperor she encountered two genii, fighting in the forest. She helped the genie who offered her his horse, Sunlight, for Sunlight was the younger, stronger brother of her horse, also a magician. Having won Sunlight, she had to outwit the genie's mother, who suspected she was a girl and just the wife for her son. With the help of her wise horse the princess managed to evade all the tests set for her, even though the genie's mother was still convinced she was a girl.

On the way to court she saw a golden curl lying in the road, and asked Sunlight if she should take it. He replied that either taking it or not taking it would cause remorse, so she might as well take it. And she did, winding it around her neck.

At the emperor's court the princess was welcomed by the

emperor and made one of his pages. There she was praised for her good nature, charm, and ability to cook, which surpassed the palace cook's abilities. But soon someone noticed the golden curl, and told the emperor his new page carried a curl of the legendary golden-haired Iliane. He demanded that the page find and bring Iliane to him, or die.

With the help of Sunlight, the princess found Iliane, where she had been hidden by a genie in the island swamps of the sea. Disguised as a charming merchant, the princess lured Iliane to her ship with a pair of golden slippers, then fled with her prize, who was happy to escape the genie. Pursued by the genie's mother, they flung behind them first a stone, which became a mountain, then a brush, which became a forest, finally Iliane's betrothal ring from the genie. When the ring was thrown, a huge tower sprang up, with the ring at its top, which caught the genie's mother and held her fast. Breathing fire, she leaped from it and fell to her death. Now, following Sunlight's advice, the princess rode back and placed her finger on top of the shrinking tower, which disappeared, leaving the magical ring on her finger.

Once back at the palace, Iliane was courted by the emperor, whom she did not love. She asked him to capture her stud of magic horses, and he commanded the princess, now called Fet-fruners (meaning brave and strong), to do this nearly impossible deed. She managed to capture the horses, but now Iliane demanded that the emperor have the horses milked, to fill a bath for the two of them to bathe in and stay young. The emperor ordered Fet-fruners, who was beginning to feel exploited, to do this. With the help of a miraculous rain, which froze and held the mares still, the princess was able to do this deed also. But her ordeals were not yet ended.

As the emperor still courted Iliane, she asked him to get her a flask of holy water from a church beyond the river Jordan. Then she would marry him. Once again he sent Fet-fruners, who was warned by Sunlight that this would be her most difficult task, but she must not be afraid, "for the hour of the emperor has struck."

Guided by Sunlight, "who was not a wizard for nothing," the princess managed to steal the holy water from under the watchful eyes of the hermit and the nuns who guarded it night and day. As she rode away on Sunlight, the hermit cursed the thief, praying that if a man, he become a woman, and if a woman, she become a man. In either case, the hermit thought this to be the most severe punishment he could invoke.

But punishment, like appearance, is a subjective matter. The princess, realizing she was finally the man she was pretending to be, was delighted. When she returned to the emperor's court, looking every inch a brave young man, the emperor thanked him and named him successor to the throne.

Now Iliane took her revenge on the emperor for all the troubles he had caused Fet-fruners. Ordering the great bath to be filled with mare's milk, she invited the emperor to don a white robe and join her in the bath. When they were both up to their necks in mare's milk, she sent for her chief horse, who breathed fresh air over her from one nostril, and a fiery blast over the emperor from his other nostril. The emperor was shriveled on the spot, leaving a tiny pile of ashes.

After the mysterious death of the emperor and his splendid funeral, Iliane sent for Fet-fruners and asked him to marry her, for it was he who had accomplished her rescue and all the tasks she had demanded of the emperor, he whom she wished to have as her husband.

> "Yes, I will marry you," said the young man, with a voice almost as soft as when he was a princess. "But know that in our house, it will be the cock who sings, and not the hen!"

When I first read this fairy tale in the early seventies, I was teaching women's studies. It seemed to me that it might have originated among early feminists, expressing the long-suppressed yearning of girls to ride out and slay dragons with their swords, instead of staying home quietly and embroidering. As I explored the then-unfamiliar terrain of women's literature with my students, we realized that these yearnings had not been invented by twentieth-century feminists. They were the inevitable feelings of women whose spirits had not been crushed in early childhood, who wanted to be whole human beings, not limited by repressive roles. Medieval women were accused of witchcraft and killed, only for showing their fearless spirits. One woman, seen riding a board on a surging river, was killed by the soldiers who saw her. Her body was left to rot on the shore. In times when women are forbidden to be their whole selves, one option is to appear as men, to dress and act accordingly, with the fantastic wish of actually becoming the more privileged sex.

The story of Fet-fruners, with its long, detailed descriptions of the various ordeals the princess must undergo before she is miraculously transformed, resembles other tales in which the hero is male from the outset, a "dummling" who prevails on account of his good heart. In the case of the princess, her success is dependent on her wise horse, who constantly counsels her, and on her own courage and stamina. But her eventual triumph is achieved through the agency of a "real" woman, Iliane, who uses her beauty and cunning—traditional feminine tools—to get rid of the old emperor and raise her beloved Fet-fruners to be her consort and ruler.

Fet-fruners is able to carry out her deceit only by showing extraordinary courage, wisdom, and strength, both natural and supernatural, and above all, humor, which permeates the story. Her most persistent foes are older women, the mothers of the genii.

Fet-fruners's principal allies are horses, symbols to so many young women of their own animal spirits, loved before any lover appears. Horses are sacred symbols in many cultures, associated with the sun (hence Sunlight's name), with fertility, with mother goddesses, with intuitive knowledge and prescience, with chaos itself, the origin of the universe.

In this story both the princess and Iliane have special, magical relationships with horses, which indicates that their union also will be very special. Neither is a conventional woman, and both have traditional "feminine" qualities—Iliane loves beautiful things, Fet-fruners is an excellent cook. Their union begins with a mysterious coincidence, for Fet-fruners finds Iliane's golden hair lying in the road, and is warned that it will cause trouble whether she leaves it or takes it. If this kind of trouble crosses one's path, one might as well take it up, because if it is ignored it will somehow crop up anyway.

The story is interesting for its omissions as much as for its contents. The word "beautiful" appears only twice in the story, once to describe the slippers the princess brings for Iliane, and once when the emperor addresses Iliane as his "beautiful dove," little suspecting the trap his dove is setting for him. Neither the princess nor her sisters nor Iliane is described in the tale as beautiful, nor are the genii's mothers called ugly. Women's appearance, so frequently described in fairy tales, is a missing element in this one, which in fact hinges on the ability of Fet-fruners to maintain her appearance as a boy until she in reality becomes one, and then her appearance is celebrated, every inch a prince.

This is the crux of the tale. The princess must be exceptionally brave and able to get past her own father in his various disguises, just to embark upon her quest, which would be the birthright of any son. Then she must deal with the suspicions of the genie's mother, and then conceal her female self from the other pages at court, all in addition to the feats of heroism that she is routinely expected to execute. I am reminded of the famous saying of the Canadian Charlotte Whitton, who was once mayor of Ottawa: "Whatever women do they must do it twice as well as men to be thought half as good. Luckily it's not difficult."

Because all her heart and soul are focused on carrying out her promise to her father, the princess has no interest in anything else, not beauty nor riches nor marriage. For her, precious goods are simply a means to capture Iliane, which the emperor has commanded her to do. By carrying out all his commands she wins his kingdom and his bride, without striving to do so. All things come to the one who is single-minded in her pursuit of wholeness.

As in many other fairy tales there is no question of romantic love between the princess and Iliane, whose name, reminiscent of the Greek Ilione, evokes patriarchal wars for power, symbolized by control of a beautiful woman. Since there is no relationship between the two women until one of them becomes a man, the story can be seen as embodying deep cultural taboos against love between women. It also shows yearnings for romance as well as power on the part of women whose identities are not encompassed in traditional feminine roles, who yearn for wholeness and independence.

Since first reading this story I have thought that beneath all cross-dressing there must be a similar urge to wholeness, to embrace the part of oneself that is not recognized by others. Because this is such a forbidden act, it often requires humor and lightness in order to succeed. Here the relation between appearance and reality, at its most playful, is most profound.

PASSING

The concept of "passing" is familiar to women and men of different backgrounds. Sometimes a way of seeking wholeness, it can also be a way of trying to conform to externally imposed standards. Light-skinned people of color pass as white; Jews pass as Christians; old people pass as young; lesbians and gay men pass as straight; women, for centuries, have passed as men, and men have passed as women. Passing may be seen as living a lie, denying one's own identity, or it may be seen as surviving, even growing, in a hostile environment.

In our quest for wholeness we adopt all sorts of survival strategies concerning our appearance, sometimes with awareness, sometimes unconsciously, always with some degree of courage. It takes courage to pursue wholeness in a repressive culture. Sometimes, the strategies we adopt involve considerable creativity.

A story from northern China, "The Wife Who Became King," tells of a woman who disguises herself as a man in order to travel safely, as she flees from a king who has kidnapped her

from her husband on account of her beauty. Having demonstrated her bravery many times on her journey, she arrives at a
kingdom where the king has just died, and she is chosen to be
the new king. Eventually her husband arrives seeking her, and
she counsels him to disguise himself as a woman. She is then
able to marry him, and she finally reveals the whole story to
her loving people, who ask her to remain as their queen, her
husband to be her consort and their king. In this story the
ancient tradition explicitly honoring the wisdom and strength
of women is stronger than in Fet-Fruners's story, where the
impress of centuries of women's subjugation is clear. Where all
women are subjugated, the clearest path to power is simply to
be a man.

In earlier centuries women were not prosecuted for loving
other women, but if one of them took the role of a man, and
dressed like a man or wore a dildo, that woman would be prosecuted. Even now, a woman may get away with wearing men's
clothes, provided they make her look attractive to men.

GENDER BOUND — LESBIANS AND APPEARANCE

Women who have facial hair and allow it to grow are often
objects of ridicule, even violence, and are criticized by other
women at least as much as by men. Implicit in these criticisms
is fear, the fear of blurring and transgressing boundaries assumed for so long to be morally right, the fear of being branded
"unwomanly," the fear of being associated with, thought of as,
worst of all treated as a lesbian, a role that defies the very basis
of patriarchy, male dominance over women.

Lesbians have as wide a range of concerns and interests in
appearance as heterosexual women. Most lesbians I know are
interested in appearance for the same reasons as heterosexual
women: they want to be attractive to others; they want to look
desirable; they want their appearance to make a statement to
the world; they want to hide behind appearance, and so forth.

Older lesbians, like some older heterosexual women, tend
to relax their concerns about appearance, and they get more

support from other lesbians for this than heterosexual women get from most men. There is a certain distinction attached to being older (but not too old!) in lesbian communities. But lesbians who associate primarily with other lesbians also tend to have concerns about appearance that may be unformulated but are still very strong, for instance, that they should not look conventionally feminine, or if they do, it should be with an element of irony or parody, or understood as "passing" because of jobs or other strategic considerations.

Many lesbians say that being with women frees them from concern about appearance, or at least from the worries about aging, weight, and conventional beauty that plague heterosexual women. But fashions and attractions based on appearance seem as prevalent in lesbian communities as in straight communities. Lesbian fashions these days have as wide a range as any other fashion, from expensive elegance to sleaze and grunge to hippie or alternative. Some lesbians think a lot about appearance and some think very little. Some, but not all, lesbian women expect their partners to look a certain way, and find their own identities bound up in their partners' appearance, as do heterosexual men and women.

Although there is still considerable interest in "femme" and "butch" roles among some lesbians, lesbians often feel freer than heterosexual women to dress comfortably and functionally in the company of their partners and friends, less motivated to wear high heels, restrictive clothing, or a lot of makeup, except where professional concerns intervene.

But when the issue is one of "passing," other considerations enter in. Now the discussion is not about attachment to appearance but about survival, just as it is when people speak of "passing" as a member of any dominant group. One woman said to me that lesbians internalize "vigilance around survival, because we're more marginalized by the dominant power group—it's an issue of safety." She continued, "Once a man finds out about a woman's lesbianism, then there is no chance of protection from other men." Another woman who has to dress conservatively for her job (that is, in feminine style) says she thinks of it as being in drag. This woman's partner loves to wear frilly dresses. She thinks they give her the advantage of shock power, because she is very intelligent and articulate, and no one expects her to be that way when they first see her.

Lesbians have long used codes based on appearance, speech, and behavior in order to find each other in situations where it is not safe to appear openly as lesbians. This is still the case in many places. In urban areas with large lesbian communities the heritage of codes has contributed to a wide range of experiment and playfulness in dress and appearance, also to lively debate among lesbians about what is politically or aesthetically acceptable. One woman refers disparagingly to what she calls "downwardly mobile," "sloppy" lesbian style; another is critical of women she calls "yuppie" lesbians.

There are so many differences among lesbians that I sometimes think the one commonality apart from sexual orientation is that every lesbian I know thinks she is not typical and cannot speak for other lesbians. This may be characteristic of a marginalized population, especially since it takes so much courage to be open about one's lesbian or gay orientation when homophobia runs so deep.

There is no single lesbian perspective on appearance. But appearance is a matter of great interest to many lesbians, in ways that illuminate what appearance means to all women. Maggie, my "oldest living friend," as we affectionately call each other, agreed to speak with me for this book about some issues of appearance as they have related to her life as a lesbian.

MAGGIE: APPEARANCE WAS MY FIRST LINE OF DEFENSE

Maggie and I recently recalled her coming-out to me, in 1966, in New York City, in the kitchen of the small apartment I shared with my husband. I had invited her and her "friend" to a party and Maggie was explaining that they might not come, as they weren't getting on very well. She said she wanted me to know that they were more than just friends. I said I had always known that about Maggie, that that was a choice I understood she had made. Looking back from the vantage of middle age, Maggie now says, "You seemed to think it was easy. I was amazed that my anguish didn't show." And I say, "I imagine I didn't want to see your anguish. It would have meant I'd have to deal with your pain, and also look at my own choices."

Maggie remembers that, as a college student in New York City in the sixties, she chose to dress in a boyish mode, partly to make herself unattractive to men, to divert unwelcome attention.

"I knew," she says, "that appearance was my first line of defense."

"Was that problematic for you?" I ask.

"Only in the sense of wondering if I was a real woman, entitled to walk along the street. Once a man in a delivery truck hollered across the street at me, 'Are you a boy or a girl?' I hollered back, 'Why do you have to know?' "

Maggie's story brings up deep feelings for me. I realize how much my own self-presentation has to do with a traditionally feminine image, how unconscious I am of how important it is for me to look "like a woman," how deep these assumptions go.

In high school Maggie dated boys and tried hard to be like other girls. "But I had already kissed and cuddled with a girl and knew that that was very wonderful, and that I had the same feelings with boys. I still wanted to fit in, and curled my hair laboriously, but I wouldn't wear makeup or nylons, and I remember wondering whether I qualified as a girl. It was a great relief to me to break through to the idea that, whatever I did, I was part of the definition of a girl. But I couldn't talk to anyone about it. It was a very shameful question."

"All this stuff," she muses, "leaks out through your appearance."

Later, in the business world, Maggie remembers wrestling with the dictates of "career-gal" appearance. She wore dresses and makeup, and was surprised when a gay man at the office picked her out as his confidante. It was 1969 and he was telling her about what had happened at the Stonewall Inn the night before, when for the first time gays had fought back and demonstrated against police harassment in New York. She said, "How did you know I'm a lesbian?" He said, "Buddiness! You don't flirt."

But other men were not so sensitive. One executive welcomed her to his office with, "What can I do for you, you delectable creature?" Maggie says her greatest desire about her appearance was to let men know, "I'm here on business." But she was keenly aware that sexual attractiveness is one of the criteria for a woman's success on the job. When she left a long-time job in a publishing house, one reason was that she didn't care to dress for the part of the executive woman, the next rung on the ladder. "When you get dressed in one of those power outfits and go into a meeting with some potentate," she says, "there are three of you in the room. You, your outfit, and the potentate. You watch the potentate talking to your outfit."

Maggie and I have had similar issues about clothes, but I realize that I haven't until now identified the strong role played by sexual attractiveness in so-called "power outfits." I say to Maggie that I think a woman who wears sexually provocative clothing to work must feel very powerful, if she is really uninterested in turning men on. It's a matter, we decide, of being able to turn "fuck me" into "fuck you!" and carrying it off with style in order to survive.

Maggie's story brings out something heterosexual women might take for granted, that the pursuit of male attention is an expected part of a woman's role in the business world.

Once again, thinking about appearance brings up the question: Who is looking? And what is the connection between power and appearance? What options are open to the woman who needs to disidentify with her feminine appearance?

DISGUISES

There are many hidden aspects of the self that may be outwardly assumed, like the magical pelt of the Imbula in the South

African story of "Mulha." Shape-shifting and disguise of all
sorts are common in fairy tales, and one common motif is the
disguise that hides a woman's beauty, assumed voluntarily, like
the disguise of the crazy beggarwoman assumed by Sun Pu-erh.
The disguise is associated with initiation, marking the transition
from maidenhood to womanhood, when a young woman must
become acquainted with the shadowy aspect of her own nature;
or the transition from the comfortable life of a woman in middle
age to the riskier adventures of a woman facing the limitations
of life as she ages.

As well as representing lesser-known aspects of the self,
disguises help in the shamanic task of eluding jealousy, for shamans understand that illnesses and troubles are often caused by
jealous spirits wreaking vengeance on otherwise fortunate people. Jealousy is usually an element in fairy tales that stress
appearance—the beautiful princess has to contend with a jealous stepmother or stepsister; and disguise is an equally common
motif—she must escape jealousy, elude the danger associated
with beauty, or do both. This is my retelling of a German fairy
tale from the Grimms' collection—"Allerleirauh" is the story
of a young woman who disguises herself to escape danger and
to evade the jealousy of those among whom she hides.

ALLERLEIRAUH

Once there was a king whose beautiful golden-haired wife lay
dying. She made him promise he would never marry another
woman except one just as beautiful and golden-haired as herself.
After some years the king's council urged him to remarry, but
although he searched widely, there was no one just as beautiful
and golden-haired as the queen.

One day the king realized that his daughter had grown into
a woman just as beautiful and golden-haired as her mother, and
he fell violently in love with her. Against the advice of his council, he determined to marry the girl.

The king's daughter, appalled by her father's intention and
hoping to put him off, said that before she would marry she

—— must have three gowns, one gold like the sun, one silver like
the moon, a third like the stars in the night sky, and a cloak
made of skins from every animal in the kingdom. She thought
this would be impossible, and would prevent her marriage, but
the king ordered the tasks done, and far too soon he spread
before her the three gowns and the furred cloak.

In despair, the king's daughter decided to run away. She put
the three gowns in a nutshell, along with three golden treasures,
a ring, a spinning wheel, and a reel. She disguised herself with
soot on her face and arms, covered herself with her fur cloak,
and left at night, hurrying through the forest until she had left
her father's kingdom. Then she slept in a hollow tree, until she
was found the next day by another king and his men, whose
dogs barked at her. When asked who she was she replied she
was a poor creature with no parents, and so they took her back
to help in the castle kitchen and sleep in a stable. Because of
her coat of many skins they called her Allerleirauh.

One night the king held a great ball, and Allerleirauh begged
the cook to let her go watch for a bit. He gave her half an hour,
so she hurried to wash off the soot that covered her and took
her gown of gold like the sun out of her nutshell. She appeared
at the ball like a vision of splendor, and the king thought he
had never seen anyone so beautiful. But after one dance she
disappeared.

Allerleirauh ran back to her stable, took off her beautiful
gown, covered herself with soot, and wrapped herself in her fur
cloak. Then she returned to the kitchen, where the cook asked
her to make the soup while he went to watch the ball. She made
a bread soup as she had learned as a girl, and slipped into the
tureen her gold ring.

The king had never tasted such good soup, then he found
the gold ring, and sent for the cook. Terrified at this royal
summons, the cook, out of his own fear, threatened to give
Allerleirauh a beating if it turned out she had dropped a hair
in the soup. But the king wanted to know who had made this
delicious soup, and who had dropped the gold ring into it. Allerleirauh was brought, but said she knew nothing, and was
good for nothing, and so nothing happened.

The next time the king gave a ball the same things took place. Allerleirauh was given half an hour by the cook, she put on her gown of silver like the moon and danced with the king at the ball. Then she disguised herself again, went back to the kitchen, and cooked a soup. This time she dropped her golden spinning wheel into the tureen. Again the king sent for the cook and for Allerleirauh; again she said she knew nothing and was good for nothing, and nothing happened.

The third time Allerleirauh wore her gown like the stars in the night sky. But she overstayed her time, and rushed back with no time to change, so she pulled her cloak over her gown and hastily rubbed soot on her face and hands. She didn't notice that the king had slipped the gold ring on her finger while they were dancing, and she forgot to put soot on that finger. When she cooked the soup for the king she dropped her golden reel into the tureen.

This time when the king summoned her he saw the gold ring on her white finger, and pulled off her cloak to reveal the starry gown and her golden hair. When the soot was washed away, her beauty shone out, and the king asked her to marry him, which she did, and so they lived happily ever after.

In this northern European story beauty is defined by white skin and golden hair, and something indescribable, which all agree upon. White skin is associated with purity; gold refers to treasure as well as to yellow, northern hair. The princess's beauty brings her into great danger, since, according to her mother's dying wish, only someone just as beautiful and golden-haired as the queen may marry the king. Now any number of creative possibilities were open to the king, once he realized that only his daughter was as beautiful and golden-haired as her mother. He could have decreed that the man his daughter chose to marry would be king in his stead. He might have named his daughter the reigning queen, and left her free to choose a consort. He might have taken his dying wife's words metaphorically, and followed a spiritual path instead of seeking another queen. However, the king, like the stepmother in "Snow White," having no intention of relinquishing his power, instead

—— fell violently in love with his own daughter, meaning he fell lustfully in love, and thereby violated a great taboo of patriarchy.

Father-daughter incest is probably the most common form of incest in modern times, reversing the mythological underpinnings of mother-son incest, according to which the goddess-queen took on ever younger consorts as her lover-son. The reversal under patriarchy is parodied in December-May stories, such as the one in Chaucer's *Canterbury Tales,* in which an old man's lust for his young bride makes him an object of ridicule. But for centuries it has been common for old men to marry very young women, and for fathers to molest their daughters, the former an open prerogative of patriarchy, and the latter a closely guarded secret. An early version of Grimm in English translation (1876) deletes the incest motif from the story of Allerleirauh and substitutes the idea that her father decided to marry her to his eldest councilor, an idea that delighted the old man and horrified the young woman.

Andrew Lang repeated his bowdlerization of the older story when he included it in his *Green Fairy Book.* But the incest motif appears in other versions of the tale, for instance, the Egyptian story called "The Princess in the Suit of Leather," in which the daughter, horrified at her father's proposal of marriage, escapes from his palace and then has a rough coat made of leather, in which she disguises herself and goes on to an adventure similar to Allerleirauh's. In this story the blame for the incest idea is placed on an old woman, who is subsequently punished by death, while the father is forgiven and reconciled with his daughter and her new husband.

The criterion for beauty in the Egyptian tale is not golden hair but the slim ankle of the queen, whose dying request is that her husband find a wife around whose ankle the queen's jeweled anklet will close. Again we see that while standards of beauty may shift according to culture, the idea that a woman must fulfill certain requirements to be beautiful is cross-cultural.

Golden-haired Allerleirauh makes a strange request to forestall her father. She wants three gowns, one like the sun, one like the moon, and one like the stars, and a cloak made of furs from all the animals in the kingdom. This is the request of a woman striving to encompass all of nature in her being, knowing the task is impossible, but still striving for wholeness. Each gown represents a different role, a different aspect of her womanly nature. The cloak of many different furs is still another aspect of Allerleirauh's identity, the most important of all. Her father has the impossible task accomplished. Once she has all these keys to wholeness in her pocket, the princess must use them, and to be free to do so she must leave her father's kingdom.

Off she goes, to become an orphan of the universe, a poor girl with neither father nor mother, her beauty safely hidden from danger under soot and her animal-fur cloak. She survives with all her talents hidden, and then she brings them out and gives them away, one by one, until they come back to bless her with marriage to a king more suited to her.

When asked who she is, Allerleirauh repeats that she is a poor child with neither mother nor father. What is true is that her mother is dead and her father, by requiring that she sacrifice herself to his need for control, has ceased to be a good father. Covered by soot from the fire and by skins from every animal in her father's kingdom, she becomes a creature of the earth. From such base material the alchemists of the middle ages made their spiritual gold. In similar ways shamans in other traditions cover themselves or their clients with earth or clay, often burying them in pits in the ground, covered with branches.

This motif is present in Sun Pu-erh's story, for she smears her face and clothing with a piece of charcoal before leaving her husband's home. Mossycoat, whose beauty shines through her ordinary dress, is covered with grease by the jealous servants in the kitchen where she works. The wicked queen in "Snow White" dyes her skin to disguise herself as an old gypsy peddler and so deceive her stepdaughter. "Mulha" is covered with the hairy red pelt of the Imbula. This is the equivalent of the descent into the underworld found in so many stories, sometimes associated with evil, always associated with power. Without this connectedness with animal life and death, with the cycles of nature and subterranean recesses, golden treasure, itself mined from the bowels of the earth, will not shine forth.

The disguise of a beautiful woman as someone barely human, close to animals, covered with dirt or ashes, appears in many stories, including the well-known story of Cinderella. It is close to the experience of women who, for many reasons, cannot acknowledge or have no access to their own beauty, or understand their physical beauty as a source of shame, trouble, or danger. But it also reflects old shamanic traditions in which women became healers and wise women, after undergoing initiatory rituals that confirmed their connection with the earth and its elements. The roots of these shamanic traditions go back to the old Goddess religions.

Another story based on this motif of a young woman's disguise, collected by Andrew Lang, is "The Maiden with the Wooden Helmet," a story from Japan. In this story the heroine's mother, on her deathbed, fearing for her daughter's safety, instructs her to place a wooden helmet on her head, so as to hide her remarkably beautiful face. The girl goes forth to earn her living, hidden and protected by the wooden helmet, which becomes attached to her head and cannot be removed until she has married in accord with her mother's guidance as revealed in a dream. Once the wedding toast has been drunk the helmet bursts apart and falls to the ground, letting fall precious stones, and revealing the young woman's incomparable beauty.

"Allerleirauh" is a story of a woman's development. The men in the story are secondary characters: the old king, bound by his promise to his dying wife and his lust for his daughter; the young king charmed by the appearance of Allerleirauh, the delicious soup she cooks, and the golden treasures she drops into the soup. It is Allerleirauh who is at the center of the story, working out the challenge her mother left for her. She is the soul yearning for wholeness, using disguise and changing roles in order to become her whole self.

This is such a simple concept, so difficult to live. That one must give up all attachments and descend into original nature in order to find oneself is a concept common to all religions, told in numerous stories and legends, out of which many mysterious rituals and ceremonies have evolved. This is the meaning of the dying queen's request, for the second marriage she referred to was a spiritual marriage, not one that could be made on earth. The treasure represented by golden hair and the golden objects the princess takes with her is spiritual treasure (but also quite literal and material). By taking his wife's request only literally, and by ignoring his daughter's needs to be treated as a person, the king abandons his own inner nature, and exposes his daughter to trials and tribulations, which turn out to be initiatory for her.

Allerleirauh disguises herself and, when questioned, repeatedly says that she knows nothing and is good for nothing except to have boots thrown at her head. By so doing she takes on the role of the dummling or fool, often played by a young man in fairy tales. The spiritual nature of this fool is summed up in the words of the Taoist teacher Wang Ch'ung Yang, who says:

> You may say that I am stupid, ignorant, and dull-witted. Why am I stupid? Because in my stupidity I do not know how to desire and covet. Why am I ignorant? Because in my ignorance I am not rashful and impatient. Why am I dull-witted? Because of my dull wits I am incapable of fabricating schemes to outwit and outdo others. Being stupid and ignorant has made me impervious to the attraction of material things. You may think this is strange, but I am merely teaching you to be stupid, ignorant, and dull-witted.

Allerleirauh is the wise fool commemorated in the Tarot deck, the figure who has shed self-importance and who takes refuge in invisibility. This is another paradoxical lesson for women, who often assume the role of ignorance unconsciously rather than with awareness. It is easy for women to be stupid and ignorant in a culture that assumes we are naturally that way. To assume the role with awareness is to transcend it, just as Sun Pu-erh assumes the role of an ugly madwoman to find freedom.

By taking her destiny into her own hands, and then trusting in fate to reveal her next step, Allerleirauh follows her mother's request in the spirit, rather than the letter. She doesn't leave her treasures behind; rather, she conceals them in a nutshell, for these are treasures of the spirit rather than of the body. On her body she wears soot and the fur of many creatures. Her initiatory journey of survival is like the Dreamtime walkabout, the initiation rite of Australian aborigines. Going forth from all she knows, and taking with her only what she can carry or wear, she is still at home, because she inhabits the magical world of dreaming.

I have been struck by the echoes of these traditional tales in stories I hear from women I know. You might say, thinking of the mythical dimension of our lives, that we all assume our physical appearance as an initiatory disguise, and drop it when the time comes to show forth our true faces, the original face of the Zen Buddhist koan, the one we had before our parents were born.

THE BODY AS DISGUISE

Many women experience their own bodies as a disguise—the body itself is like Allerleirauh's coat of skins. The danger and victimization experienced by some women as a threat from outside is felt by others somatically, as illness or as dissociation from the body, which may be manifested as an eating disorder or as self-mutilation. While it is relatively easy to recognize the issues of appearance related to eating disorders and mutilation, the subtle connections of appearance issues with grave illnesses are not always recognized. The deprivation of power that goes along with treating a woman as an ornament may evoke reactions deep in a woman's body.

In some cases it seems possible for a woman to reclaim the power of which she has been deprived. The following story is about a woman who has, since childhood, perceived herself to be alone and in danger from the world, and who is in the process of transforming her own situation.

SOPHIE

When I first saw her, she was bent almost double on her crutches, hobbling along with distorted movements, supported by people on both sides. Once she sat down in our group, and settled herself, I was startled by the contrast between her painful movements and the radiance of her face in repose. We were at an open community meeting of the Process Work Center of Portland, attended by staff, students, clients, and visitors, who sometimes come from faraway places. Sophie had come all the way from Poland to Portland, to study process work and to find out more about her own illness.

Sophie told me, after I had gotten to know her better, that as a child she longed to be ill, so that she would get the attention and affection she desperately craved from her older sister and her parents. When she turned sixteen, Sophie was diagnosed with rheumatoid arthritis, a progressive disease, which, at her present age of thirty-two, has her confined to a wheelchair, or walking with difficulty on crutches.

All during her childhood in Poland, Sophie says that her older sister and her teachers told her, often indirectly, that everything about her was ugly. She says that her mother was cold and distant, and that her father, while warm and affectionate, looked to his daughters for the warmth he didn't get from his wife. Sophie remembers her father's begging her as a child to smile for him, and cursing her as a devil when she did not smile. She says that he supported her intellectual growth and helped her to believe in her intelligence, but not in her personal worth or attractiveness.

As a child Sophie felt isolated, even from her playmates, afraid and ashamed. She felt that her teachers treated her worse than the other students because of the way she looked. She wore ill-fitting hand-me-downs, which were mended and often stained, and she was constantly ashamed of her appearance and her clothing. At age seven, she dreamed that she had a wonderful ruffled white dress, and this dream gave her great pleasure.

She remembers two sources of pleasure in her childhood— playing with dolls and acting in the community-center play *Cinderella.* Sophie says she was considered too ugly for the coveted role of Cinderella, a role given to her older sister. Sophie, who was complimented as a talented actress by the director, played, according to need, three different roles: the two stepsisters and the stepmother. She says that in such role play she could express the whole of her being, could feel, as she seldom did, fully alive.

Sophie has that rare quality of face that film directors dream of discovering. She reminds me of the luminous actress Falconetti in Dreyer's classic film *La Passion de Jeanne d'Arc.* And yet she tells me that when she looks in the mirror she sees a swollen face, with eyes that are too small, thin lips, an ugly smile. She sees ugliness, but she repeats to herself, "For me, you *are* beautiful." She has decided to love herself, from the inside, as a whole person. In this way she seeks to fill the void she experiences in the outside world.

When I told Sophie the story of Allerleirauh, she nodded in recognition. She knows this story of a woman in disguise, humiliated and humble, spending many hours and days alone. She says that within her own self, Sophie, there is the persona of a queen, and when she shows this persona to me her whole figure opens up, even her arthritic hands spread wide, and her face is radiant. At such moments she is transcendently beautiful. She says she feels limitless inside.

Since she has been working on this issue of appearance and inner worth in relation to her illness, Sophie says that her movements have become more limber. She is now able to get up from her chair without help, to go downstairs with her crutches, which was impossible before. This rather startling change followed Sophie's participation at a process work seminar, where she received individual therapy sessions and also took part in exercises and group study of physical symptoms.

As a young girl, Sophie gained weight, mostly, she told me, from eating to console herself for her loneliness. She says she was about fifty pounds overweight. In Poland, she said, it is quite unacceptable for a young woman to be overweight, and this, she believed, kept men away from her. She was not aware that this is a great problem for women in the West also. As she has worked with her sense of self-love, watching her diet because of her illness, she says she has lost weight quite naturally.

Sophie and I discussed the curious phenomenon of her changed experience as she moved between Poland and other countries. Sophie left Poland in her late twenties, and went to Egypt to do archaeological work. There, away from her family and her home culture, she first started to lose weight, and had her first experience of being attractive to men. She says she feels more alive when she is abroad, and more attractive. In Poland, at least until now, Sophie has hardly ever heard that she is beautiful, or even attractive. Abroad, even among other Poles, she is frequently complimented. She believes beauty comes from the inside, that if you change internally your appearance will also change.

As we spoke, Sophie showed me how she held herself as a child, head lowered, looking up fearfully. I could see, as she did this, how people could have missed her beauty. I could also see the posture of her illness, beginning even in childhood. A few moments later, speaking of how she has learned to love herself and believe in her own wholeness and beauty, Sophie was transfigured. I understood why she had once yearned to be an actress, and why she described herself as being able to take different roles fluidly when acting in plays as a child.

Because of her illness, Sophie spends most of her time alone in her Warsaw apartment, working as a translator. She dreams of recovering her health, of traveling, and of finding a way to express herself fully, and she hopes that by continuing to love herself and work on herself she will cause her dreams to become reality.

Something she said toward the end of our talk stays with

me, as I think of other women I know who have struggled with painful body issues and felt pressure to conform to cultural standards that seem wrong for them. "Power," says Sophie, "is boiling in me."

Sophie's story resonates for me on many different levels, for the beauty she so craves and desires is also a source of great pain and jealousy. It is her own sense of personal power, boiling and contained at great cost within her, that is trying to emerge in all its queenly magnificence. Disguised, it may appear even in the constricted, painful movements of illness.

The oldest rituals involve the use of disguise, makeup, masks, and costumes, which imitate the spirits being invoked. Now that mask making and costuming have become popular as therapeutic exercises, many Westerners have had the experience of feeling free to experiment with their identities by changing appearance dramatically, socially, for costume parties or at Halloween, or in the context of workshops or theater. It is easy enough to imagine how such changes of appearance could have developed as rites of initiation, or shamanic rituals designed to evoke power. The power evoked comes from the hidden aspects of the self, the shadowy parts, which can best be represented in wild masks and costumes. Such rituals are still invoked in many parts of the world during religious and spiritual festivals—in India, Africa, and China; in Brazil and Louisiana and Switzerland in the Christian (formerly pagan) tradition of Mardi Gras or Fasnacht, the beginning of Lent.

Fasnacht in Switzerland is especially interesting because this is the one time of the year when conservative, conventionally sober Swiss bankers and housewives dress in wild, often artistically inspired costumes, makeup, and masks, traditionally made by themselves at great expense of time and labor, and cavort alongside artists and rebels in socially sanctioned drunken revelry in the streets and squares of Swiss cities and towns.

Playing at dressing up and costuming are good rehearsals for the fluidity in changing roles so crucial to becoming the whole self. But for all the reasons we are exploring, which have to do with the ambivalence of the concept of women's appearance—such as the insistence on youthful, slim, white beauty, the identification of such beauty with "true" womanhood, the reality of human jealousy, and the implicit disempowerment of women that accompanies patriarchal myths of appearance—many women have a terrible time creating and then dropping our identities as beautiful or ugly, young or old.

Whether it is in finding the support of another, a woman or a man whose love is not conditional upon appearance, or in questioning the assumptions of the mainstream about color or ethnicity or some other physical trait, or in accepting the changes of age, most women learn against the grain to define ourselves in ways other than through our appearance. The odd thing about this is that the learning, while often painful and unwelcome, may be the most freeing action of our lives.

Modern media influence our sense of identity and possibility, and so women look to the media for change, while finding problems there, ranging from underrepresentation to misinformation to the promotion of violence and prejudice.

II

MOVING

IMAGES AND

MASS MEDIA

If this book is made into a film, the child can't just have a pretty face. That could jeopardize the film. There's something else at work in this child—something "hard to get around," an untamed curiosity, a lack of breeding, a lack, yes, of reticence. Some Junior Miss France would bring the whole film down. Worse: it would make it disappear. Beauty doesn't act. It doesn't look. It is looked at.
　　　　　—Marguerite Duras, *The North China Lover*

"Don't blame me for the way I look—I was drawn this way."　　　　　—Jessica Rabbit, *Who Framed Roger Rabbit*

Much of our current obsession with appearance is rooted in our experience with mass media, the images we see in magazines, in movies, and on television, those hypnotic images that enter our dream worlds, stand behind us when we gaze into the mir-

ror, hover in critical judgment as we compare ourselves with
others.

Much more detailed and specific than the images of fairy
tales, the images of the media ask to be matched, and they defy
our greatest efforts to match them. Women who would never
dream of aspiring to skin that is literally as white as snow look
in dissatisfaction at skin that is normally blemished, at cellulite,
at wrinkles, which never appear on the airbrushed perfection
of magazine models or under the studio lights trained on carefully made-up movie stars. Normal fat deposits are pinched
with horror by the thinnest women, comparing themselves with
models who appear to have no fat whatsoever. As for hair, what
modern woman has not had a "bad hair day"? An older African
American woman said to me wistfully that she's wished all her
life she had hair that swings from side to side, like the white
women's hair in television ads for shampoo and conditioners.

Mass media are constructed from appearances, but from a
surprisingly narrow band of appearances. The range of wom-
en's images in the media is much narrower than the range of
men's images. While we see much more attention paid to wom-
en's bodies than to men's, it is always young, slim women's
bodies that are shown. When was the last time you saw, in a
commercial movie, a woman's leg with spider veins creating a
mottled design? How many sex scenes have you seen in which
a woman's fleshy thighs and ample buttocks are caressed lov-
ingly by her partner? How many women over the age of forty
have you seen cast in romantic roles? The grammar of commercial film with regard to images of women is very specific
and not the least bit "natural." It can be broken down into
basic kinds of shots—the close-up: profile, three-quarter, or full
face; the medium shot: clothed, semiclothed, or nude; and the
long shot: clothed, semiclothed, or nude—and it is based on
the apparently seamless presentation of youthful female beauty.

IMAGES OF WOMEN: THE FACE, SEEN IN CLOSE-UP

*One day, I was already old, in the entrance of a public
place a man came up to me. He introduced himself and said,*

"I've known you for years. Everyone says you were beautiful when you were young, but I want to tell you I think you're more beautiful now than then. Rather than your face as a young woman, I prefer your face as it is now. Ravaged." —Marguerite Duras, *The Lover*

The human face fascinates me. Sexuality, intimacy, affection, friendship, solitude, pleasure, pain, spiritual wholeness, personal power—all of these can be read on the map of the human face seen in close-up.

The power of the close-up, in photography and in film and television, is enormous. It is said that in the first days of cinema audiences ran screaming from the theater at the sight of what appeared to be a gigantic severed head. It was the close-up that created the worldwide reputations of the stars: Garbo, Dietrich, Bogart—legendary names. Charlie Chaplin and Buster Keaton, both masters of pantomime and action-based humor using full-figure shots, also used the close-up to great effect.

Unlike portraits in oils and early photographs, cinematic close-ups zoom in relentlessly on the face, sometimes, especially in television, cutting off part of the head and the chin in what is called an extreme close-up. One aspect of the close-up is its merciless exposure of age. Although a young face can, with skillful makeup, sometimes pass for an older one, I have never yet seen an old face made significantly younger in close-up, except by the use of blurred lenses for a dreamlike effect.

Greta Garbo, known simply as The Face, refused to be photographed or to appear in films after the age of thirty-six. Marlene Dietrich, on the other hand, appeared in public, draped in white fur and exposing her still-glamorous legs as well as her heavily made-up face, well into old age. For these stars, the litmus test of their stardom, regardless of snowy bosoms and long, elegant legs, has ultimately been the close-up.

A history of narrative in television and popular movies could be written entirely in terms of the aging of stars' faces, those who age publicly and those who do not. Such a history would reflect the interests of many moviegoers, who are unaware of the director or writer as a creative force behind the film, but who go to see their favorite stars, tracing their careers over time.

The advantage of such absorption in a star's career may be the chance to witness the star's transformation in a range of different roles. The disadvantage is the tendency to discount the appearance of those who are not stars, ordinary people like oneself. The Russian film director Sergei Eisenstein created some of his most powerful images by using close-ups of the faces of nonactors, people whose faces he found cinematically interesting and representative of the great ethnic range of the Russian people.

THE FACE AND THE FIGURE

Long before photography was invented, the fascination of the female face was a subject for stories and myths: Helen of Troy, the face that launched a thousand ships; Medusa, whose face turned men who looked upon it to stone. The face is the cornerstone of identity, symbol of the ego. The face is a mask, a façade, a map, mysterious, naked, revealing, and deceptive.

The development of interest in the face, like the development of interest in the beauty of women, followed the establishment of patriarchy and the rise of individualism. The twenty-thousand-year-old sculpture known as the Venus of Willendorf is faceless, an image of the female body with a stylized head, adorned with seven rings, sexuality and procreation personified and worshiped as a goddess. Other extant images of ancient goddesses have faces, some of them exquisite. One image, a delicately carved head with all features except the mouth, dates back twenty-two thousand years. But for the most part these faces, like the faces of gods, are archetypal rather than individual, with abstract, stylized features. Sometimes they are the faces of birds or animals. The faces of the old goddess sculptures, like their bodies, suggest meaning and power, rather than beauty as a decorative function.

There is a tension between ideal beauty and individuality in an admired woman's face. Men's faces are said to have character. Images of women's faces, even when the women are not models, are reproduced in the mass media because of their agreed-upon beauty, except in the unusual cases of women who are world leaders, such as Golda Meir and Indira Gandhi, or acknowledged great thinkers and writers, such as world economist Jane Jacobs and writer Toni Morrison. What constitutes a beautiful face has been a subject for poets and aestheticians and, most recently, cultural anthropologists. There is widespread agreement that certain faces are beautiful, for instance that of Greta Garbo and the ancient face of Nefertiti, but beyond that tacit agreement the debate about the elements of beauty, in nature as in art, has never been resolved.

The "great beauties" of the era of mass reproduction have in common, along with their acclaimed flawless skins, "classic" noses, large and well-modeled eyes, photogenic bone structure and pleasing proportions, some quality of individuality, uniqueness, irregularity, something that makes each particular face memorable. This quality, like Garbo's nose or Dietrich's cheekbones, may appear mainly as a photographic artifact, an effect created by lighting and camera angle, and only tangentially related to the woman's everyday appearance. This is the quality our dreams hook onto, this difference, this break in the regularity of the same classic harmonies found in all "beautiful" faces.

The other quality these famous women have in common is that they are all accustomed to presenting their faces to the gaze of a camera or an audience, and so they share a certain look that contains the awareness of being looked at. I see a difference in photos of stars and models, on the one hand, and photos of indigenous individuals in Africa, Asia, and Australia, on the other, people unaccustomed to posing for cameras, who may look quite candidly at the camera as at another person, or look inwardly or at something, without the consciousness of their own images which is so common in people who have been raised in an age of universal cameras.

The impact of the media on our imaginations is undeniably

enormous. We are accustomed to seeing still, posed faces, even in the movies. In everyday life, when I meet someone for the first time, forming an immediate impression based in large part on appearance, I am often amazed at the way this first impression changes as I get to know the person. Nothing changes more than my sense of face, as we sit close together, talking intimately, or as I see someone from a distance, in a crowd, recognizing me and breaking into a smile, or harboring some cloudy resentment, perhaps ignoring me, or unaware of me, absorbed in something else, talking to someone else. The information available to me in an individual face is constantly changing, and the more information I get, the less meaningful are such categories as beauty and ugliness, except as momentary descriptions. This flow of experience is constantly contradicted by the images of the media, whether in still photographs or in movies.

Women's beauty in the media has two major and sometimes competing elements, the face and the figure, by which I mean the image of the face and the image of the body, frozen representations of a manipulated moment, seen from a particular angle, under a particular light. Women suffer extraordinary regimes of diet and exercise in order to look like the lean models in magazines and movies; women spend great sums of money on cosmetics and treatments to emulate the flawless faces on magazine covers and movie posters.

Because there is such an emphasis on the production of beauty, the relationship between face and figure is seldom clear. One woman's face can be cut out and placed on another woman's body. The faces of Greta Garbo and Marlene Dietrich were superimposed on images of the Mona Lisa and other famous paintings by film-studio publicity agents. Bodies are sculpted by exercise and draped with clothing to create fashionable figures. Faces, even made up in ritualized ways, express more individuality than bodies.

Still, with all my understanding and skepticism about techniques of producing beauty, I occasionally find myself gazing at a young woman in a café or a restaurant, stunned by the way she looks, moves, smiles. And I imagine how she would look in a photograph, or on film. It is as if a film had come alive, as if my childhood dream of the MGM lion charging out of the screen had substance, for these young women are as influenced by the images of the media as I am. Their look is only partially their own, shaped as it is by all the other looks they have pored over and which they emulate.

As I examine my own relationship with these hypnotic images in the mass media, I notice a tendency to pathologize the relationship, to see myself as somehow neurotic in my fascination. My opposite tendency is to embrace my fascination, to defend the aesthetic value of the images, and ignore the ways in which they lead me to devalue myself. Keeping my sense of self-acceptance while continuing to enjoy my fascination with the media and with the media-influenced faces I see around me requires a degree of detachment, an ability to honor myself while admiring others. Sometimes I feel like a pair of disembodied eyes, gazing at the parade around me.

THE MIRROR

Before the age of mechanical reproduction, which made such images widely available, there were portraits for the rich and mirrors or reflections in windows or water for all. We gaze at our own faces and figures in mirrors, almost always in private. In public restrooms I notice myself and other women in front of mirrors washing our faces, combing our hair, applying makeup, but very seldom simply looking at ourselves. It is too private an action, making us too vulnerable. We focus instead on self-adjustment, improvement, and we look at clothing, hair, makeup. And yet narrative film is filled with images of women looking at themselves in mirrors, sometimes alone, but often in the presence of friends or lovers.

As I write, my eyes are drawn to a photo on my desk, a snapshot I took recently of myself, using a flash and the reflection in my bathroom mirror. Wanting to finish the roll of film in my camera, I took the picture casually, glancing through the lens, then holding the camera lower than my chin to get my face in the picture. The top of my head is cut off and the flash is a streak of light, which tears the middle of the image. But my face appears clear, if dim, behind the vivid flash. What I see is myself looking at something, in this instance an image of myself.

I am riveted by this image. A woman looks at herself in the mirror. A woman takes a snapshot of herself looking at herself in the mirror. The ultimate in narcissism? And yet the look I see in my eyes is one of interested detachment. My relationship is with the camera, the mirror, and my own image, in the mirror and on film. All is contained, orderly, except for the wild flash of light that sears the image. I see in this photo the past twenty-odd years of feminist media work as it has intersected with my life, as I have identified myself as an academic, as a filmmaker, as a therapist and writer. The image itself is dim, brown, peaceful, detached. The flash of light is intense and foregrounded. It splashes out into the picture, chaos without apparent pattern.

Just behind this photo is another, a similar one I took a month earlier. In this other photo the camera is in front of my left eye, obscured by the flash. My right eye and the right side of my face are clearly lit, and the lines are emphasized by the makeup my friend has just applied. The effect is quite different. In this photo I look more of a photographer, more interested in the picture I am taking and perhaps less interested in my own image. The splash of light covers my eye, nose, and forehead. It is more central to the image, less of a disruption.

If this were a movie, the camera would now zoom into the splash of light in the second photo, and the image would dissolve to another image, of a woman, myself, twenty years younger, sitting at a typewriter rather than a computer. I was writing my first article, about images of women in movies and fiction. The basic idea was that we project onto people we consider Other, different from ourselves, qualities with which we do not identify. We make these Others into objects, denying to them the status of perceiving, feeling, thinking beings we hold for ourselves. We think of ourselves as subjects, and Others as objects. In white culture, people of color are Other. In patriarchal culture, women are Other, for the dominant subject is male. Men and women both tend to identify with the male subject and project Otherness onto the female object. The act of noticing this identification and projection is the beginning of the awareness that eventually can change the entire cultural system. It is in the areas of art and mass media that most attention has been given to these issues.

BUTTERFLIES AND LIPSTICK

Contemporary mass media, including movies, television, radio, and print media, are areas where trivial concerns intersect with global and spiritual matters, and everything is potentially significant. Like the butterfly of chaos theory, which flutters its wings in China and triggers an unpredictable pattern of events, which may culminate in a hurricane elsewhere in the world, something so apparently insignificant as the color of lipstick may have enormous ramifications.

Causality is not very important in chaos theory because it has no predictive abilities. The ability to recognize patterns and attractors, elements to which energy is attracted, is crucial. We might say that beauty and privilege are attractors in our chaotic global system, concepts that attract energy, around which great patterns swirl.

It is for this reason that the appearance of women is so interesting to consider, now, at a time when great disorder is felt in the world, and when we suffer as a planet from realistic fears of destruction. Globally, we on this planet fear and mistrust disorder, whether or not we believe in an implicit universal order, such as that described by physicist David Bohm. But the social "orders" we have known have concealed great violence and suppression, especially of women. Virginia Woolf summed up the pent-up rage of many women when she spoke of the romantic heroine depicted in novels who in reality was routinely "beaten and flung about the room." Order, to a physicist or a mystic, may mean a deep, inherent pattern. Patriarchal

order is more a matter of control, or domination of one person
or group by another.

Concealment of violence has depended in part upon the correct appearance of women. So long as warlords and dictators,
kings and presidents have been able to display their women,
appropriately groomed and costumed, their claims to have established order seemed true. Conversely, wartime rape of
women has been a tactic of military terror since the time of the
first invasions. So long as women have, in the interests of supporting the present "order," sent their husbands, lovers, and
sons, and sometimes their daughters and even themselves, off
to war, war itself, the greatest man-made disorder in the world,
has been supported by those who suffer most from it and gain
the least.

Given the paradoxical relationship of women and war,
whereby women are penalized by our supposed lack of suit-
ability for active combat, and victimized for exactly the same
reason, the relationship of women with issues of war in the
media is fascinating. During the 1991 Gulf War there was a
general absence of women's participation in the constant bar-
rage of media analysis of military events, striking even in contexts where women have not played a major role as experts and
commentators. But the few women in active combat received
intense media attention, as did the bizarre situation of U.S. military men required to put away their pinups because of Saudi
Arabian censorship.

The Pentagon was more interested in censoring images of
war-related violence. Judging by the heavily censored U.S. media coverage during the brief period of the attack, no women
and very few humans were even hurt in this war, which appeared to take place between rockets and tanks in an abstract
video realm. But the human toll, which emerged later when
media crews were finally able to show what had happened from
the bombings, was very severe.

Given the overall context of U.S. news reporting, veteran
public television reporter Charlayne Hunter-Gault is a media
heroine, an African American woman who has conquered

heavy odds to become a role model for women aspiring to careers in broadcast journalism.

BEAUTY AND DISORDER IN THE NEWS

Charlayne Hunter-Gault undertook an investigative series of direct reports from Somalia for the *MacNeil-Lehrer News Hour*, after the United States under the Bush administration sent troops into Somalia. She interviewed generals and American soldiers, Somali leaders and people on the street, and she went into centers where starving children were being fed and tended by international relief workers. The pictures shown were not pretty, and Hunter-Gault spoke directly about the feelings and experiences these pictures created in her, as she stood in the midst of civil unrest and famine.

In one instance she visited a center for children in Baidoa, run by the international relief agency Concern. She spoke with the center's director, a young Irish nurse, twenty-six-year-old Michele Mackin, from Belfast. Surrounded by skeletal children and their caretakers, Hunter-Gault asked the young nurse if her presence with her television crew was an intrusion, an additional burden to people already pushed beyond their limits. The nurse replied that the story needed to be told, and that the people in the center understood that. This interchange is not typical of broadcast news interviews in stressed areas. The interview took place in December 1992.

In the spring of 1993 Hunter-Gault went back to Somalia, and again interviewed Michele Mackin, who was now heading a number of relief and training centers for Concern, in Mogadishu. Since the last show, Mackin's friend and colleague, Valerie Place, had been killed in an ambush by bandits. Questioned by Hunter-Gault, Michele Mackin spoke of her fear and personal insecurity as symptomatic of the generally unstable conditions, also of her guarded hopefulness now that the worst of the famine was over, and people were returning to their villages. She told one particularly disturbing story of a mother who agreed to nurse an orphaned baby and did so until she discovered the baby was from an enemy clan. The woman then starved the baby to death, returning it to the center to die in the nurse's arms.

As Mackin told the story, I was shocked to notice my split reactions. My attention was focused on the story she was telling, its implications for understanding the depth and intensity of clan warfare and what lengths women and men will go to for revenge. I was also aware of the irony that Michele Mackin, who remarked that the Somalis have a lot to learn about getting along, is herself from Belfast in Northern Ireland, where getting along is not always the primary mode of interaction. But another side of me was equally drawn to the fascinating faces of Michele Mackin and Charlayne Hunter-Gault.

I was once more struck with the way Hunter-Gault appeared in the African climate, how she adapted herself to her surroundings and was dressed for the heat and circumstances, with little makeup, her hair blowing in the breeze, looking very much like and unlike any reporter, by which I mean any male reporter, in a disturbed location. She is a striking woman in her fifties, very photogenic, a powerful woman. As for the nurse, a young woman with the sort of face one sees in old European movies, I was fascinated, as I always am, by a haunting face. I also wondered if Mackin's image was a factor in drawing Hunter-Gault and her crew back for a second interview.

I can imagine the story conference that took place in Washington before Hunter-Gault went back to Somalia, the very good intentions of the producers to get the story that would have the most impact, effect change the fastest, enlist the hearts and minds of the American people. The nurse's visual appeal and her articulateness make her an excellent spokeswoman for people in a desperate situation. Is she therefore a better spokeswoman than an attractive African nurse or a less photogenic nurse? Is she a better counterbalance to the older, African American attractiveness of Hunter-Gault? I have no simple answer to these questions. Were I in Hunter-Gault's place I would probably have made the same decision she made, to use a woman's appearance for its best and highest purpose, the evocation of compassion in the world. I imagine that she has no more illusions than I do about the ultimate power of a woman's face to effect lasting change.

Turning from the misery depicted in news stories and glimpsed on city streets, men and women alike seek solace in the glamour of advertisements and romantic adventures. Is this why ugliness is so blatantly absent from television commercials, miniseries, and talk shows? Recently we have been seeing the phenomenon of commercials that use problematic social situations to sell products, for instance, an ad that shows a child with Down's syndrome and his mother, used to sell laundry stain remover. But such ads still carefully select the images that indicate social awareness without disturbing the viewer's willingness to watch.

The role played by the ugly witch or ogre or monster in fairy tales is relegated by television and many popular movies to the horror genre, in which ugliness is a matter of lavish special effects, and to news shows, where the ugly realities of war, famine, and domestic violence are carefully framed and edited for viewer consumption. Some of the most powerful images in documentary history are photographic and cinematic images of war, poverty, and disease. Are they beautiful or ugly, these images? Or are they beyond standards of beauty and ugliness? What is their relationship to the experience they claim to depict? What is our relationship to the images, and to the experience behind them?

These questions about images and reality, similar to recurring questions about appearance and reality, are fascinating and have multiple possibilities of response. Sometimes a story or a movie seems to use such questions as a springboard for an imaginative journey into the unknown, like *Alice in Wonderland* or *The Wizard of Oz*, a movie that functions very like a fairy tale in its accurate reflection of a collective idea. Like *Alice*, *The Wizard of Oz* uses a young girl as its protagonist, a choice well suited to the examination of strange appearances, reality, imagination, and power.

THE WIZARD OF OZ *VERSUS* THE RUBY SLIPPERS

Dorothy is a young white girl in sepia-toned Kansas, sur-rounded by busy sepia people in a large sepia landscape. She is stocky and well scrubbed, with a brave spirit and a wonderful voice. Her closest companion is her little dog, Toto, threatened with dog murder by the villainous Miss Gulch. Dreaming of a different life somewhere over the rainbow, Dorothy and Toto are rescued from Kansas and Miss Gulch by a tornado, which takes them and the house up, up, up and over the rainbow, into the beautiful, green and fruitful, but also perilous, land of Oz. Their crash-landing squashes one of the two powerful and wicked witches of Oz, the Wicked Witch of the East, who has, until now, ruled over the Munchkins.

When Dorothy arrives in the Technicolor land of Oz and inherits the ruby-red shoes of the witch she has inadvertently killed, she learns from Good Witch Glinda that not all witches are, in Dorothy's words, "old and ugly." "Only wicked witches are ugly," says Glinda firmly. Women's beauty is a moral im-perative in the land of Oz, and *The Wizard of Oz* is, among other things, about a young girl's initiation into the perils and demands of womanhood. This is a territory with a clear, if dan-gerous, map. The only women Dorothy gets to know in Oz are the witches. Good witches wear glittering gowns, ride in colored bubbles, speak in genteel accents, and have long curly hair. Bad witches ride broomsticks, shriek and cackle, have green faces, and appear in red puffs of smoke.

When Dorothy and her mates arrive in Oz, seeking the il-lusory wizard who will give them their heart's desire, they are first taken to a Wash and Brush center where each is groomed according to physiognomy and gender. Dorothy's attendants, and those of the Cowardly Lion (who, as played by Burt Lahr, has strong affinities with a drag queen), look remarkably like beauty-parlor attendants, and Dorothy and the Lion both emerge with curled hair and ribbons, which Dorothy retains until her return to childhood in Kansas.

The choice of Judy Garland to play Dorothy, with her pow-

erful singing voice and strong persona, turned out to be a perfect expression of this moment of transition. Like Snow White,
and like most movie heroines, Judy Garland's Dorothy is in the
Maiden stage of life. Her famous red shoes are ancient images
of the menarche, representing female power, for which the
dried-up wicked witches yearn, and which Dorothy must learn
to recognize and use.

The Wizard of Oz is also about the transition of Hollywood
movies from black-and-white to color. The change takes place
when Dorothy opens the door of her Kansas farmhouse and
steps out into glowing Technicolor, to discover that she has
inadvertently become a heroine to the Munchkins. From now
until her return to the sepia tones of Kansas, color will play an
important part in Dorothy's journey, creating the feeling tone
of the movie, of illusion, magic, and the uses of power. The
Ruby Slippers glow in Dorothy's darkest moments.

Although the movie seems tame by current standards, it was
a searing memory of my childhood. The terrifying moment
when the Wicked Witch of the West, grinning her sinister,
green-faced grin, throws a fireball at the Scarecrow caused me
at the age of six to dive under my seat and caused my cousin
Susie to throw up, thereby horrifying my father, who had taken
us to a matinee and never again, as I remember, took us anywhere by himself. And when Dorothy melts the wicked witch
by throwing a bucket of water over her, my young protofem-
inist heart almost burst with relief and pride.

But it never occurred to me to wonder about the mysterious, endless fascination of the Ruby Slippers, which the wicked
witch wanted so badly, which I wanted so badly, and which
turned out to have the power everyone had attributed to the
Wizard, who was nothing but an affable American humbug. An
artistic humbug, with the talent and vision to create a greenlit
version of Hollywood in Oz, but nevertheless, a humbug. A
wise humbug, who knew that what we seek is within us, knew
it in others if not in himself, but still a humbug. The real power,
unmistakably female, is in the Ruby Slippers. They finally, with
the guidance of Good Witch Glinda, allow Dorothy to go

home, presumably a wiser and more self-reliant Dorothy than the one who left Kansas in the eye of a cyclone some unspecified time ago. What Dorothy says she has learned from her adventure in Oz is this, "If I ever go looking for my heart's desire again, I won't look any further than my own backyard." All Dorothy has to do now is click her ruby heels three times and repeat, with feeling, "There's no place like home." (But will she now leave Kansas, and go to Hollywood, Chicago, or New York, if not for her heart's desire, then for the glamour of Technicolor?)

The Ruby Slippers echo the terrible red shoes of Hans Andersen's fairy tale, also the red-hot shoes in which the wicked stepmother of Snow White was forced to dance to her death. The remarkable achievement of *The Wizard of Oz* for postpatriarchal mythmaking is the transformation of the perilous red shoes of patriarchal lore into the powerful Ruby Slippers, which witches covet and a young girl learns to retain and use for her own purposes. These Ruby Slippers were not in Frank Baum's children's story on which the movie script was loosely based; in his story the shoes are silver, as they are in Sidney Lumet's remake of the story with an all-black cast, *The Wiz* (1978). They didn't turn into ruby until the fourth version of the first film's script. As Salman Rushdie remarks in his wonderfully detailed examination of the movie for the British Film Institute, this is truly an example of Hollywood filmmaking at its most collective, for numerous directors, writers, and editors had their hands in the making of *The Wizard of Oz.* Perhaps this is why the movie has such a fairy-tale feel to it—like fairy tales it was honed and polished by many reshapings.

Frank Baum wished to create what he called "a modernized fairy tale, in which the wonderment and joy are retained and the heartaches and nightmares are left out." He therefore mentioned but refrained from bringing to life the power of the wicked witches, saying only that the Wizard was quite afraid of them.

What Baum failed to understand was the importance of acknowledging the power of violence and the shadow side of human nature in stories for young children. The movie picked up what Baum's story omitted, adding the powerful Ruby Slippers and the green-faced glory of Margaret Hamilton as the Witch, who, when Dorothy throws a bucket of water at her, laments as she melts down into a puddle, "Who could have thought a little girl like you could destroy my beautiful wickedness?"

ERIN: A SPIRIT TO BE IN TOUCH WITH

Dreaming of the Ruby Slippers, I wonder, remembering my childhood models in Nancy Drew, Jo March, and Dorothy, what comparable role models young girls have now. Thirteen-year-old Erin tells me that *The Wizard of Oz* is one of her favorite movies, along with *Now, Voyager* and all of Whoopi Goldberg's movies, especially *Sarafina!* I'm surprised and delighted to hear her choices—I'm partial to *Sarafina!* myself, an innovative South African movie, which combines Hollywood-style musical sequences with tough docudrama. Whoopi Goldberg plays a schoolteacher who is arrested and later killed in prison by the South African police. Sarafina is one of her students, a young African girl who dreams of movie stardom, but must deal first with poverty and life under apartheid, then with the harsh realities of arrest, imprisonment, and torture in a South African prison, along with thousands of other African children. To look at *Sarafina!* after watching *The Wizard of Oz* is to witness the global context for Hollywood dreams. There are no Ruby Slippers for Sarafina; instead she dresses herself as Nelson Mandela, and, accompanied by the one child her age left in Soweto, she sings and dances a song of liberation, not over the rainbow, but in her native land. Erin loved *Sarafina!*, which she says was a very "heavy" movie. Like me, she also loves comic books—her favorites are *Donald Duck* and *Wonder Woman.* She thinks most of the superhero comics are chauvinistic. I agree, and we raise our eyebrows in mutual understanding.

Erin is an attractive, very slim young woman of mixed Mexican and Anglo-Irish descent. The variety of her outfits reflects the thrift-store fashions of her peer group and her own whimsical imagination. Sometimes she wears a long skirt with clunky boots and paints her short fingernails green. Sometimes she wears oversize, baggy sweatshirts and torn leggings. When I compliment her on her appearance, she grins, and I have a glimpse of a mischievous sprite peering at me from another world, which she inhabits.

Erin is spending her summer vacation writing a horror story along with her best friend. She loves reading Christopher Pike's teenage horror stories, and describes the typical plot: a bunch of kids hang out and one of them goes crazy. As for current movies, she loved *Jurassic Park,* but also "cheap, weird horror movies that don't really scare you." She says, grinning, "What are movies for if not to excite?"

Erin and her friends like to experiment with their appearance. "There's a fashion revolution—the hippie thing, the grunge thing, gloom 'n' doom." She'd like to try putting her long brown hair into complicated braids, but she can't afford to have it done professionally. She thinks she's pretty now, and that she might be beautiful when she's older. She'd like to be elegant, and cites Judy Garland in *The Wizard of Oz:* "She's got elegance in her voice . . . even if she had one penny to her name, she'd be rich."

Listening to her, I imagine that Erin is like one of my fairy-tale heroines, dissatisfied with a stay-at-home life, looking for adventure, and, just now, having to express those longings through her clothes and appearance. But what would she do if she were really free?

I ask Erin what it means to be beautiful, and she hesitates. "Beautiful, wow! Who's beautiful? It's such a big thing to be beautiful. 'Beautiful' is such a strong word." She says she and her friends experiment with makeup and call each other "Bootifull." Erin says with decision that fashion models aren't beautiful because they all look alike, that Audrey Hepburn was beautiful, that dark-skinned women can be beautiful, also large women. She thinks her grandmother, my friend Diane, is a beautiful, large Mexican American woman at fifty-two.

What doesn't Erin like about herself? The freckle on the end of her nose and her feet, which she says have knobby toes. She worries about aging: "What happened to being six and swinging from my big tree? I worry that life is passing me by." What is she missing? "All the good movies." (Erin's been sick for a week.) I try to remember what life was like when summer vacation stretched indefinitely ahead and time was slow in the summer. What stops Erin now from swinging from a tree, living each moment to its fullest? She dreams of her future, misses her past, but where is Erin now?

Erin wants to own an exotic pet shop in Hawaii, or else be an architect, or a cartoonist. She says expansively, "I want to go to Harvard, I want to make something of myself." She doesn't think she'll find somebody to love truly until she's older—someone she'll live with for the rest of her life, "someone who's spiritually there. You have to know who you are, be able to be alone with yourself. That means you have a spirit to be in touch with."

In what wild thicket does Erin's spirit hide now? I wonder what Erin would do if she were to go crazy, follow her adventurous spirit, become the heroine of her own story. At her age, young women in some indigenous cultures go off on their own vision quests. At her age, fairy-tale heroines are often faced with perilous adventures. But Erin's adventures are still in her imagination, in her complex world of school and family relationships, and in her mirror, her place of reflection and possibility. The trickster spirit that appears in her clothing and attitudes is also reflected in the stories and movies she loves, in her changeable moods and her ready wit. At Halloween she and a friend create costumes based on one of their imaginary characters, who has his own distinctive language and way of walking. Will the world offer Erin a way of using her creative, unpredictable trickster energy?

Erin at thirteen holds a mirror to me. I catch glimpses in her of the fluid being who also lives in me, one of the spirits with whom I sometimes come in touch.

Mirrors were thought of by some ancients as soul-catchers,

but they turned out, in many instances, to be tricksters. A Chinese story associated with the Yellow Emperor tells of how, at the beginning of time, the mirror world interacted freely with the world of human beings. Mirror beings were quite different from humans, and there was a great deal of coming and going between the worlds, with mirrors serving as gateways. But the humans were afraid that the mirror people would take over, and that chaos would prevail. The mirror people were quintessential tricksters, and the very basis of their world was chaos. And so the Yellow Emperor wove a spell to bind the mirror people in their world and to compel them to imitate the movements of human beings. But the spell will not last forever. One day, as the spell weakens, the forms in our mirrors will begin to shift and change, and slowly the mirror people will take on their own chaotic, turbulent life, bringing their spirits into our world once again.

Dreaming into Erin's choices of movies and books, I notice my own underlying belief, that contemporary mass media act like trickster mirrors to our culture, rendering some parts with apparent faithfulness, others with manipulation, and others not at all. There are disorder and patterns of disturbing beauty that form and reform as we gaze upon them. What will we do with such wealth, and such disturbance?

12

STORYTELLING

All the important questions of my life multiply faster than any answers I can find, a realization that fills me with hope and uncertainty. Questions, asked in a spirit of inquiry, open the way to creative answers, to storytelling with its possibilities for the reinvention of reality.

The myths we live by can be double-edged swords, oppressing us with culturally generated stereotypes, and offering great power to us if we can recover their archetypal power for our own uses. Storytelling is an essential tool for the explorer of myths. The universal impulse to tell stories derives in part from the need to frame and shape our most personal, problematic material. We find inspiration in stories, and the glorious thing about stories is that we can always retell them, changing them to suit our needs and our creative spirit.

It is the creative and exploratory act of telling old stories in the light of our own lives, and retelling our own life stories, that helps us to become our whole selves. By joining in the act of storytelling, we formulate a new relationship with the roles found in the stories, a relationship that allows us to explore the roles in depth, and to go beyond any one role in our understanding of the whole story.

Just as, in working with our dreams, we can try out each of the roles in the dream, moving from our tendency to identify only with the dreamer, so in working with stories we can imagine ourselves as the hero and also as the villain, as the beautiful princess and as the wicked stepmother, even as the magical horse or the mysterious wizard. The greater our ability to move fluidly from one imaginary role to another, the greater our ability to perceive the whole, the world presented by the story. This world is a metaphor for each one of us as a totality, and for the world we each inhabit. In retelling stories from this perspective of the whole, we reinvent the world as well as ourselves.

This act of reinventing the self and the world is part of every young person's initiation into adulthood. In the case of women living within patriarchy, it is always a radical act.

Since the time of Inanna's sojourn under the apple tree, and despite the enormous restrictions on women's imaginations imposed by patriarchy, young women have dreamed of going forth and founding their own visionary cultures, risking and confronting death in the process, the archetypal heroic enterprise. Inanna got the *Me,* the laws of civilization, and brought them back to her Sumerian people. Esther's goal was very much more restricted than Inanna's, but still she risked death for the salvation of her people. Snow White descended into the world of death, and returned to take on what leadership she could in her changing culture. Mulha learned the magic hidden in the Imbula's pelt, and became a woman of honor among her people. These were Maidens who went on heroic journeys.

We also have models of heroism in older women. As a mature woman, a mother, Inanna risked losing everything when she descended into the underworld. Nangsa Obum flew in the mountains after she had borne and nurtured her son and endured violence and even death in her marriage. Nangsa's Western scribe, Tsultrim Allione, a woman and mother in her own middle age, has dedicated her life to offering spiritual leadership to women. Florinda Donner-Grau and other women of her tradition have made their own stories available to the world, and now teach widely. Clarissa Pinkola Estés has brought her vision of the Wild Woman and the stories upon which her vision is based to a large audience. These women exemplify the wise Mother, moving toward the greater wisdom of the Crone, achieved by Sun Pu-erh, a woman who had passed the age of childbearing when she decided she would do anything, even die, to seek enlightenment. Their stories are nourishment for hungry souls.

We delight in reading and listening to stories from all over the world, but we each have a story of our own, which is woven from all the stories we've heard and witnessed in our lives, and which, like the mirror people of the Chinese legend, is capable of taking on a turbulent, unpredictable life of its own, reflecting not merely our surface but the depths that connect us with the whole world. In the preceding chapters I have offered some versions of my own story, in the hopes of provoking you, my readers, to think of your stories, and how accurately they reflect your surface and your depths at any moment. I find for myself that having access to my storytelling capacity is my greatest protection against the menacing critic who is only one of the characters living in the mirror, but a powerful and disturbing one.

I TELL MORE OF MY OWN STORY, WITH A FEW CHANGES

Dear reader, having begun my second half-century, resembling my old friend Beatrice's colorful portrait of me more every day, I change my disguise and my role almost at will. I enjoy enormous freedom from the tyranny of my own image. Privileged to have work independent of dress codes and company pressures, I choose my appearance according to my mood and my schedule.

Some days I am a motherly, nurturing therapist with a mischievous gleam in my eye. Some days I am a hermit, writing with my door closed, dressed in whatever sweatshirt comes to hand. Some days I dress to kill, and go out to slay demons in the world. One of my favorite disguises lately is that of gardener, with muddy boots, gloves, and baggy pants. My hair is cut to emphasize the streaks of white that showed up recently, but I dreamed of having pink hair like my artist friend Polly, and maybe I'll do that, just to try.

My t'ai chi practice has taught me not to wear anything that restricts circulation in my body, a rule that has meant throwing out most of my old wardrobe but still allows me enormous choice of daily disguise. Disguises these days are functional, related to my activities, but the relationship is sometimes whimsical.

Of course, not everyone is satisfied. My friend Mary Ellen says I don't know a thing about makeup, and I'm never happy when someone "does" my face. The trouble is that the stuff doesn't transform me—I just look like myself with too much makeup on. Most people think I could stand to lose some weight, but my t'ai chi friends think I still have some to gain. I notice that my widened hips allow me greater freedom of movement, give me more solidity and flexibility. Some days I feel huge, the two sizes I've gained feel more like ten, and I lumber along the street like an ogress. Other days I feel light and springy in my black-and-white Converse sneakers with the red shoelaces, young and filled with energy.

The nice thing about being over fifty is that my appearance is no longer the defining aspect of my identity. I still care enormously about my appearance, more than I like to admit. I still rely heavily on the approval of those closest to me. But I am clearer now about who it is I am trying to satisfy, to whose standards I need to react.

MY MOTHER, THE EXPERT

As an educated urban woman, I have access to stories and fairy tales from all cultures, to movies as they appear in local theaters and as they turn up on videotape in rental stores, to books, paintings, TV shows, theater, to the daily spectacle that appears in newspapers, magazines, and outside my window. But there is still within me a critical, sometimes nagging voice, which repeats the mottoes I learned as a child and tells me I'll never measure up. The voice is often like my mother's. Who decides what influences me, and how? Who is the expert who says this is authentic, this is the standard, this is true and this false?

As a child and as a young woman, I suffered from having others' standards imposed on me. I suffered from my mother's constant retelling of her personal stories, without apparently noticing the negative feedback from my sister and me. Through my formal education I strove to become the expert who could influence the setting of standards, and the artist who could set my own. I was a rebel, but a halfhearted one, because I cared so much about what people thought of me. Learning to balance the feedback of others with my own experience comes slowly for me.

There is an expert who lives in each of us, a real expert who knows when a story or an image represents something deep, hidden, something yearning for recognition, something which accurately reflects our own experience, or which maps unknown territory so that we can explore it. Sometimes we need to tell and retell a story, until it is integrated and no longer needed.

When I think of my mother's story in this light I realize the value for me of telling her story, like my own, from several different perspectives.

There is the perspective of the little girl who was my mother, who was often hungry, sometimes for food but more often for affection. For her, clothes and a beautiful figure meant a way to get recognition from the world, and when these failed her, eating became her greatest delight. There is the perspective of the little girl who was her daughter, me, seeing in my mother a huge, terrifying, insatiably hungry witch, who tried to devour me and then my sister, living her life vicariously through us. There is the perspective of the old woman my mother became just before she died, looking back on her life with peaceful eyes, remembering my father's love for her and her many friendships, telling me, at our last meeting, as I was saying good-bye to her, a sexual joke, then looking at me with a wicked gleam in her eye and saying, "You don't get it!"

The joke my mother told me as she lay dying was this: An old woman was traveling by train, in a sleeping compartment. She prepared for bed, not realizing that the man across from her was watching through the opening in her curtains. First she removed her wig, and put it on the shelf. Then she took out her false teeth, and put them in a jar on the shelf. Then she removed her glass eyes, and put them in their container on the shelf. Next came her prostheses, one for each breast. One by one the old woman unstrapped her artificial legs and arms, and placed them on the shelf. And she was quiet. But after a few moments the man called across to her, "Okay, there's one thing more to come—hand it over!"

My mother told me this story and looked at me expectantly from her hospital bed in my sister's house. But I didn't laugh. I was thinking of a child's book my son had when he was small, called *The Man Who Gave Himself Away*. It was a beautiful story about a man who gave his clothes and his few belongings away to other people, then his body parts to the animals of the forest, and finally his voice to the wind.

My mother's story was very moving for me. It made me think about what it meant to her to be a woman, old and dying as she was. My mother had false teeth, eyeglasses, a wig, and a prosthesis, all of which she had laid aside before these last weeks in bed. Now the very last thing was her woman's body, her organs, her belly, her vagina, my entranceway into the world, the site of her lovemaking with my father. She told me that my father and her mother were waiting for her on the other side of a stream—she had dreamed this a year earlier, and in

—— her dream she told them she wasn't quite ready to cross over. Now she was getting ready.

My mother's story also reminded me of another story she had once told me, about how, when she was a little girl, one of the boys in her school convinced her that he had a powerful telescope, which could see through walls, and which he used to spy on her. My terrified mother undressed in her closet, huddled down, hoping that the boy's telescope couldn't find her.

Dreaming into the myth of my mother's life revealed by these two stories of voyeurism, I imagine that there was something about my outgoing, loud mother that was very shy and introverted, also something that wanted her to express her most private thoughts. I think that for most of her life she had no outlet, no creative way of working with this private, shy part. My mother cared terribly about appearances, and suffered from her own appearance for the greater part of her life. She was unable, until just before her death, to take on the role of the one who looks, and drop the role of the one who is looked at, and judged.

Before she told me the joke, my mother said something that I think was the most difficult and profound thing she ever said to me. She said, "When you were a child, I was in awe of you, your command of language was so amazing. But now there is a balance between us. I have come into my own sense of myself."

Until a few days before she said good-bye to me and slipped into her final coma, which lasted two weeks, my mother still had some concern for her appearance. She had us wash and comb her hair, and trim her toenails, but she kept her long fingernails, although they had grown thick and yellow. Then she stopped caring how she looked, probably for the first time since she was a small child. She opened her eyes one day and looked at the flowers and plants outside the window, at the sparkling waters of the bayou overlooked by her room in my sister's house, and she said, "How beautiful. I must remember to open my eyes more often." That was the first time in my life I heard my mother comment on the beauty of nature.

In those few days before she died my mother became the beautiful woman she had dreamed of being all her life. Her beauty, which came from her transfigured spirit, drew people to her, as she had always dreamed of having people drawn to her. The nurses who cared for her asked my sister to call them when my mother's end approached, so they could come and sit with her.

The wicked witch of my childhood and early adulthood was my mother. She became the wise woman I had longed for, but only in the last moments of her life. Yet these last moments were enough to transform all that had gone before.

My mother's legacy to me has nothing to do with conventional images of nurturance or loving motherhood. In my dreams of her now, she is ahead of me and beyond me, going off on her own, inspiring me to do the same. I realize I have yearned all my life to be the shining spirit my mother became on her deathbed. My mother's obsession with appearance, and mine, have been at heart a longing for beauty, which has little to do with appearance and everything to do with freedom of spirit.

CODA

13

ORIGINAL

FACE

I have spent many years exploring my interests in beauty and in creativity. My own development now has more to do with my relationship to ugliness, with madness, pain, and suffering, with the Taoist story of Sun Pu-erh, and how she used the disguise of an ugly madwoman to attain enlightenment. Sun Pu-erh's teacher said of her, "If she is not mad, how can she become immortal?" Only by dropping, at least for a moment, my identity as an attractive woman, only by exploring my own ugly face, only by seeking the spirit that informs my obsession with appearance can I find my immortal self, the self that is beyond appearance, what the Buddhists call Original Face.

As I prepare to do this, I think of the story of Ch'iu Ch'ang-Ch'ung in *Seven Taoist Masters.* One of the seven disciples who eventually became immortal, Ch'iu Ch'ang-Ch'ung had the most arduous path in his earthly life. At one point he was told by a man who studied faces that he was destined to die of hunger, that he would not achieve enlightenment in this life, and that it was useless for him to resist his destiny. Despairing, Ch'iu Ch'ang-Ch'ung tried to commit suicide by hanging himself. He made several attempts, but each time heaven intervened, and finally a god came disguised as an herb gatherer to set Ch'iu Ch'ang-Ch'ung straight. He explained that the face is only a reflection of the mind, or heart, and that destiny is determined not by external appearances but by our actions. He rebuked Ch'iu Ch'ang-Ch'ung for forgetting his training:

> You are supposed to be trained in the path of the Tao and yet you fell into the clutches of external forms and let your attachment to appearance ruin you. As a Taoist adept, you should know that immortality is within the reach of everyone and that it is up to our own efforts to make it a reality. You should know that it is not the "destiny" written on your face that determines whether you will achieve enlightenment but the effort that you make.

Ch'iu Ch'ang-Ch'ung resumed his meditative practice, determined to overcome the "monsters of the mind," which afflicted him. He finally achieved enlightenment and became an advisor to the emperor before ascending to heaven to join the other Immortals.

Bearing his experience in mind, I approach the study of my own mental monsters with a hope for eventual detachment. The best way I know to achieve detachment is to study, even embrace my monsters, those things that disturb me the most, finding out what meaning they have to offer. Many of my monsters live in mirrors, as well as in my dreams.

LOOKING AT MY UGLY FACE

I meditate on my appearance. What disturbs me the most? My full breasts and full figure to match, with a full moon face. I

have always disliked this fullness, always longed for lean elegance, like Audrey Hepburn or Georgia O'Keeffe. I've never
thought of the value of fullness, nor have I identified with being
full, full of thoughts, of mischief, of malice, even of revenge, of
fun, full of ideas and love and wild impulses, full even of energy
and determination! And yes, full of shit, blood, and piss. This
seems like someone else I am describing. But I can imagine how
I really am speaking of myself. To be full is wonderful and
dangerous; it also contains the possibility of being empty, a
possibility of increasing interest to me. What would it be like
to alternate between states of fullness and emptiness? This is
one aspect of the old metaphor of woman as vessel or container,
like the crucible or cauldron of the alchemist or witch.

I look at my skin, thick and large-pored. I, of course, would
like to have fine, delicate skin. But to have thick skin is not a
bad idea in many of the situations in which I find myself, metaphorically as well as literally. This is also a quality with which
I don't tend to identify. I think of myself as being thin-skinned,
easily bruised. I often feel that way, but I also notice that I have
a tendency to go looking for trouble, even to feel exhilarated
in the midst of an argument. I need to be thick-skinned.

My skin, like my middle-aged body, is full of blemishes.
Well, I am clearly full of blemishes, and they annoy the hell
out of me. I have a terrible temper and a monstrous ego. I am
often impatient, and I tend to interrupt. I am stubborn and lazy,
and I resist change. What a drag, and what a potential pleasure!
Mother Nature herself must rejoice in her myriad blemishes.
How important it is for me to remember my own blemishes
before I give way to my more critical impulses, to remember
that I am also imperfect!

But my acceptance of imperfection is still incomplete. In
order to look at my naked body I have to make a conscious
effort, and then I have a conversation with myself about the
new folds of skin around my middle, the brown spots and
moles that have recently appeared here and there, the veins, the
sags. I am particularly horrified by the spider veins, which crawl
and bulge on my legs, so that I avoid going bare-legged even

on the hottest days of summer. I remind myself to notice my overall shape, the tendency to movement, how my body changes as I move. Staring at my spider veins I imagine tattooing my legs all over to match the pattern of the veins. I notice that each patch of veins has its own unique pattern, and I begin, slowly, to see them in decorative terms.

My skin has many colors, ranging from pale ivory around my eyes through light beige, various shades of pink and red, light-brown freckles and spots, light-green veins, and purple, blue, and red arteries. I am a white woman of many colors. Those that disturb me are the extremes, the lightness and the weirdness of color, which, when I think in terms of an artist's palette, are actually fascinating. I look again at Beatrice's oil portrait of me, and I realize that she used all those colors to create the impression of my skin thirty years ago, long before I ever noticed them.

The colors of my skin are easier for me to accept than the lightness. It is the lightness, the pale ivory color, which I associate with whiteness, with being a white woman, pale-skinned, lacking in depth, in definition, lacking soul. (Soul conjures up a rich darkness in my racialized imagination.) I've never had the complexion that is called, poetically, "milk-white," and until recently when I've become sensitive to the sun, I've always exposed my skin as much as possible, hoping to get a tan, to darken my skin.

Probing far into the background of my white heritage, I consider that it comes from the North, from cold winter lands, places I associate with silence and remoteness, with the fierceness of conquering tribes, with hardship and survival. I need the strength of a survivor to deal with the complexities of my heritage, for part of that heritage is racism.

I am defensive about my whiteness, about my legacy of privilege and the hurt it has brought to others. But if I were really to follow my own disturbing lightness of skin, I would notice a tendency that I have to disappear in times of stress. I have known myself to become invisible, a quality that has often bothered me. But there is something useful as well as self-protective in this invisibility, something I could use more consciously, allowing my small self to disappear and my awareness of the whole to take over. As a facilitator and leader in groups, this quality has many uses, but only if acknowledged alongside other qualities, for instance, my weirdness and my passions, which show in my changes of color. If I can really leave myself aside, and put the ebb and flow of my passions at the service of the whole, without ownership or attachment, that is a way of honoring my paleness and neutrality as well as my colorful nature.

Appreciating this part of me, I can then own up, more consciously, to the everyday privilege I enjoy because I am pale, because I am white. It is not customary to acknowledge our privileges, to explore this aspect of oppression. I have the privilege of being invisible. I can, mostly, shop where I like, eat where I like, live where I like. Realizing this privilege, I want, greedily, to have even more privilege, to feel comfortable in neighborhoods where my skin is lighter than everyone else's. For that to be the case, everyone would have to share my privilege. It would have to be acknowledged by all as a human right, due to everyone who is born human on this planet.

I know my own face better than almost anything else. Yet, asked to describe myself, I hesitate. I have no words for my face. I notice I am reluctant to find words. My face is round, with a slightly pointy chin and a high forehead. My eyes are wide-set, hazel, changing color from a range of greens to browns. I have folded eyelids, more so on the right than the left, which, along with wide cheekbones, give an Asian cast to my face. My nose is short and tilts up slightly, and I have an old scar, an indentation just above the tip of my nose. My mouth now in middle age is rather small, and fine lines gather above my upper lip. Between my eyes I have two vertical lines, which deepen and lighten according to my intestinal health and emotional states. The fine lines around my eyes intensify when I smile or squint.

I read over what I have written and I wonder if anyone would get a picture from these words. They have very little relation, for me, to the image I see in the mirror. To achieve that I would have to use more metaphoric terms. My face is impish and also withheld. I can look maternal and nurturing, with a foreboding twinkle. My face is deceptive, unnerving to those who fail to notice the gimlet quality of my glance, or the way I hold my mouth. I am a bundle of mixed signals.

I once spent ten days on a farm without once looking into a mirror or seeing a mass-produced image. It was a happy time in my life, and part of the happiness had to do with the way I was experiencing myself, from inside, from my body feelings, and from outside, in terms of how other people related to me. I was sated with visual feedback, and needed this respite. Since that time of learning to live without mirrors, I sometimes allow myself to experience my own face from the inside, to feel myself looking out through my eyes, noticing how I hold my mouth, how my cheeks feel, how my nose looks (I just see the tip of it), how my hair brushes my cheeks, and how the breath I take in connects my face with my whole body. This experience of my face is quite different from seeing myself in a mirror or in a photograph. When I feel my own face in this way, I look differently at other people's faces, wondering how they feel from inside.

I often wish I had "good bones," by which I mean elegant, photogenic bones, clearly defined cheekbones, a chiseled nose, and so forth. Slim ankles. Lately, with osteoporosis threatening to haunt my older age, I value strong, elastic bones, bones with plenty of density and the resilience not to break easily. I don't want to identify with the weakness of my bones, any more than I want to identify with the blemishes of my skin. To identify with my weakness would mean, for me, to be more humble and realistic about what I can't do well, to give way to others who are more capable than I, to seek help and coalition when I need it, not to imagine I can save the world or myself single-handedly. It would mean to acknowledge my biggest weakness, my tendency to inflation and arrogance.

When I look at my facial bone structure, I see that my lines tend to blur, especially on film or videotape. I associate this blurry vagueness with indecisiveness, also with being short-sighted. The world often looks to me the way I look when I catch myself unaware, blurry, like images seen through moving water. According to the Chinese study of facial characteristics called Siang Mien, my face shape is called the Moon. It is associated with water, which is able to change course, to flow into any container. This face shape is also associated with greed. I am greedy for many things, for food, for comfort, for love and affection, for knowledge and the wisdom to use it. I think, if I were to attain the wisdom and love I crave, my other cravings might not be so strong.

Vagueness is a quality of my face with which I don't much identify, as I have sharp opinions and can be very insistent about them. But I have my own vague states, and when I think about them I realize that these are the beginnings of something more meditative and detached. Entering into the vagueness deliberately, I find a state of consciousness in which I come close to a sense of Original Face. This is a sense of my own nature, a state I experience first in feeling, then visually. The feeling is something like sinking down into myself, allowing my breathing to settle, going deep down, taking time inside, finding quietness.

After a while in such a state, when I look out at the world from deep inside, I see people and things differently than I do in my everyday states. It's as if I were looking through water, which acts as a lens, making some things clear and others remote. It's easier for me to understand what is happening, and I have very little to say about it. I feel for the suffering around me. But I am also at once empty and full. Empty of my usual emotions, full of something like well-being, or joy.

This state unites and transforms the most disturbing aspects of my appearance. In it I am an empty vessel full of awareness, invisible and detached.

After this descent into myself I return to my everyday awareness. I am sometimes beautiful, and sometimes ugly. I disturb myself and suffer from my own sense of my shortcomings. I am vague, sharp-tempered, stubborn, affectionate, impossible. I am an ordinary woman, with the world inside me.

APPENDIX:

WORKING ON

YOURSELF ALONE

PREPARING TO WORK ON YOURSELF—
A PRELIMINARY NOTE

Working on yourself is a process-oriented concept that means following your own experience with awareness, focusing on what disturbs or interests you, noticing and describing your experience in sensory-grounded terms, amplifying your experience, and noticing edges. An edge is a boundary to your known experience. Whenever you work on yourself you will, sooner or later, feel confused, or bored, or sleepy, or you'll go into a trance, or you'll find yourself thinking, This is too weird, or I can't do this. You've come to a personal edge. The biggest step to take is just to notice that you have come to an edge. Then you can explore it, go back and forth, notice what keeps you from going over the edge, notice what draws you to it. Being compassionate to yourself is a great help, especially when you're at an edge. Don't feel you have to go over the edge. Whatever you do is just right!

WHY WORK ON APPEARANCE?

Why do it? After all, appearance issues bring up our worst fears and insecurities. Why not just repress them and go shopping, or have a coffee or something sweet? If you've read through this book, though, you know that the roles associated with appearance are connected with power and creativity, and can enrich our lives, if we can get to the spirit behind the roles. By focusing on those aspects of appearance that disturb or attract us, we get right to the concrete details of beauty or ugliness in ourselves, and the different relationships we have with these roles.

INNER WORK ON APPEARANCE

These are exercises to do alone, in a room by yourself, with a large mirror handy. Keep this book open and try doing each exercise, step by step, as you read. Suggested time allotments are in parentheses.

I. YOUR FACE (5–10 MINUTES)

1. First, *find a comfortable position,* then close your eyes and *notice what is going on inside.* Are you seeing something with your inner eye? Are you having a body feeling, such as heat, cold, or pressure? Are you hearing something, or thinking of a conversation or story in your mind? Are you noticing any little movements in your body? You may be having more than one experience. Just notice what is happening.

2. Now, *focus on your face,* keeping your eyes closed. What does your face feel like? With your eyes closed, imagine what your face looks like from the outside. Can you move parts of your face? Go ahead and move what you can, your eyebrows, your nose, your mouth. Play with your jaw, your chin, your tongue. Notice stiffness or other sensations.

3. *Make up a story* about this face. What kind of a face is this? To whom does it belong? What is the history and future of this face?

II. YOUR BODY (10 MINUTES)

1. *Look at yourself,* at your hands, your arms, your breasts and belly, your torso, hips, legs, feet. What do you see? What do you like? What disturbs you?

2. *Choose one aspect of your body,* something you like or something you don't like, something that attracts your attention.

3. *Focus on this one thing,* and ask yourself, What is it that attracts my attention? What is the quality that I like, or that disturbs me? As you focus, notice how you experience it. Is it something you see, hear, feel, or is it something about movement?

4. *Amplify your experience.* If seeing, see it in great detail. If hearing, hear the tone of voice, the rhythm and pace of it, who is speaking. If feeling, be precise. Where and what are you feeling? If movement, notice it and exaggerate it.

5. *Now add a channel of perception.* If you are seeing or feeling, add movement. If you are already moving, add sound. Involve your whole body in this exploration. Find out, through movement and sound, what sort of character emerges from this quality you are working with. (For example, if you are working with large breasts, and you notice first how they look, try finding out how they move. Move your whole body the way your breasts move. Make a sound to go with the movement. Who is this, moving and making these sounds?)

III. WORKING ON YOURSELF (20–30 MINUTES)

1. *Look at your whole self,* every part you can see. Now look in the mirror at your face. Notice what you like and what disturbs you. Look at your whole body, turn, look at your back, the parts you can't see by just looking at yourself. Notice how you move and how you hold yourself.

2. *Choose one aspect of your appearance,* just one, something about your face, your hair, or your body. Something that attracts your attention, something you like, or something you don't like. It can be something you've chosen before, or a new thing. This will be the focus of your inner work.

3. *Focus on this one thing,* and ask yourself, What is it that attracts my attention? What is the quality that I like, or that disturbs me? How do I experience it? Is it something I see, hear, feel, or is it something about movement?

4. *Amplify your experience.* If seeing, see it in great detail. If hearing, hear the tone of voice, the rhythm and pace of it, who is speaking. If feeling, be precise. Where and what are you feeling? If movement, notice it and exaggerate it.

5. *Switch channels of perception.* If you are seeing something, try hearing it, or telling yourself a story about it. If you are having a feeling, try moving in a way that matches the feeling, or make a picture of the feeling, and so on. Be sure to match the original experience. For example, if you are seeing a big red splotch, make sure the movement you make or the story you tell goes along with red splotchiness. Try as many channels as you can, and be sure to try one you're not familiar with—movement if you're shy about moving, a story if you're shy about words, etc.

6. Once you have explored this aspect of your appearance in several different ways, ask yourself, *What is it about this thing that I could use,* in my relationships, in my work, or somewhere in my life? How could I use it? What would that be like?

7. *Use your creativity now:* tell yourself a story, or draw a picture, or choreograph a dance, or make up a song about this wonderful terrible thing, this eye or nose or wrinkle or pimple, or whatever it is that encapsulates something you need.

8. Try it out. Try integrating this into your life. Let me know what happens. I'd love to hear from you.

You can try these exercises over and over, especially the last one. Sometimes focus on an aspect of your appearance, or someone else's appearance, that disturbs you. Sometimes focus on something that attracts you. Either will yield results for noticing what in you needs more attention, cultivation, amplification.

As a process worker I have studied and taught ways of working alone, or inner work, a skill that is useful for people who don't always have access to a therapist or supportive friend, who would like to develop the inner life. If you find this idea appealing, I recommend the following books for developing inner work skills:

Arnold Mindell, *Working On Yourself Alone: Inner Dreambody Work* (London: Arkana, Penguin, 1990).

Arnold Mindell and Amy Mindell, *Riding the Horse Backwards: Process Work in Theory and Practice* (London: Arkana, Penguin, 1992).

NOTES

These notes are an accompaniment to the text, listed by page number without corresponding page citations. The text may be read without reference to the notes.

p. 4: "You will meet with perils . . ." Eva Wong, trans. *Seven Taoist Masters: A Folk Novel of China,* p. 57. The characters in *Seven Taoist Masters* are historical figures who lived in the eleventh century after the Common Era. The story was written down about 1500 A.C.E.

p. 14: "For her, clothing was fashion . . ." For a cultural and historical context for this issue, see Ewen and Ewen, *Channels of Desire: Mass Images and the Shaping of American Consciousness,* 2nd ed. "While sweatshop labor dampened the hopes of many who had sought a land of freedom, there were other, provocative elements of urban America that encouraged one to 'dress for success.' Forsaken in the promised land, working people saw mass-produced fashions as one key to the mastery of a new world. The terms of that world can be reduced to a single word: *appearance*," p. 140.

p. 17: "a movie about beauty, ugliness, and the cycles of nature." *The Secret Garden,* directed by Fred Wilcox, produced by Clarence Brown, 1949.

p. 20: "principles of internal alchemy . . ." See Eva Wong trans., ed. *Cultivating Stillness: A Taoist Manual for Transforming Body and Mind.*

p. 21: "In *Keltie's Beard, a Woman's Story* . . ." 1983, 16mm, distributed by Filmmakers Library, New York.

p. 22: "Dr. Arnold Mindell, who developed from his clinical practice as a Jungian analyst the theory of process-oriented psychology . . ." See books by Mindell listed in the Bibliography.

p. 25: Marguerite Duras, "Leontyne Price," *Outside: Selected Writings,* p. 181.

p. 25: "beauty is a demon . . ." Carlos Castaneda, *The Eagle's Gift,* p. 271.

p. 28: "the ancient history of Halloween . . ." Barbara Walker, *The Woman's Encyclopedia of Myths and Secrets.* New York: Harper & Row, 1983, p. 372.

p. 28: "We were radical in our fantasies . . ." For research-based accounts of young girls' often radical reactions to mainstream culture, see Carol Gilligan, *Women, Girls and Psychotherapy: Reframing Resistance.*

p. 29: "When she leaned against the apple tree . . ." Diane Wolkstein and Noah Kramer, *Inanna: Queen of Heaven and Earth,* p. 12.

p. 29: "properly 'kept covered.' " Agnola Firenzuola, *On the Beauty of Women,* First Dialogue, p. 31.

p. 29: "Of all these 'other parts . . .' " A curious and revelatory moment in cinematic history was created by Anne Severson when she used extreme close-ups in glowing color of women's vaginas to create her controversial short silent film, *Near the Big Chakra* (1972, distributed by Canyon Cinema in San Francisco). Severson gave the same absorbed attention to the female vagina that thousands of filmmakers have devoted to the female face, with very different results. Extreme reactions, ranging from utter silence to lewd remarks from an all-male audience, to an actual riot, were provoked when the film was shown.

The recognition of the intense repression our culture applies to women's own visions of our sexuality inspired Severson to make the film. The direct impetus for the film came about when Severson's teenage daughter was lounging in the nude one day. Severson found herself staring at her daughter's vagina, and realized that she had not done so since her daughter was a baby, and, more importantly, that both she and her daughter were embarrassed by her doing so. MacDonald, "Demystifying the Female Body: Anne Severson—Near the Big Chakra; Yvonne Rainer-Privilege," *Film Quarterly*, Fall, 1991, pp. 18–32.

p. 30: "I will decree a sweet fate for him." "The Courtship of Inanna and Dumuzi," Wolkstein and Kramer, *Inanna: Queen of Heaven and Earth*, p. 44.

p. 31: "One main characteristic of patriarchy . . ." See Anne Baring and Jules Cashford, *The Myth of the Goddess, Evolution of an Image;* Riane Eisler, *The Chalice & the Blade: Our History, Our Future.*

p. 32: "some agreement, as well as considerable debate, about the time preceding patriarchy." See, for instance, Baring and Cashford, *The Myth of the Goddess;* Eisler, *The Chalice & the Blade;* Gadon, *The Once and Future Goddess;* Gimbutas, *The Goddesses and Gods of Old Europe, 6500–3500 B.C.: Myths and Cult Images,* and *The Language of the Goddess;* Stone, *When God Was a Woman;* Barbara Walker, *The Woman's Encyclopedia of Myths and Secrets.*

p. 32: "the triple deity was conceived as mother, father, and son." Baring and Cashford, *The Myth of the Goddess,* p. 187.

p. 33: "the old stereotypes of ugly wicked witches still persist." Movies provide the imaginary field where caricatured witches, as in *The Witches of Eastwick,* appear, only to be countered by such remarkable portrayals of old women as Jeanne Moreau's in *The Summer House,* Lillian Gish and Bette Davis in *The Whales of August,* and the wonderful cast of *Strangers in Good Company.* See also Donnelly, *Women and Aging;* Scott-Maxwell, *The Measure of My Days;* Walker, *The Crone, Woman of Age, Wisdom, and Power.*

p. 34: "And was hung from a hook on the wall." Wolkstein and Kramer, *Inanna: Queen of Heaven and Earth,* p. 60.

p. 34: " 'Take Dumuzi away!' " Ibid., p. 71.

—— p. 34: "I turn the male to the female." Esther Harding, *Women's Mysteries, Ancient and Modern*, p. 159.

p. 35: "The *Enuma Elish* . . ." For further discussion and the context of cultural violence and displacement, see Baring and Cashford, *The Myth of the Goddess.*

p. 36: "Esther won 'favour in [Ahasuerus's] sight' " . . . *Holy Bible,* King James version, *Esther* 4, 5.

p. 36: "Esther dressed herself in splendor . . ." Goodspeed, *The Apocrypha, an American Translation*, p. 171.

p. 36: "a new idea into the Bible . . ." Tikva Frymer-Kensky, *In the Wake of the Goddesses: Women, Culture and the Biblical Transformation of Pagan Myth*, attributes this idea to the influence of the Greeks.

p. 37: "Inanna was a highly unusual goddess . . ." Ibid.

p. 38: "A woman's beauty is associated with her sexual appeal . . ." See Elissa Melamed, *Mirror Mirror: The Terror of Not Being Young.* She remarks on "the fertility-linked secondary sexual characteristics we call beauty," p. 40, and traces the difficulties encountered by women as these youthful qualities fade.

p. 38: "lesbians . . . have been condemned as a threat to society." The treatment of lesbians is typically separate from the treatment of male homosexuals. In their discussion of beauty among the ancient Greeks, Claudia Brush Kidwell and Valerie Steele point out the influence of what they call "homophilia," without noting that Greek culture represented a transition from Goddess worship to patriarchy: "For the ancient Greeks, a certain type of young male body was regarded as ideally beautiful. Greek statues of rather heavy-set goddesses were intended to be beautiful, but the overwhelming emphasis was on male beauty, an estimation that was related to the practice of homosexuality and a generalized cultural homophilia." From Kidwell and Steele, *Men and Women, Dressing the Part*, p. 17.

p. 41: "in which women certainly excelled . . ." There is now a large body of writing on this subject. See, for instance, Baring and Cashford, *The Myth of the Goddess;* Gadon, *The Once and Future Goddess;* Walker, *The Woman's Encyclopedia of Myths and Secrets,* and see their excellent bibliographies for further reading.

p. 41: "Women, once the bearers of medical wisdom . . ." See Barbara Ehrenreich and Deirdre English, *For Her Own Good.*

p. 42: "My hair is short and kinky . . ." Alice Walker, *The Color Purple*, p. 229.

p. 43: "femininity is constructed, at the expense of women's fullest development." Susan Brownmiller, *Femininity*.

p. 43: "The beauty myth . . ." Susan Faludi, *Backlash: The Undeclared War Against American Women*. Wolf, *The Beauty Myth: How Images of Beauty Are Used Against Women*.

p. 44: "the irony of wanting to approximate White standards of beauty . . ." Paula Giddings, *When and Where I Enter: The Impact of Black Women on Race and Sex in America*, p. 185 ff.

p. 45: "we long for an aesthetic of blackness—strange and oppositional." bell hooks, *Yearning: Race, Gender, and Cultural Politics*, p. 113.

p. 46: "some of the concerns I have [about white racism] . . ." For another personal account of whiteness, see Judith Levine, " 'White Like Me: When Privilege Is Written on Your Skin,' " *Ms.*, March–April 1994, pp. 22–24.

p. 48: "my own assumptions about appearance . . ." The retrenchment of the Black Power movement in the seventies, in the face of police violence and a general American shift to political conservatism, was accompanied by a change in middle-class African American fashions, away from large Afros and African costume, toward more "mainstream" standards of appearance. In the nineties there is a resurgence of ethnic fashion, and African American women in the professions and in the media are wearing elaborate braids and dreadlocks, large earrings and necklaces. Perhaps most important, there is increasingly open discussion of the politics of color within the African American community.

On February 15, 1994, Oregon Public Broadcasting aired a documentary called *A Question of Color,* in which filmmaker Kathe Sandler examines "color consciousness" in the African American community, especially in terms of the European standard of beauty for women.

p. 51: "supported . . . by family and/or community." See Lena Wright Myers, *Black Women: Do They Cope Better?*, cited by Barry Glassner, *Bodies, Why We Look the Way We Do and How We Feel About It*, p. 76. Also see Jacqueline F. Brown, "Helping Black Women Build High Self-Esteem," *American Counselor,*

1993, 2: 9–12, and Gloria Joseph and Jill Lewis, *Common Differences: Conflicts in Black & White Feminist Perspectives.*

p. 55: "the influence of fashion magazines . . ." The February 1994 issue of *Femina,* printed in Bombay, featured an article called "Grow Younger As You Age," which used Western examples of fit older women and men to inspire Indian women to keep themselves looking and feeling young. The same issue also featured a section called "International Trends 1994–'95—a New Column from Paris!"

p. 56: "fairness, lightness of skin, ranked highest." Anuradha's points are illustrated by the ads in the Indian fashion magazines she sent to me after her return to Bombay. From the beauty-contest focus of *Femina* to the emphasis on women's independence seen in *Savvy,* the ads remain the same. They feature dark-haired, light-skinned women with European features, aquiline noses, the same wide smiles, full lips, sultry eyes, and currently fashionable cosmetics that are found in European and American fashion magazines. Some wear saris, some are shown in Western dress, some have jeweled caste marks and pierced noses, but any could appear in *Harper's Bazaar* or *Vogue,* depending on the ethnic flavor of the issue. These models are very different from the women who appear in the photos accompanying the articles in *Savvy*—women who tend to be larger, less glamorously dressed and made up. The models would fit in with almost any assemblage of fashionable beauties anywhere in the world. The women in the news photos are distinctively Indian in appearance, and represent a wide range of ages, body shapes, and sizes. In other words, Indian women's magazines are strikingly similar to Western women's magazines, selling a global standard of beauty along with its products, tailoring articles to local tastes.

p. 56: "A high school principal in Alabama . . ." Kendal Weaver for AP, "High School Principal Suspended for Alleged Racial Slur," *The Oregonian,* Tuesday, March 15, 1994. Principal Hulond Humphries was suspended pending an investigation after students complained that he tried to forbid interracial dates at their prom and told ReVonda Bowen she was a "mistake."

p. 56: "thousands of black women were impregnated by their white masters." See Margaret Busby, ed., *Daughters of Africa,* passim; hooks, *Yearning: Race, Gender, and Cultural Politics,* p. 57 ff.

p. 57: "Does the change in roles represent growth or camouflage?" See below, Chapter 10, "Passing."

p. 59: " 'Black women will do incredible things to get their hair to where it ought to be.' " See also Busby, ed., *Daughters of Africa,* p. xxxxv; Giddings, *When and Where I Enter: The Impact of Black Women on Race and Sex in America,* p. 187 ff.

p. 59: "Baker still took Clorox baths in order to lighten her skin." Baker and Chase, *Josephine: The Hungry Heart,* p. 137.

p. 59: "a black woman who died from using bleach on her skin." Giddings, *When and Where I Enter,* p. 187.

p. 59: "alter almost any aspect of the face or body." Barry Glassner recounts, without comment about its racism, the story of a plastic surgeon who spoke of his satisfaction at having altered the "exaggerated African features" of a woman who wanted to be a television journalist. Glassner, *Bodies, Why We Look the Way We Do and How We Feel About It,* p. 193. In Kathe Sandler's documentary, *A Question of Color,* an African American plastic surgeon uses his African American nurse as a model to explain how he would be able to alter her African nose, to make it more European.

p. 59: "A performance artist from Paris, Orlan . . ." Susan Gerhard, "The Beauty Morph," *San Francisco Bay Guardian,* February 2, 1994, pp. 29–30; Barbara Rose, "Is it Art? Orlan and the Transgressive Act," *Art in America,* February 1993, p. 82.

p. 60: " 'They devote enormous care . . .' " Fisher, *Africa Adorned.*

p. 62: "the pain of enduring other people's withdrawal." Barbara Macdonald with Cynthia Rich, *Look Me in the Eye: Old Women, Ageing and Ageism,* Cynthia Rich, "Ageism and the Politics of Beauty," p. 144.

p. 66: "related to the menopause in terms of overall life change." See Betty Friedan, *The Fountain of Age;* Greer, *The Change: Women, Aging and the Menopause.*

p. 66: "she suffered from an eating disorder." Diana Maychick, *Audrey Hepburn: An Intimate Portrait.* Hepburn traced her eating disorder back to a time of near-starvation in her childhood during World War II in the Netherlands.

p. 66: *Whales in August,* directed by Lindsay Anderson, 1987.

p. 67: "Her story says a great deal . . ." See the television documentary, "A Tribute to Audrey Hepburn," hosted by Roger Moore, first shown by public television stations in the U.S. in August 1993. See also *The Summer House,* 1993; *Strangers in Good Company,* directed by Waris Hussein, Canada, 1991, directed by Cynthia Scott; *Enchanted April,* directed by Mike Newell, 1991.

Saying "Beauty is timeless," Jeff Cohen, managing photo editor of *Playboy,* announced a search for over-forty women for the magazine's fortieth-anniversary centerfold. "Fast Talk," *The Oregonian,* March 23, 1994.

p. 70: "the older woman becomes a 'truthteller.'" Friedan, "The Fountain of Age," p. 151. This is in marked contrast to the fears of middle-aged women discussed by Elissa Melamed in her book *Mirror Mirror: The Terror of Not Being Young.*

p. 70: "skin of different textures." Cynthia Rich, in Macdonald and Rich, *Look Me in the Eye,* p. 139.

p. 71: "tendency to trivialize and jeer at old women . . ." See Sarah H. Matthews, *The Social World of Old Women,* reviewed by Cynthia Rich in Macdonald and Rich. Matthews tells of an old woman being yelled at on the street by a young man: "Why aren't you in your grave?" Another woman was called "ugly, ugly, ugly," by small children when she smiled at them on the street.

p. 73: "dieting against the grain . . ." See Roberta Pollack Seid, *Never Too Thin: Why Women Are at War with Their Bodies.* New York: Prentice-Hall, 1989. One of my early mentors was Catherine McDermott, whose daughter Anne was my best friend in high school. In 1986 Catherine, a brilliant computer programmer and a large, active woman with five children, won an eleven-year lawsuit against the Xerox Corporation, who fired her on the grounds that she was "grossly obese." Her argument, which she sustained without a lawyer, and which she presented on television talk shows around the country, was that she was naturally large, that she ate healthily and exercised regularly, and that her size in no way hindered her ability to do the job for which she had been hired. Other women have not been so successful as Catherine in maintaining their right to their own body shapes. Her story is told in Wolf, *The Beauty Myth: How Images of Beauty Are Used Against Women,* p. 33.

p. 75: "you will dance the fire dance in iron shoes." Anne Sexton, *Transformations,* pp. 4–5.

p. 77: "Walt Disney was a conservative misogynist . . ." Ariel Dorfman and Armand Mattelart, *How to Read Donald Duck: Imperialist Ideology in the Disney Comic,* Introduction by David Kunzle. Notice the roles for female characters in Disney cartoons, even in the animal kingdom. There are no living mothers, only girlfriends and stepmothers. Bambi's mother dies at the beginning of the movie, and Snow White's mother is eliminated from the script.

p. 77: "documentary of the 1936 Olympic Games . . ." *Olympia, Part I: Festival of the Nations; Part II: Festival of Beauty.*

p. 78: "the only consideration is to make them look young and lovely." Müller, *The Wonderful, Horrible Life of Leni Riefenstahl.* Hitler, who had his own screening room, was a great admirer of Disney and of Riefenstahl. Her film, *Triumph of the Will,* 1936, filmed at the Nazi Party Congress of 1934, is considered by some film historians to be the greatest propaganda film ever made. It presented a romantic vision of a "pure" Aryan Germany. Today, the same mythic underpinning allows the word "cleansing" to be used as a euphemism for genocide. While it may seem to be an extreme leap from the cute animation of "Snow White" to the horrors of fascism, it is important to remember that fascism in Germany was, in its early stages, embraced wholeheartedly by many people as a celebration of "Aryan" ideals, embodied in such fairy tales as "Snow White" and "The Blue Light," subject of Riefenstahl's first film as a director. Riefenstahl was Disney's guest when she visited Hollywood in 1939. See Sontag, below.

Fascism sees beauty as an attribute of the superior race, and ugliness is assigned to supposedly inferior races. Beauty is the possession of the powerful, and ugliness is the lot of the powerless. But this opposition is unstated. Those designated inferior according to race or physical disability are never represented in such systems as powerless, but rather as evil, jealous, and untrustworthy. Riefenstahl insists that her depiction of beautiful bodies in *Olympia* was distasteful to Hitler because black athletes were shown winning medals and glorified alongside white athletes. Later in her life she went to Africa and photographed the Nuba, people who, like the Wodaabe, believe that they are the most beautiful in the world.

p. 78: "This apparently innocent love of beauty . . ." Susan Sontag wrote about Riefenstahl's book of photos of the Nuba as extending the Fascist aesthetic, which she sees epitomized in Riefenstahl's earlier work. Sontag's extended essay on Riefenstahl, called "Fascinating Fascism: I," first appeared in the *New York Review of Books* in 1975, and was included with other essays in her collection *Under the Sign of Saturn* in 1980.

p. 78: "Here is my retelling of the tale written down by the Grimm brothers." I consulted the following editions: Grimm, *Stories,* London, 1876, and *The Complete Grimm's Fairy Tales,* Stern, ed., Margaret Hunt, trans., New York, 1972.

p. 81: "Oya, powerful Yoruba Goddess." See Judith Gleason, *Oya, in Praise of the Goddess.*

p. 81: "The wild boar was an early sacrificial god surrogate . . ." Barbara Walker, *The Women's Dictionary of Symbols & Sacred Objects.*

p. 82: "The Seven Sages . . ." Ibid.

p. 82: "The stepmother is an example of what Jung called the Terrible Mother . . ." See C. G. Jung, *Symbols of Transformation,* 5, and *The Archetypes and the Collective Unconscious,* 9.1.

p. 87: "the denial of passage or change curses a woman and kills her spirit." Clarissa Pinkola Estés, *Women Who Run with the Wolves: Myths and Stories of the Wild Woman Archetype.*

p. 88: "Women who suffer as their youth fades . . ." In the movie *American Heart* (1993), a Seattle woman who dances topless to support herself and her two children is told by her teenage daughter, "You're just jealous of me because you're old and ugly!" The mother makes no reply in this movie, which portrays the underside of the city romanticized in the better-known *Sleepless in Seattle.*

p. 88: "understand her jealousy as zeal . . ." I am grateful to Arnold Mindell, who pointed out this connection between jealousy and zeal, words that derive from the same root.

p. 89: "The jealousy of women toward women . . ." For a discussion of the changing relationships of (mostly white) mothers and daughters see Kim Chernin, *The Obsession: Reflections on the Tyranny of Slenderness* and *The Hungry Self: Women, Eating & Identity.* For more cross-cultural discussions of these issues see Lyn Brown and Carol Gilligan, *Meeting at the Crossroads: Women's Psychology and Girls' Development,* and Joseph and Lewis, *Common Differences: Conflicts in Black & White Fem-*

inist Perspectives. For a discussion of the psychology of girls as they enter adolescence, especially in relation to older women, see Gilligan, *Women, Girls and Psychotherapy: Reframing Resistance.*

p. 89: "frequently encountered situation in which a woman is shamed and humiliated by another woman . . ." In cultures where women have been severely repressed, it is usual for the repression to be enforced by other, usually older, women, for instance, in the case of foot binding in China, or female circumcision in African tribes. On the latter, see Alice Walker and Pratibha Parmar, *Warrior Marks: Female Genital Mutilation and the Sexual Blinding of Women.* On footbinding, see Howard S. Levy, *The Lotus Lovers: The Complete History of the Curious Erotic Custom of Footbinding in China.*

p. 90: "it is in the retelling, the honoring of our own narrative influences . . ." Jungian scholar Marie-Louise von Franz said firmly that in order to analyze a fairy tale you must first read a great many, so as to know all the variations on a particular theme or motif that come up in a particular tale. It is certainly helpful, when thinking about one fairy tale, to be aware of fairy tales in general, and von Franz herself, with her vast knowledge, contributed a lot to the understanding of fairy tales as maps of the human psyche. Bruno Bettelheim recognized the value of the changes children make in retelling fairy tales. He saw that this process reflects the way fairy tales have evolved and changed in human history. We adapt stories and movies and experiences to fit our own needs of the moment. See Bettelheim, *The Uses of Enchantment: The Meaning and Importance of Fairy Tales,* and Marie-Louise von Franz, *Interpretation of Fairy Tales.*

p. 96: "These stories can and should be written and rewritten . . ." In the tradition of fairy tales themselves, which varied from one generation of tellers to the next, contemporary writers, notably Anne Sexton and Angela Carter, have experimented with transforming the old stories. See Carter, *The Bloody Chamber and Other Stories,* and Sexton, *Transformations.*

p. 97: " 'No, Monsieur, I did, because I was afraid he would kill her.' " Marguerite Duras, *The North Chinese Lover,* p. 153.

p. 99: "Perhaps the very first form of sacrifice was menstrual blood . . ." Lara Owen, *Her Blood Is Gold: Celebrating the Power of*

Menstruation; Penelope Shuttle and Peter Redgrove, *The Wise Wound: The Myths, Realities, and Meanings of Menstruation.*

p. 99: "the shame attached by Christianity to her sex and to her beauty." For a discussion of the Christian concept of shame as developed by Augustine, see Elaine Pagels, *Adam, Eve, and the Serpent,* p. 111 ff.

p. 100: " 'and her crotch he used to support the sky.' " From *The Enuma Elish,* in Thorkild Jacobsen, *The Treasures of Darkness: A History of Mesopotamian Religion,* cited by Baring and Cashford, *The Myth of the Goddess,* p. 279.

p. 102: "Nangsa Obum was beaten . . ." Tsultrim Allione, *Women of Wisdom.*

p. 102: "Susanna in her bath . . ." in Edgar J. Goodspeed, *The Apocrypha, an American Translation.*

"From early church times . . ." For two wide-ranging accounts of cultural attitudes toward women and sexuality in the medieval church, see Ewa Kuryluk, *Veronica and Her Cloth,* and Aline Rousselle, *Porneia: On Desire and the Body in Antiquity.* An excellent critical examination of the history and implications of the church's attitude toward sexuality is found in Pagels, *Adam, Eve, and the Serpent.*

p. 102: "the acceptance . . . of violence toward women . . ." An unusual examination of this issue in the context of the African practice of female circumcision is found in Alice Walker, *Possessing the Secret of Joy,* and her subsequent book on the subject, Walker and Parmar, *Warrior Marks.*

p. 102: " 'how can she become an immortal?' " Wong, *Seven Taoist Masters,* p. 58.

p. 103: "she bit the girl in the arm." Ibid., p. 59.

p. 103: "the punitive and often violent nature of methods . . ." The first comprehensive feminist critique of psychiatry was published by Phyllis Chesler in 1972. Work that has built on her critique and incorporated subsequent understandings from feminist research include Elaine Showalter's study in 1985 and Peter Breggin's chapter "Suppressing the Passion of Women," in *Toxic Psychiatry.* See Chesler, *Women and Madness;* and Showalter, *The Female Malady: Women, Madness and English Culture, 1830– 1980.*

p. 106: "social standards of appearance." Doris Lessing wrote a detailed and perceptive account of a woman's encounter with the pressure of such standards as she approached her own older age, an account that Germaine Greer refers to frequently in her book on menopause as a time of change for women, *The Change: Women, Aging and the Menopause.* Lessing, *The Summer Before the Dark.*

p. 105: "Jean Rhys's twentieth-century telling . . ." Rhys, *Wide Sargasso Sea.*

p. 105: " 'I learned to talk about what was going on.' " Transcript of *Dialogues with Madwomen,* directed by Allie Light, distributed by Light-Saraf Films, 264 Arbor Street, San Francisco, CA 94131.

p. 106: "Behind these practical ideas is an approach to the extreme states . . ." For an extended, clinically based discussion of ways of supporting and picking up the information contained in extreme states, see Arnold Mindell, *City Shadows: Psychological Interventions in Psychiatry.*

p. 106: "goddess worship in ancient China." Verified in private conversation with Eva Wong, translator of *Seven Taoist Masters* and *Cultivating Stillness,* September, 1993.

p. 108: "the illusions of sexual attractions and desire." Wong, *Seven Taoist Masters,* p. 111.

p. 109: "two people playing with each other like children." Ibid., pp. 115–16.

p. 110: "intelligent human beings." Ibid., p. 116.

p. 110: "one's own original nature . . ." This complex concept is fundamental to the school of Taoism called Return to Earlier Heaven, or Wu-Chi, which is the school from which my teacher, Moy Lin-shin, derives his lineage. For an introductory account of this school and the concept of original nature, see Wong, *Cultivating Stillness: A Taoist Manual for Transforming Body and Mind.*

p. 110: "are like borrowed jewels . . ." *Song of Nangsa Obum.* From Allione, *Women of Wisdom.*

p. 112: " 'delog' or wise soul . . ." This is an exception to the tradition of death and reincarnation in Tibetan Buddhism. The delog returns to her original body because her allotted time on earth is not up.

p. 113: " 'you cannot hold me.' " Allione, *Women of Wisdom,* pp. 124–25.

—— p. 115: " 'Nothing was missing in her costume.' " Ibid., p. 69.

308 p. 117: "deliberately mistaken for 'true nature.' " Brownmiller, *Femininity*, p. 183.

p. 118: "stories of childhood abuse . . ." Alice Miller is one of many feminist therapists who have written about this subject. Miller, a former psychoanalyst, repudiated psychoanalysis because of the distortion she believed it brings to the subject of childhood abuse. See Miller, *The Drama of the Gifted Child; Thou Shalt Not Be Aware: Society's Betrayal of the Child; For Your Own Good: Hidden Cruelty in Child-Rearing and the Roots of Violence; Banished Knowledge*. See also Florence Rush, *The Best Kept Secret: Sexual Abuse of Children*, and Jeffrey Masson, *The Assault on Truth: Freud's Suppression of the Seduction Theory*. See also Sigmund Freud, "The Etiology of Hysteria," *CPW*.

p. 119: "It is while finding these long-buried longings . . ." For resources on healing from abuse, see Ellen Bass and Laura Davis, *The Courage to Heal: A Guide for Women Survivors of Child Sexual Abuse*, and Judith Herman, *Trauma and Recovery*.

p. 119: " 'in which I delight.' " Duras, *The Lover*, pp. 3–4.

p. 122: "Duras used a male narrator . . ." In an unpublished interview with Duras, conducted in Paris in June 1973, and subsequently revised and approved by her, I spoke with her about this use of male narrators. She was surprised at my observation, and, after some thought, said she used male narrators "because the narrative mode is a masculine mode. . . . To narrate something, to tell a story, one must be rational, logical, moving in a very clear, ordered space. . . . And the women in my books are marked by schizophrenia, or by paranoia, they are in complete confusion. They are in the night. Therefore they cannot narrate with clarity." From *Women Imagine Women*, unpublished ms.

p. 123: " 'yet in activity there is stillness.' " Wong, *Seven Taoist Masters*. p. 74.

p. 126: "channels of perception . . ." A clear and useful description of this idea, which is central to process work, can be found in Mindell and Mindell, *Riding the Horse Backwards: Process Work in Theory and Practice*.

p. 131: "the dumbest privilege there is." Florinda Donner, *Being-in-Dreaming: An Initiation into the Sorcerer's World*, p. 58.

p. 131: "shamanic traditions from all over the world offer possibilities . . ." See Arnold Mindell, *The Shaman's Body.* Also see his bibliography. The classic study of shamanism is Mircea Eliade, *Shamanism, Archaic Techniques of Ecstasy.*

p. 133: "having done some inner work by now . . ." For a useful introduction to inner work, see Arnold Mindell, *Working on Yourself Alone: Inner Dreambody Work;* also see the appendix on inner work at the back of this book.

p. 134: " 'my limited self.' " Private correspondence, July 26, 1993.

p. 141: "Remnants . . . can be traced in the tarot deck . . ." See Barbara Walker, *The Secrets of the Tarot.*

p. 142: "the demonstrations and pickets and writings from all perspectives." See Robin Morgan, ed., *Sisterhood Is Powerful,* p. 521, for a feminist account of the first protests against the Miss America pageant.

p. 145: "all the movie stars were white." Dorothy Dandridge was the only black female star of the fifties who was in any way comparable in youthful glamour to the many white stars. She was restricted to roles in films that emphasized her racial background, such as *Imitation of Life,* 1959, directed by Douglas Sirk, and *Porgy and Bess,* 1959, directed by Otto Preminger.

p. 146: "the moral standards for women's appearance have varied widely." See Anne Hollander, *Seeing Through Clothes,* and Alison Lurie, *The Language of Clothes.*

p. 147: "Diamonds Are a Girl's Best Friend" by Jule Styne and Leo Robin, in *Gentlemen Prefer Blondes,* directed by Howard Hawks, 1953, Twentieth Century-Fox.

p. 150: "a hostile newspaper journalist suggests . . ." Leonard Pitts, Jr., "In Terms of Afterlife, Madonna Is No Elvis."

p. 150: "a fantasy." Madonna, *Sex.*

p. 153: "the vitality of the struggle." Gertrude Stein, *How Writing Is Written* in *Previously Uncollected Writings,* p. 154.

p. 158: "Just as the scientists studying chaos . . ." James Gleick, *Chaos: Making a New Science.*

p. 158: " 'the most beautiful women.' " Madame de La Fayette, *The Princess of Clèves,* p. 17.

p. 160: "A South African story, 'Mulha' . . ." Ethel Johnston Phelps, *The Maid of the North: Feminist Folk Tales from Around the World.* "Mulha" is retold from *Fairy Tales from South Africa,* Sarah Bourhill and Beatrice Drake, 1910.

p. 163: "a privilege hoarded by Mulha and the old woman . . ." What happens to the old woman when Mulha regains her true form? This story, like many other traditional tales, reflects a cultural attitude toward the old, especially old women, which sees them as dispensable, often objects of derision or ridicule.For other examples, see Carter, *The Old Wives' Fairy Tale Book.*

p. 163: "She is an initiatory figure for Mulha, . . ." I am grateful to Arnold Mindell for pointing out the importance of the chief's sister in this story.

p. 164: "a dream figure, a hairy monster who lived in the basement . . ." Sara Halprin, "Preparing for Death and Planning to Live, an Interview with Marianne Pomeroy," *The Journal for Process-Oriented Psychology,* 1993, 5. Subsequent quotations are also from this interview.

p. 166: "She says that her life now . . ." Ibid.

p. 168: "she prayed, not for sight in that eye, but for beauty . . ." Alice Walker, *In Search of Our Mothers' Gardens,* "Beauty: When the 'Other Dancer Is the Self.' "

p. 168: "in one poem I compare . . ." Halprin, "Geography of the Body Geography of the Spirit," *Porter Gulch Review,* 1988, p. 21.

p. 172: "Callas," Duras, *Outside: Selected Writings,* p. 207.

p. 172: "the heroine or hero deals with ugliness in someone else." A notable exception is "The Ugly Duckling," best known in the version told by Hans Christian Andersen, in which appearance is used as a metaphor for belonging, and it is clear that ugliness is the same as strangeness, or otherness.

p. 173: "Rackham used a long French version of the tale . . ." *The Arthur Rackham Fairy Book.*

p. 175: "but only by following a demanding spiritual path." In her high moral stance, Beauty is similar to the heroine of Madame de La Fayette's novel *The Princess of Clèves* (1678), who refuses to follow her passion for the man who loves her because of her allegiance to her husband, even after her husband dies, and even though her beloved is a man of rank and status equal to her own, a consideration of the utmost importance in these paradoxical tales of the bourgeoisie, in which a spiritual disdain for worldly things coexists with great respect for the arrangements of the world as it is.

p. 179: " 'Her face seemed more animal than human.' " Phelps, *The Maid of the North*, p. 37.

p. 179: " 'a string of horrible curses echoing behind him.' " Ibid., p. 40.

p. 180: "the marriage of Gawain and the lady Ragnell." Ibid., p. 44.

p. 181: "literally, a burning issue." Barbara Walker, *The Woman's Encyclopedia of Myths and Secrets.*

p. 181: ". . . an impeccable spiritual warrior . . ." For more detailed examinations of the role of the spiritual warrior, see Carlos Castaneda, *Tales of Power,* and Arthur Mindell, *The Shaman's Body.*

p. 183: "As Mari danced . . ." For an account of Mindell's work with physical symptoms, see Arthur Mindell, *Dreambody: The Body's Role in Revealing the Self* and *Working with the Dreaming Body.*

p. 183: " 'Mossycoat.' " Retold by Carter, *The Old Wives' Fairy Tale Book.* (New York: Pantheon Books, 1990).

p. 186: Oni Faida Lampley, "The Wig and I," *Mirabella,* April 1993, pp. 144–48.

p. 191: " 'they took the ugliness in their hands . . .' " Toni Morrison, *The Bluest Eye,* p. 34.

p. 191: " 'I don't want people to see my picture.' " Erin Hoover Schraw, "Kids' Art, Sculpture Enhances Self-image," *The Oregonian,* Thursday, June 3, 1993.

p. 193: " 'If she is not careful, however . . .' " Regina Turner, "The Sexual Ordeal of the 'Ugly' Black Woman," *Black Male/Female Relationships,* 1982, 21–29, p. 28.

p. 193: "believing she was ugly." *Face,* I, 4, May/June 1993, p. 92.

p. 196: " 'Beauty's New Debate' . . ." *Harper's Bazaar,* July 1993.

p. 197: "bulge just looks better." Wendy Wasserstein, "The Wendy Chronicles: Move Over Waifs, the Bulge Look Is Here," *Harper's Bazaar,* November 1993, issue no. 3384.

p. 197: " 'a sexy and successful big girl.' " *People,* September 20, 1993.

p. 199: "Most violence against children . . ." See Judith Herman, *Trauma and Recovery;* Miller, *Thou Shalt Not Be Aware: Society's Betrayal of the Child; For Your Own Good: Hidden Cruelty in Child-Rearing and the Roots of Violence,* 2nd ed.; *Banished Knowledge;* and Steinem, *Revolution from Within: A Book of Self-Esteem.*

—— p. 200: "bell hooks's writing about the racialized context of fashion . . ." See hooks, *Black Looks: Race and Representation.*

p. 201: "Is she an enemy or an ally?" See Barbara Macdonald's essay, "The Power of the Old Woman," on knowledge of death as a key to enjoyment of life, Macdonald and Rich, *Look Me in the Eye: Old Women, Ageing and Ageism,* pp. 90–101.

p. 202: "The King Who Would Have a Beautiful Wife," Andrew Lang, *The Pink Fairy Book,* p. 164.

p. 202: "occasionally it might be fine to sit at her feet!" Shevy Healy, "Growing to Be an Old Woman: Aging and Ageism," *Calyx: A Journal of Art and Literature by Women, Women and Aging, an Anthology,* Winter 1986, vol. 9, numbers 2 and 3, p. 59.

p. 202: " 'Be quiet, you old hag!' " Agatha Christie, *The Body in the Library,* p. 142.

p. 203: "How old women see themselves . . ." See also "Age" in Chapter 1, and Elissa Melamed's discussion in *Mirror Mirror.*

p. 203: " 'Let the young ones eat their hearts out!' " Patricia Huckle, *Tish Sommers, Activist, and the Founding of the Older Women's League,* p. 13.

p. 203: "The problem for old women . . ." Baba Copper, "Voices: On Becoming Old Women," *Calyx: A Journal of Art and Literature by Women, Women and Aging, an Anthology,* Winter 1986, vol. 9, numbers 2 and 3, p. 56.

p. 204: "the very thin 'feminine' woman." See Brownmiller, *Femininity;* Chernin, *The Obsession: Reflections on the Tyranny of Slenderness* and *The Hungry Self: Women, Eating and Identity.*

p. 206: "The concern about weight as an issue . . ." In addition to the work by Brownmiller and Chernin already cited, see Charles Schroeder, *Fat Is Not a Four-Letter Word.* Also see Susie Orbach, *Fat Is a Feminist Issue.*

p. 210: " 'as tyrannical and selfish a little pig as ever lived.' " Frances Hodgson Burnett, *The Secret Garden,* pp. 1–2.

p. 211: *The Secret Garden,* directed by Clarence Brown, MGM, 1949.

p. 213: "subsequent film versions . . ." Later versions of *The Secret Garden,* which vary from the psychologically realistic BBC version of 1975 to the wooden Hollywood disaster of 1987 and the impressive new release of 1993, are entirely in color and so miss the magical contrast between the shadowed black-and-white of the scenes outside the garden and the glowing color within. The

1993 version, directed by Agnieska Holland and produced by Francis Ford Coppola, compensates for the change by using other striking visual effects, such as a dark, tunneled entrance into the garden. I can't pretend to objectivity here—while Holland's direction is strong, the version I saw in my childhood remains for me the definitive, authentic, unsurpassable version.

p. 214: "the 1945 movie *The Enchanted Cottage . . .*" Directed by John Cromwell, RKO, from a screenplay by Herman Mankiewicz, with Robert Young, Herbert Marshall, and Dorothy McGuire.

p. 214: "*Now, Voyager,* with Bette Davis . . ." Directed in 1942 by Irving Rapper for Warner Brothers.

p. 215: "*All About Eve . . .*" Directed by Joseph Mankiewicz, Twentieth Century–Fox, 1950.

p. 219: " 'What was my Face . . .' " Compiled and edited by Philip Kapleau, *The Three Pillars of Zen: Teaching, Practice, and Enlightenment,* p. 130.

p. 223: "This makeup requirement . . ." For an analysis of the meanings attached to women's choices about appearance, see Deborah Tannen, "Markers: Wears Jump Suit. Sensible Shoes. Uses Husband's Last Name," *The New York Times Magazine,* 1993. Tannen, the author of *You Just Don't Understand: Women and Men in Conversation,* argues persuasively in this article that women's appearance is "marked," carries meaning, in many more ways than men's appearance does, and that this surplus of meaning acts as a limitation for women, tending, as Tannen puts it, "to mark them for frivolousness."

p. 223: "These standards of appearance . . ." See Brownmiller, *Femininity;* Craft, *Too Old, Too Ugly, and Not Deferential to Men;* Faludi, *Backlash: The Undeclared War Against American Women;* and Jo Spence, *Putting Myself in the Picture: A Political, Personal, and Photographic Autobiography.*

p. 225: "the long period of transition into patriarchy." See Baring and Cashford, *The Myth of the Goddess,* and Stone, *When God Was a Woman.*

p. 225: "a story about the creation of humans . . ." Firenzuola, *On the Beauty of Women,* p. 16 ff.

p. 227: "cross-dressing has historically been . . ." See Marjorie Garber, *Vested Interests: Cross-Dressing and Cultural Anxiety.*

p. 227: "The Girl Who Pretended to Be a Boy." Retold from Andrew Lang, *The Violet Fairy Book,* who retold it from *Sept Contes Romaines,* by Jules Brun and Leo Bachelin.

p. 230: " 'it will be the cock who sings . . .' " Ibid., p. 344.

p. 231: "Her body was left to rot on the shore." Barbara Walker, *The Woman's Encyclopedia of Myths and Secrets,* p. 1078, cites C. L'Estrange Ewen, *Witchcraft and Demonianism.*

p. 231: "Her most persistent foes are older women . . ." In this respect her story echoes a Russian folk story about "Vasilisa the Priest's Daughter," who goes about as a man, Vasily Vasilyevitch. A "backyard witch" counsels the king about ways to find out if the young man is really a woman, but her wiles are foiled by the young woman's superior wit. Carter, *Old Wives' Fairy Tale Book.* The pattern here is that of the older woman as guardian of traditional femininity.

p. 231: "Fet-fruners' principal allies are horses . . ." Stories of the love between women and horses are ancient and universal, and extend into modern times, with Elizabeth Taylor as an equestrian child movie star in *National Velvet,* and much more explicitly, as the sensuous and frustrated equestrian wife of an army colonel in *Reflections in a Golden Eye. National Velvet* was directed by Clarence Brown, MGM, 1944; *Reflections in a Golden Eye,* based on the novel by Carson McCullers, was directed by John Huston, Warner Brothers, 1967.

p. 231: "Luckily it's not difficult." P. T. Rooke and R. L. Schnell, *No Bleeding Heart.*

p. 233: "Passing may be seen as living a lie . . ." See also above, Chapter 1, "Mixed Race and Passing."

p. 233: "The Wife Who Became King . . ." Allen B. Chinen, *Once Upon a Midlife: Classic Stories and Mythic Tales to Illuminate the Later Years.*

p. 234: "In earlier centuries women were not prosecuted . . ." See Lillian Faderman, *Surpassing the Love of Men: Romantic Friendship and Love Between Women from the Renaissance to the Present.*

p. 234: "Women who have facial hair . . ." See above, "The Personal Thread," discussion of film *Keltie's Beard.*

p. 235: "There is a certain distinction attached to being older . . ." See Macdonald and Rich, *Look Me in the Eye: Old Women,*

Ageing and Ageism, and *Calyx: A Journal of Art and Literature by Women, Women and Aging, an Anthology,* Winter, 1986.

p. 236: "Lesbians have long used codes . . ." Julia Penelope and Sarah Valentine, *Finding the Lesbians: Personal Accounts from Around the World.*

p. 239: "the transition from the comfortable life of a woman in middle age . . ." See the description of Kate Brown's experiments with appearance and disguise in Doris Lessing, *The Summer Before the Dark.*

p. 239: "shamans understand that illnesses and troubles . . ." See Mindell, *The Shaman's Body.*

p. 239: "a German fairy tale . . ." My sources for this retelling of "Allerleirauh" are Grimm, *Stories,* London, 1876, and *The Complete Grimm's Fairy Tales.* Stern, ed. Margaret Hunt, trans., New York, 1972.

p. 240: "Because of her coat of many skins . . ." The literal translation from German to English of *Allerleirauh* would be "all rough things," or "a mixture of rough things."

p. 242: "An early version of Grimm . . ." Grimm, *Stories,* 1876.

p. 242: "bowdlerization of the older story . . ." Carter, *The Old Wives' Fairy Tale Book,* and Lang, *The Green Fairy Book.*

p. 243: "Each gown represents a different role . . ." This is discussed in great detail in Marion Woodman, *Leaving My Father's House: A Journey to Conscious Femininity,* a book focused on various readings of "Allerleirauh."

p. 243: "shamans in other traditions . . ." See Eliade, *Shamanism: Archaic Techniques of Ecstasy.*

p. 244: "The Maiden with the Wooden Helmet." Lang, *The Violet Fairy Book.*

p. 245: "You may say that I am stupid . . ." Wong, *Seven Taoist Masters,* p. 71.

p. 246: "she inhabits the magical world of dreaming." On the subject of dreaming, see Castaneda, *The Art of Dreaming;* Donner-Grau, *The Witch's Dream;* and Mindell, *The Shaman's Body.*

p. 248: *La Passion de Jeanne d'Arc.* Directed by Carl Theodor Dreyer, France, 1928, with Falconetti, Michel Simon, and Antonin Artaud.

p. 249: "study of physical symptoms." Working with physical symptoms has been a central concern of process work as it has been developed by Dr. Arnold Mindell and colleagues in the past twenty years. The Lava Rock Clinics, a series of seminars held on the Oregon Coast beginning in 1991, brought together a community of patients and other participants with therapists and health practitioners to study the meaning and experience of illness and physical symptoms.

p. 252: " 'Beauty doesn't act.' " Duras, *The North China Lover*, p. 61n.

p. 252: " 'I was drawn this way.' " *Who Framed Roger Rabbit*, directed by Steven Spielberg, Touchstone, 1988.

p. 253: "How many women over the age of forty . . ." The shock value of Jeanne Moreau's extraordinary performance as a woman of advanced age and undiminished libido in *The Summer House*, 1993, is derived from this stereotype of older women. See above, Chapter 1, "Cultural Standards of Beauty: Age," for a discussion of the contemporary shift in this regard. *See also* notes for page 67.

p. 253: "The grammar of commercial film . . ." Many experimental filmmakers and a few women directors of theatrical films, such as Jane Campion, Marta Meszaros, Agnes Varda, and Lina Wertmuller, have experimented with creating a wider range of images of women and our points of view: for instance, Wertmuller's controversial fisheye close-ups of a very large woman's buttocks in *The Seduction of Mimi* (Italy, 1972); Meszaros's subjective images of a woman's body in a shower, seen from her own perspective in *Two Women* (Hungary, 1978); Campion's shot in *The Piano* (Australia, 1993) of Harvey Keitel's finger caressing the single spot of flesh exposed by a hole in the Victorian heroine's stockinged leg, and the unusual angles she used in *Sweetie;* Varda's extreme landscapelike close-ups of tiny details of her husband's body in *Jacquot* (France, 1993). However, the general parameters of mainstream media visions of women have remained very limited.

p. 253: " 'One day, I was already old . . .' " Duras, *The Lover*, p. 3.

p. 255: "One image, a delicately carved head . . ." Head of goddess, Brassempouy, Landes, France. See photograph in Baring and Cashford, *The Myth of the Goddess*, p. 9.

p. 258: "The Mirror." For a discussion of mirrors and some of their cultural reflections, see the chapter called "The Mirror" in Hollander, *Seeing Through Clothes.*

p. 259: "I was writing . . ." Barbara Halpern Martineau, "Thoughts About the Objectification of Women," *Take One* (1972). 3: 15–19.

p. 260: "Men and women both tend to identify . . ." My ideas in this early article were an attempt to integrate concepts from Simone de Beauvoir and Frantz Fanon into thinking about the representation of women. See de Beauvoir, *The Second Sex,* and Fanon, *Black Skin, White Masks.*

p. 260: "We might say that beauty and privilege are attractors . . ." On attractors, see John Briggs and F. David Peat, *Turbulent Mirror: An Illustrated Guide to Chaos Theory and the Science of Wholeness,* and James Gleick, *Chaos: Making A New Science.*

p. 260: "an implicit universal order . . ." See David Bohm, *Wholeness and the Implicate Order.*

p. 260: " 'beaten and flung about the room.' " She was referring to Trevelyan's *History of England,* which provided a very different picture of the situation of women than that depicted in fiction and poetry. Virginia Woolf, *A Room of One's Own,* p. 45.

p. 261: "So long as women have . . ." For a discussion of connections between women's roles and war, see Cynthia Enloe, "The Women Behind the Warriors," *The Women's Review of Books* (1993) X: 23–24. Also see Jean Bethke Elshtain and Sheila Tobias, *Women, Militarism, & War;* Anne E. Hunt, "On Peace, War, and Gender: A Challenge to Genetic Explanations," *Genes and Gender,* ed. Tobach.

p. 262: "In spring of 1993 . . ." MacNeil-Lehrer News Hour, April 22, 1993.

p. 264: "to effect lasting change . . ." When Hunter-Gault interviewed the centenarian Delany sisters, daughters of a freed slave and subjects of a book about their lives, she concluded her interview by asking, "What has been the cause of more difficulty in your lives, being women or being black?" Without hesitation both women replied, "Being black." And on this note Hunter-Gault ended the interview. Their biography, *Having Our Say: The Delany Sisters,* is by Amy Hill Hearth.

p. 264: *The Wizard of Oz,* directed by Victor Fleming, Loew's, 1936.

p. 267: "numerous directors, writers, and editors had their hand's ..."
Salman Rushdie, *The Wizard of Oz.*

p. 267: " 'a modernized fairy tale . . .' " Frank Baum, *The Wizard of Oz.*

p. 268: *Sarafina*! directed by Darrell James Roodt, 1992.

p. 271: "bringing their spirit into our world once again." This story is loosely based on a Chinese legend retold by John Briggs and David F. Peat in their Foreword to *Turbulent Mirror, an Illustrated Guide to Chaos Theory and the Science of Wholeness.*

p. 274: "brought her vision of the Wild Woman . . ." Estés, *Women Who Run with the Wolves.*

p. 277: *The Man Who Gave Himself Away* by Gordon Sheppard.

p. 284: " 'the effort that you make.' " Wong, *Seven Taoist Masters,* p. 139.

p. 289: "my face shape is called the Moon." Lailan Young, *Secrets of the Face; The Chinese Art of Reading Character through Facial Structure and Features.*

SELECTED

BIBLIOGRAPHY

(See also the bibliographies in the books marked with an asterisk *.)

BOOKS

Taisha Abelar. *The Sorcerer's Crossing.* New York: Viking Penguin, 1992.

Tsultrim Allione. *Women of Wisdom.* London: Routledge and Kegan Paul, 1984 (1986).

Hans Christian Andersen. *Fairy Tales.* Trans. Mrs. E. V. Lucas and Mrs. H. B. Paull. New York: Grosset & Dunlap, 1945.

Sherry Ruth Anderson and Patricia Hopkins. *The Feminine Face of God: The Unfolding of the Sacred in Women.* New York: Bantam Books, 1991.

Gloria Anzaldua, ed. *Making Face, Making Soul; Haciendo Caras: Creative and Original Perspectives by Feminists of Color.* San Francisco: Aunt Lute Books, 1990.

Jean-Claude Baker and Chris Chase. *Josephine: The Hungry Heart.* New York: Random House, 1994.

Nancy C. Baker. *The Beauty Trap: Exploring Woman's Greatest Obsession.* New York: Franklin Watts, 1984.

Lois W. Banner. *American Beauty.* New York: Alfred Knopf, 1983.

Anne Baring and Jules Cashford. *The Myth of the Goddess, Evolution of an Image.* New York: Viking, 1991.

Ellen Bass and Laura Davis. *The Courage to Heal: A Guide for Women Survivors of Child Sexual Abuse.* 2nd ed. New York: HarperCollins, 1992.

Frank Baum. *The Wizard of Oz.* New York: Rand McNally, 1987 (1900).

Simone de Beauvoir. *The Second Sex.* New York: Alfred Knopf, 1974 (1949).

Evelyn Torton Beck, ed. *Nice Jewish Girls: A Lesbian Anthology.* New York: The Crossing Press, 1982.

Frances Beer. *Women's Mystical Experience in the Middle Ages.* Rochester, N.Y. Boydell & Brewer, 1992.

John Berger. *Ways of Seeing.* London: BBC and Penguin Books, 1972.

Bruno Bettelheim. *The Uses of Enchantment: The Meaning and Importance of Fairy Tales.* New York: Alfred Knopf, 1976.

Sibylle Birkhäuser-Oeri. *The Mother: Archetypal Image in Fairy Tales.* Trans. Michael Mitchell. Toronto: Inner City Books, 1988 (1977).

David Bohm. *Wholeness and the Implicate Order.* London: Routledge & Kegan Paul, 1980.

Susan Bordo. *Unbearable Weight: Feminism, Western Culture, and the Body.* Berkeley, Calif.: University of California Press, 1993.

Boston Lesbian Psychologies Collective. *Lesbian Psychologies: Explorations and Challenges.* Chicago: University of Illinois Press, 1987.

Robert Brain. *The Decorated Body.* New York: Harper & Row, 1979.

Peter R. Breggin. *Toxic Psychiatry.* New York: St. Martin's Press, 1991.

Wini Breines. *Young, White, and Miserable: Growing Up Female in the Fifties.* Boston: Beacon Press, 1992.

John Briggs and F. David Peat. *Turbulent Mirror: An Illustrated*

Guide to Chaos Theory and the Science of Wholeness. New York: Harper & Row, 1989.

Lyn Mikel Brown and Carol Gilligan. *Meeting at the Crossroads: Women's Psychology and Girls' Development.* New York: Ballantine Books, 1992.

Susan Brownmiller. *Femininity.* New York: Paladin Books, 1986 (1984).

Frances Hodgson Burnett. *The Secret Garden.* New York: Frederick A. Stokes, 1911.

Margaret Busby, ed. *Daughters of Africa.* New York: Ballantine Books, 1992.

Joseph Campbell. *The Hero with a Thousand Faces.* 2nd ed. Princeton, N.J. Princeton University Press, 1968.

Angela Carter. *The Bloody Chamber and Other Stories.* London: Victor Gollancz, 1979.

———. *The Old Wives' Fairy Tale Book.* New York: Pantheon Books, 1990.

Carlos Castaneda. *Tales of Power.* New York: Simon & Schuster, 1974.

———. *The Eagle's Gift.* New York: Simon & Schuster, 1981.

———. *The Art of Dreaming.* New York: HarperCollins, 1993.

Chang Chung-yuan. *Creativity and Taoism.* New York: The Julian Press, 1963.

Wendy Chapkis. *Beauty Secrets: Women and the Politics of Appearance.* Boston: South End Press, 1986.

Kim Chernin. *The Obsession: Reflections on the Tyranny of Slenderness.* New York: Harper & Row, 1981.

———. *The Hungry Self: Women, Eating & Identity.* New York: Times Books, 1985.

Phyllis Chesler. *Women and Madness.* New York: Doubleday, 1972.

Allen B. Chinen. *Once Upon a Midlife: Classic Stories and Mythic Tales to Illuminate the Later Years.* New York: Jeremy Tarcher, 1993.

Agatha Christie. *The Body in the Library.* New York: Pocket Books, 1970 (1941).

Christine Craft. *Too Old, Too Ugly, and Not Deferential to Men.* Rocklin, Calif.: Prima, 1988.

—— Angela Davis. *Women, Culture, and Politics.* New York: Random House, 1989.

Madame de La Fayette. *The Princess of Clèves.* Trans. Walter J. Cobb. New York: New American Library, 1961 (1678).

Teresa de Lauretis. *Alice Doesn't: Feminism, Semiotics, Cinema.* Bloomington: Indiana University Press, 1984.

Muriel Dimen-Schein. *The Anthropological Imagination.* New York: McGraw-Hill, 1977.

Margarita Donnelly, ed. *Women and Aging. Calyx: A Journal of Art and Literature by Women.* 1986.

Florinda Donner-Grau. *The Witch's Dream.* New York: Simon & Schuster, 1985.

——. *Being-in-Dreaming: An Initiation into the Sorcerer's World.* New York: HarperSanFrancisco, 1991.

Ariel Dorfman. *The Empire's Old Clothes: What the Lone Ranger, Babar, and Other Innocent Heroes Do to Our Minds.* New York: Pantheon Books, 1983.

Ariel Dorfman and Armand Mattelart. *How to Read Donald Duck: Imperialist Ideology in the Disney Comic.* Trans. David Kunzle. New York: International General, 1975 (1971).

Colette Dowling. *The Cinderella Complex.* New York: Simon & Schuster, 1981.

Marguerite Duras. *The Lover.* Trans. Barbara Bray. New York: Pantheon Books, 1985 (1984).

——. *Outside: Selected Writings.* Trans. Arthur Goldhammer. Boston: Beacon Press, 1986 (1984).

——. *The North China Lover.* Trans. Leigh Hafrey. New York: The New Press, 1992.

——. *The Sea Wall.* Trans. Herma Briffaut. New York: Noonday Press, 1967 (1959).

Andrea Dworkin. *Right-Wing Women.* New York: Coward-McCann, 1983.

Irwin Edman, ed.). *The Philosophy of Plato: The Jowett Translation.* New York: Modern Library, 1928.

Barbara Ehrenreich and Deirdre English. *For Her Own Good: 150 Years of the Experts' Advice to Women.* New York: Anchor Press, Doubleday, 1979.

Riane Eisler. *The Chalice & the Blade: Our History, Our Future.* New York: Harper & Row, 1987.

Mircea Eliade. *Shamanism: Archaic Techniques of Ecstasy.* Bollingen

Series. Trans. Willard R. Trask. Princeton, N.J. Princeton University Press, 1972 (1951).

Mary Ellmann. *Thinking About Women.* New York: Harcourt, Brace & World, 1968.

Jean Bethke Elshtain, and Sheila Tobias, eds. *Women, Militarism, and War.* Savage, Md.: Rowman & Littlefield, 1990.

*Clarissa Pinkola Estés. *Women Who Run with the Wolves: Myths and Stories of the Wild Woman Archetype.* New York: Ballantine Books, 1992.

Stuart Ewen and Elizabeth Ewen. *Channels of Desire: Mass Images and the Shaping of American Consciousness.* 2nd ed. Minneapolis: University of Minnesota Press, 1992.

Lillian Faderman. *Surpassing the Love of Men: Romantic Friendship and Love between Women from the Renaissance to the Present.* New York: William Morrow & Co., 1981.

Susan Faludi. *Backlash: The Undeclared War Against American Women.* New York: Crown Publishers, 1991.

Frantz Fanon. *Black Skin, White Masks.* New York: Grove Press, 1967.

Beatrice Faust. *Women, Sex, and Pornography.* Harmondsworth, England: Penguin Books, 1981 (1980).

Agnolo Firenzuola. *On the Beauty of Women.* Konrad Eisenbichler, Jacqueline Murray, trans. and eds. Philadelphia: University of Pennsylvania Press, 1992 (1548).

Angela Fisher. *Africa Adorned.* New York: Harry Abrams, 1984.

John Carl Flügel. *The Psychology of Clothes.* New York: International University Press, 1930.

Merle A. Fossum and Marilyn J. Mason. *Facing Shame: Families in Recovery.* New York: W. W. Norton, 1986.

Ruth Frankenberg. *White Women, Race Matters: The Social Construction of Whiteness.* Minneapolis: University of Minnesota Press, 1993.

*Rita Freedman. *Beauty Bound.* Lexington, Ky.: D. C.: Heath, 1986.

———. *Bodylove: Learning to Like Our Looks and Ourselves.* New York: Harper & Row, 1988.

Sigmund Freud. "The Etiology of Hysteria," *The Complete Psychological Works of Sigmund Freud.* Vol. 3. Trans. C. M. Baines. Standard Edition. London: Hogarth Press, 1888.

Betty Friedan. *The Fountain of Age.* New York: Simon & Schuster, 1993.

Tikva Frymer-Kensky. *In the Wake of the Goddesses: Women, Culture and the Biblical Transformation of Pagan Myth.* New York: Free Press, 1992.

Elinor Gadon. *The Once and Future Goddess.* New York: Harper & Row, 1989.

Jane Gaines and Charlotte Herzog. *Fabrications: Costume and the Female Body.* New York: Routledge, 1990.

Marjorie Garber. *Vested Interests: Cross-Dressing and Cultural Anxiety.* New York: Routledge, 1992.

Paula Giddings. *When and Where I Enter: The Impact of Black Women on Race and Sex in America.* New York: William Morrow, 1984.

Carol Gilligan. *In a Different Voice: Psychological Theory and Women's Development.* Cambridge, Mass.: Harvard University Press, 1982.

Carol Gilligan, Annie G. Rogers, and Deborah L. Tolman, eds. *Women, Girls and Psychotherapy: Reframing Resistance.* Binghamton, N.Y.: Harrington Park Press, 1991.

Marija Gimbutas. *The Goddesses and Gods of Old Europe, 6500–3500 B.C.: Myths and Cult Images.* London: Thames and Hudson, 1982.

———. *The Language of the Goddess.* San Francisco: Harper & Row, 1989.

Daniela Gioseffi. *On Prejudice: A Global Perspective.* New York: Doubleday, 1993.

Barry Glassner. *Bodies, Why We Look the Way We Do and How We Feel About It.* New York: G. P. Putnam, 1988.

Judith Gleason. *Oya, In Praise of the Goddess.* Boston: Shambhala, 1987.

James Gleick. *Chaos: Making a New Science.* New York: Viking Penguin, 1987.

Laurence Goldstein, ed. *The Female Body: Figures, Styles, Speculations.* Ann Arbor: University of Michigan Press, 1991.

Edgar J. Goodspeed. *The Apocrypha, an American Translation.* New York: Vintage Books, 1959.

Judy Grahn. *Blood, Bread, and Roses: How Menstruation Created the World.* Boston: Beacon Press, 1993.

Miriam Greenspan. *A New Approach to Women and Therapy.* New York: McGraw-Hill, 1983.

Germaine Greer. *The Female Eunuch.* New York: McGraw-Hill, 1971 (1970).

———. *The Change: Women, Aging and the Menopause.* New York: Fawcett Columbine, 1993 (1991).

Susan Griffin. *Woman and Nature: The Roaring Inside Her.* New York: Harper & Row, 1978.

The Brothers Grimm. *Stories.* London: George Routledge & Sons, 1876.

———. *The Complete Grimm's Fairy Tales.* Trans. Margaret Hunt. New York: Random House, 1972 (1944).

Felix Guirand, ed. *New Larousse Encyclopedia of Mythology.* London: Paul Hamlyn, 1972 (1968).

Emily Hancock. *The Girl Within.* New York: Fawcett Columbine, 1989.

M. Esther Harding. *Women's Mysteries, Ancient and Modern.* New York: Harper & Row, 1971.

Amy Hill Hearth. *Having Our Say: The Delany Sisters.* Mount Vernon, N.Y.: Kodansha, 1993.

Carolyn Heilbrun. *Toward a Recognition of Androgyny.* New York: Harper/Colophon Books, 1973.

Judith Herman. *Trauma and Recovery.* New York: Basic Books, 1992.

Anne Hollander. *Seeing Through Clothes.* New York: Viking, 1978.

bell hooks. *Yearning: Race, Gender, and Cultural Politics.* Boston: South End Press, 1990.

———. *Black Looks: Race and Representation.* Boston: South End Press, 1992.

Patricia Huckle. *Tish Sommers, Activist, and the Founding of the Older Women's League.* Knoxville, Tenn.: University of Tennessee Press, 1991.

Anne E. Hunt, ed. *On Peace, War, and Gender: A Challenge to Genetic Explanations. Genes and Gender.* New York: Feminist Press, 1991.

Thorkild Jacobsen. *The Treasures of Darkness: A History of Mesopotamian Religion.* New Haven, Conn.: Yale University Press, 1976.

Gloria I. Joseph and Jill Lewis. *Common Differences: Conflicts in Black & White Feminist Perspectives.* Boston: South End Press, 1981.

—— C. G. Jung. *Collected Works of C. G. Jung.* Bollingen Series XX. Trans. R. F. C. Hull. Princeton, N.J.: Princeton University Press, 1972.

Philip Kapleau, ed. *The Three Pillars of Zen: Teaching, Practice, and Enlightenment.* Boston: Beacon Press, 1967.

Melanie Kaye-Kantrowitz and Irena Klepfisz, eds. *The Tribe of Dina: A Jewish Women's Anthology.* Montpelier, VT.: Sinister Wisdom Books, 1985.

Claudia Brush Kidwell and Valerie Steele. *Men and Women, Dressing the Part.* Washington, D.C.: Smithsonian Institution Press, 1989.

Maxine Hong Kingston. *The Woman Warrior: Memoirs of a Girlhood Among Ghosts.* New York: Alfred Knopf, 1976.

Nora Scott Kinzer. *Put Down and Ripped Off: The American Woman and the Beauty Cult.* New York: Crowell, 1977.

Madonna Kolbenschlag. *Kiss Sleeping Beauty Good-bye.* New York: Doubleday, 1979.

Ewa Kuryluk. *Veronica and Her Cloth.* Cambridge, Mass.: Basil Blackwell, 1991.

Andrew Lang, ed. *The Violet Fairy Book.* London: Longmans, 1902.

——, ed. *The Green Fairy Book.* London: Longmans, Green, 1914.

——, ed. *The Pink Fairy Book.* London: Longmans, 1916.

Gerda Lerner. *Black Women in White America: A Documentary History.* New York: Random House, 1992 (1972).

Doris Lessing. *The Summer Before the Dark.* New York: Alfred Knopf, 1973.

——. *A Small Personal Voice.* New York: Alfred Knopf, 1974.

Howard S. Levy. *The Lotus Lovers: The Complete History of the Curious Erotic Custom of Footbinding in China.* Buffalo, N.Y.: Prometheus, 1992.

Lucy R. Lippard. *From the Center: Feminist Essays on Women's Art.* New York: E. P. Dutton, 1976.

——. *Overlay: Contemporary Art and the Art of Prehistory.* New York: Pantheon, 1983.

Anita Loos. *"Gentlemen Prefer Blondes": The Illuminating Diary of a Professional Lady.* London: Brentano's, 1926.

Alison Lurie. *The Language of Clothes.* New York: Random House, 1981.

Barbara Macdonald and Cynthia Rich, eds. *Look Me in the Eye: Old Women, Ageing and Ageism.* San Francisco: Spinsters, 1991.

Madonna. *Sex.* New York: Warner Books, 1992.

Wendy Maltz. *The Sexual Healing Journey: A Guide for Survivors of Sexual Abuse.* New York: Harper Perennial, 1992.

Jeffrey Moussaieff Masson. *The Assault on Truth: Freud's Suppression of the Seduction Theory.* New York: Farrar, Straus, & Giroux, 1984.

Sarah H. Matthews. *The Social World of Old Women.* Beverly Hills: Sage Publications, 1979.

Diana Maychick. *Audrey Hepburn: An Intimate Portrait.* London: Birch Lane Press, 1994.

Colin McDowell. *Dressed to Kill: Sex Power & Clothes.* London: Hutchinson, 1992.

Elissa Melamed. *Mirror, Mirror: The Terror of Not Being Young.* New York: Simon & Schuster, 1983.

Maurice Merleau-Ponty. *The Primacy of Perception and Other Essays.* Northwestern University Press, 1964.

Alice Miller. *The Drama of the Gifted Child.* Trans. Ruth Ward. New York: Basic Books, 1981 (1979).

———. *Thou Shalt Not Be Aware: Society's Betrayal of the Child.* Trans. Hildegard and Hunter Hannum. New York: Farrar, Straus & Giroux, 1984 (1981).

———. *For Your Own Good: Hidden Cruelty in Child-Rearing and the Roots of Violence.* Trans. Hildegard and Hunter Hannum. 2nd ed. New York: Farrar, Straus & Giroux, 1984 (1980).

———. *Banished Knowledge.* Trans. Leila Vennewitz. New York: Doubleday, 1990 (1988).

Kate Millett. *Sexual Politics.* New York: Doubleday, 1970.

———. *The Looney-Bin Trip.* New York: Simon & Schuster, 1990.

Arnold Mindell. *Dreambody: The Body's Role in Revealing the Self.* Boston: Sigo Press, 1982.

———. *River's Way: The Process Science of the Dreambody.* London: Routledge & Kegan Paul, 1985.

———. *Working with the Dreaming Body.* London: Routledge & Kegan Paul, 1985.

———. *The Dreambody in Relationships.* London: Routledge & Kegan Paul, 1987.

———. *City Shadows: Psychological Interventions in Psychiatry.* London: Routledge & Kegan Paul, 1988.

——— ———. *The Year I: Global Process Work.* London: Arkana, Penguin, 1989.

———. *Working on Yourself Alone: Inner Dreambody Work.* London: Arkana, Penguin, 1990.

———. *The Leader As Martial Artist.* New York: HarperSanFrancisco, 1992.

———. *The Shaman's Body.* New York: HarperCollins, 1993.

Arnold Mindell and Amy Mindell. *Riding the Horse Backwards: Process Work in Theory and Practice.* Penguin: Arkana, 1992.

Thomas Moore. *Care of the Soul: A Guide for Cultivating Depth and Sacredness in Everyday Life.* New York: HarperCollins, 1992.

Cherrie Moraga and Gloria Anzaldua, eds. *This Bridge Called My Back: Writings by Radical Women of Color.* New York: Kitchen Table: Women of Color Press, 1983.

Robin Morgan, ed. *Sisterhood Is Powerful.* New York: Vintage, 1970.

Toni Morrison. *The Bluest Eye.* New York: Holt, Rinehart & Winston, 1970.

———. *Tar Baby.* New York: Alfred Knopf, 1981.

———. *Jazz.* New York: Alfred Knopf, 1992.

———. *Playing in the Dark: Whiteness and the Literary Imagination.* Cambridge, Mass.: Harvard University Press, 1992.

Lena Wright Myers. *Black Women: Do They Cope Better?* Englewood Cliffs, N.J.: Prentice-Hall, 1980.

Erich Neumann. *The Great Mother: An Analysis of the Archetype.* Trans. Ralph Manheim. 2nd ed. Princeton, N.J.: Princeton University Press, 1963 (1955).

Susie Orbach. *Fat Is a Feminist Issue.* New York: Berkeley Books, 1978.

Lara Owen. *Her Blood Is Gold: Celebrating the Power of Menstruation.* New York: HarperSanFrancisco, 1993.

Elaine Pagels. *Adam, Eve, and the Serpent.* New York: Random House, 1988.

Camille Paglia. *Sexual Personae, Art and Decadence from Nefertiti to Emily Dickinson.* New York: Vintage Books, 1991.

———. *Sex, Art, and American Culture.* New York: Vintage Books, 1992.

Julia Penelope and Sarah Valentine, eds. *Finding the Lesbians: Personal Accounts from Around the World.* Freedom, Calif.: The Crossing Press, 1990.

Sylvia Brinton Perera. *Descent to the Goddess, A Way of Initiation for Women.* Toronto: Inner City Books, 1981.

Ethel Johnston Phelps. *The Maid of the North: Feminist Folk Tales from Around the World.* New York: Holt, Rinehart & Winston, 1981.

Jill Purce. *The Mystic Spiral.* New York: Thames and Hudson, 1974.

Arthur Rackham, ed. *The Arthur Rackham Fairy Book.* London: George C. Harrap, 1933.

Jean Rhys. *Wide Sargasso Sea.* New York: Norton, 1967 (1966).

James Riordan. *An Illustrated Treasury of Fairy and Folk Tales.* London: Hamlyn, 1986.

P. T. Rooke and R. L. Schnell. *No Bleeding Heart.* Vancouver, B.C.: University of British Columbia Press, 1987.

Aline Rousselle. *Porneia: On Desire and the Body in Antiquity.* Trans. Felicia Pheasant. Oxford: Basil Blackwell, 1988 (1983).

Lillian Rubin. *Women of a Certain Age.* New York: Harper & Row, 1979.

Florence Rush. *The Best Kept Secret: Sexual Abuse of Children.* New York: McGraw-Hill, 1981.

Salman Rushdie. *The Wizard of Oz.* London: British Film Institute, 1992.

Charles Roy Schroeder. *Fat Is Not a Four-Letter Word.* Minneapolis: Chronimed, 1992.

Florida Scott-Maxwell. *The Measure of My Days.* New York: Penguin, 1979 (1968).

Roberta Pollack Seid. *Never Too Thin: Why Women Are at War with Their Bodies.* New York: Prentice-Hall, 1989.

Adam Sexton. *Desperately Seeking Madonna.* New York: Delta, 1993.

Anne Sexton. *Transformations.* Boston: Houghton Mifflin Company, 1971.

Gordon Sheppard. *The Man Who Gave Himself Away.* Montreal: Harlan Quist, 1971.

Elaine Showalter. *The Female Malady: Women, Madness and English Culture, 1830–1980.* New York: Pantheon, 1985.

Penelope Shuttle and Peter Redgrove. *The Wise Wound: The Myths, Realities, and Meanings of Menstruation.* Rev. ed. New York: Grove Press, 1986.

June Singer. *Seeing through the Visible World: Jung, Gnosis, and Chaos.* San Francisco: Harper & Row, 1990.

——— Susan Sontag. *Under the Sign of Saturn.* New York: Farrar, Straus & Giroux, 1980.

Jo Spence. *Putting Myself in the Picture: A Political, Personal, and Photographic Autobiography.* Seattle: The Real Comet Press, 1988.

Gertrude Stein. *How Writing Is Written.* Vol. II of *Previously Uncollected Writings.* Los Angeles: Black Sparrow Press, 1974.

Gloria Steinem. *Revolution from Within: A Book of Self-Esteem.* Boston: Little, Brown, 1992.

Merlin Stone. *When God Was a Woman.* New York: Harcourt Brace Jovanovich, 1978 (1976).

Carole S. Vance, ed. *Pleasure and Danger: Exploring Female Sexuality.* Boston: Routledge & Kegan Paul, 1984.

Marie-Louise von Franz. *Interpretation of Fairy Tales.* Dallas: Spring Publications, 1970.

———. *The Feminine in Fairy Tales.* Dallas: Spring Publications, 1972.

Alice Walker. *The Color Purple.* New York: Harcourt Brace Jovanovich, 1982.

———. *In Search of Our Mothers' Gardens.* New York: Harcourt Brace Jovanovich, 1983.

———. *Possessing the Secret of Joy.* New York: Harcourt Brace Jovanovich, 1992.

Alice Walker and Pratibha Parmar. *Warrior Marks: Female Genital Mutilation and the Sexual Blinding of Women.* New York: Harcourt Brace, 1993.

Barbara Walker. *The Woman's Encyclopedia of Myths and Secrets.* New York: Harper & Row, 1983.

———. *The Secrets of the Tarot.* San Francisco: Harper & Row, 1984.

———. *The Crone, Woman of Age, Wisdom, and Power.* San Francisco, New York: Harper & Row, 1985.

———. *The Women's Dictionary of Symbols & Sacred Objects.* San Francisco, New York: Harper & Row, 1988.

*Naomi Wolf. *The Beauty Myth: How Images of Beauty Are Used Against Women.* New York: William Morrow, 1991.

Diane Wolkstein and Samuel Noah Kramer. *Inanna: Queen of Heaven and Earth.* New York: Harper & Row, 1983.

Eva Wong, trans., ed. *Seven Taoist Masters: A Folk Novel of China.* Boston: Shambhala, 1990.

———, trans., ed. *Cultivating Stillness: A Taoist Manual for Transforming Body and Mind.* Boston: Shambhala, 1992.

Marion Woodman. *Leaving My Father's House: A Journey to Conscious Femininity.* Boston: Shambhala, 1993.

Virginia Woolf. *A Room of One's Own.* London: Penguin, 1963 (1928).

Lailan Young. *Secrets of the Face: The Chinese Art of Reading Character through Facial Structure and Features.* Boston: Little, Brown, 1984.

JOURNAL ARTICLES

Judith Myers Avis. "Perspectives on Sexual Abuse and Violence within Families in North America." *Journal of Feminist Family Therapy,* Vol. 4.3/4 (1992): 87–100.

Sandra Bartky. "Women, Bodies and Power: A Research Agenda for Philosophy." *APA Newsletter on Feminism and Philosophy,* 89.1 (1989): 78–82.

Jacqueline F. Brown. "Helping Black Women Build High Self-Esteem." *American Counselor,* 2. Winter, no. 1 (1993): 9–12.

Carole M. Counihan. "Never Say Diet." *Women's Review of Books,* XI.3 (Fall) (1993): 19–20.

Mary Crane. "Wild Flowers and Bearded Ladies." *Newsletter on Feminism and Philosophy,* 91.2 (1992): 51–52.

Cynthia Enloe. "The Women Behind the Warriors." *The Women's Review of Books,* X.5, February (1993): 23–24.

Sara Halprin. "Geography of the Body/Geography of the Spirit." *Porter Gulch Review,* Spring-Summer (1988): p. 21.

———. "Preparing for Death and Planning to Live: An Interview with Marianne Pomeroy." *The Journal for Process-Oriented Psychology,* 5.2, Fall-Winter (1993).

Scott MacDonald. "Demystifying the Female Body: Anne Severson —*Near the Big Chakra;* Yvonne Rainer—*Privilege.*" *Film Quarterly,* 45.1 (Fall, 1991) 18–32.

Barbara Halpern Martineau. "Thoughts about the Objectification of Women." *Take One,* 3.2 (1972): 15–19.

Susan Sontag. "The Double Standard of Aging." *Saturday Review of Literature,* September (1972).

Robert Staples. "The Role and Importance of Beauty in the Black Community." *Black Male/Female Relationships,* 7 (1982): 32–40.

——   Regina Turner. "The Ordeal of the 'Ugly' Black Woman." *Black*
332   *Male/Female Relationships*, 6 (1982): 21–29.

MAGAZINE AND NEWSPAPER ARTICLES

Judy Bachrach. "A Certain Age." *Allure,* April 1993.

Jacqueline Carey. "Social Roots." *Allure,* January 1993: 40.

Patti Doten. "Breast Cancer's Cover Girl." *The Oregonian,* August 23, 1993: C1.

Susan Gerhard. "The Beauty Morph: Orlan Makes a Feminist Spectacle of Herself." *San Francisco Bay Guardian,* February 2 1994.

Kathy Healy. "Plastic Surgery Addicts." *Allure,* April 1993: 80.

Amy Hempel. "Beauty Marks." *Allure,* March 1993: 94.

Oni Faida Lampley. "The Wig and I." *Mirabella,* April 1993: 144–48.

Judith Levine. " 'White Like Me: When Privilege Is Written on Your Skin.' " *Ms.,* March-April 1994: 22–24.

Jill Neimark. "Change of Face . . . Change of Fate." *Psychology Today,* May-June 1994: p. 42.

Judith Newman. "Eye Hopes." *Mirabella,* May 1993.

Leonard Pitts, Jr. "In Terms of Afterlife, Madonna Is No Elvis." *The Oregonian,* Knight-Ridder News Service, Thursday, September 2, 1993.

Barbara Rose. "Is It Art? Orlan and the Transgressive Act." *Art in America,* February 1993, p. 82.

Phil Rosenthal. "Is the Material Girl Really Showing Signs of Cracking?" *The Oregonian,* May 20, 1993: C5.

Erin Hoover Schraw. "Kids' Art, Sculpture Enhances Self-Image." *The Oregonian,* June 3, 1993: C2.

Deborah Tannen. "Markers: Wears Jump Suit. Sensible Shoes. Uses Husband's Last Name." *The New York Times Magazine,* June 22, 1993.

Sallie Tisdale. "A Weight That Women Carry: the Compulsion to Diet in a Starved Culture." *Harper's,* March 1993: 49–55.

Andrew Ward. "Picture Perfect." *The Washington Post,* September 7, 1993.

Kendal Weaver, "High School Principal Suspended for Alleged Racial Slur," *The Oregonian,* March 15, 1996.

Marilyn Murray Willison. "A Second Look." *Allure,* February 1993: 72–79.

ACKNOWLEDGMENTS

First thanks go to my teachers. Master Moy Lin Shin first drew my attention to the story of Sun Pu-erh, which inspired me to write this book, and he recommended that Eva Wong translate *Seven Taoist Masters* into English, thereby making it accessible to me and many others. Dr. Arnold Mindell, who developed the theoretical framework I have applied to my study of appearance, encouraged me in the early, middle, and late stages of writing.

Many friends and colleagues have read various sections of the manuscript in various stages, and have helped with their comments and encouragement. Special thanks to Jan Baross, Kathy Barry, Ruby Brooks, Liz Campbell, Barbara Douglas, Emetchi, Marge du Mond, Susan Hall, Gladys Johnson, Allie Light, Amy Mindell, Lara Owen, Alice Anne Parker, Anne Stadler, Tonda Thomas, and Nisha Zenoff. Elizabeth Behnke, John Johnson, Martha Keaner, Catherine Duncan, and Francis Martineau were helpful resource people.

Thanks also to the patient reference staff at Portland's Multnomah County Library. In writing this book I relied on the wisdom of many who wrote before me, especially the women who invented feminist scholarship and women's literature, old and new—my references are in the footnotes and bibliography, but I want to note this debt here, for we do not work in a vacuum.

I am very grateful to the women, more than the number who finally appear in the book, who shared their stories with me, read over what I wrote about them, and made helpful suggestions: Freude Bartlett, Susan Barton, Hattie Brown, Sophie Brykczynska, Anuradha Deb, Andrea Debnam, Catherine Hogue, Allie Light, Dao Thi Mai, Beverly Michaud, Marlene Moore, Chris Moyers, Erin O'Shea, Marianne Pomeroy, Jacqueline Posey, Mari Quihuis, Kana Riley, Marian Tobler, Justine Toms, Seema Weatherwax, Waynelle Wilder and Fawn Yacker; and in memoriam, Renée Howell.

Freude Bartlett has been a constant support, editorial guide, and fount of wisdom during the long process of writing and rewriting. Thanks to Lara Owen for introducing me to Marian Young, who has been a wonderful and calming influence as well as an excellent agent. Thanks to all the staff at Viking, especially Beena Kamlani, production editor extraordinaire, and Mindy Werner, my eagle-eyed and stalwart editor.

Noah Martineau, my son, has been showing me new ways of looking at people and the world since he came into it, and I am grateful for his creative eye and his loving belief in me.

My sister, Cher Sauer, has encouraged me and believed in me all along, and she is the reader for whom this book was written.

Herb Long, my husband and friend, helped me to write this book by doing all the things a wife is often expected to do for her preoccupied husband; and, in crossing this gender boundary, he showed himself to be fluid as well as strong, graceful, and tender.

For spiritual sustenance I am grateful to the memories of Beatrice Macdonald, Violet Dreschfelt, my mother and father, my grandmother Rebecca and great-grandmother Sarah.

INDEX

Numerals in **bold** type represent sections or chapters devoted to the entry.